PRAISE FOR *BETTER GOOD*

"Scott Curran has been in the trenches of public service and knows how to get results. *Better Good* not only lays out *what* you need to do to make a difference in your life and in the world, but also the very crucial *how*."

—President Bill Clinton, 42nd president of the United States and founder and board chair of the Clinton Foundation

"A simple and powerful road map for anyone ready to turn what they have into real impact."

—Scott Harrison, founder and CEO of Charity: Water and *New York Times* bestselling author of *Thirst*

"*Better Good* strips away the celebrity halo and billionaire mythology around doing good. This isn't a book for saints or saviors—it's for you and me, regular people, ready to make a real difference with what we already have, right now."

—Ann Lee, CEO and cofounder, CORE

"Everyone needs to read this book. Simply put, it's the *Atomic Habits* of doing good."

—Dr. David Fajgenbaum, bestselling author of *Chasing My Cure* and cofounder of Every Cure

"Generous, grounded, and refreshingly free of pedantic lectures. Curran trusts you to act, and then hands you the tools to do it well. A sharp guide for anyone ready to stop spectating and start building something meaningful."

—Amanda Litman, cofounder and president of Run for Something and author of *When We're in Charge*

"This book is grounded in real experience, hard-earned lessons, and practical leadership. Curran has created a powerful playbook for anyone serious about turning values into action and building organizations that support the communities they serve."

—Nishant Roy, chief impact officer of Chobani

"*Better Good* should be taught in schools and inscribed in every organization charter. Everyone should pick up this book to think about how they can do 'better good' in all arenas of their life."

—Alex Amouyel, president and CEO of Newman's Own Foundation and author of *The Answer Is You*

"Offering both insight and inspiration, Curran's simple framework shows how everyone—from seasoned business leaders to first-time volunteers—can use the tools they already have to make a real impact."

—Rajiv J. Shah, author of *Big Bets*

"In the chaos of modern life, we forget that doing good doesn't need to be a daunting task—but guidance helps, and Curran provides us with a road map to be the best version of our best selves."

—Kelly Leonard, vice president of The Second City; author of *Yes, And*; and host of the *Getting to Yes, And* podcast

"*Better Good* reframes impact not as the responsibility of a select few, but as an opportunity for all of us to make a difference."

—Julie Gehrki, president, Walmart Foundation, and senior vice president, Philanthropy, Walmart Inc.

"I've seen what drives real impact in business, government, and philanthropy. Scott Curran has captured it—and made it usable for everyone. *Better Good* is the leadership book this moment calls for."

—Robert A. "Bob" McDonald, eighth secretary of Veterans Affairs; retired chairman, president and CEO, Procter & Gamble; and chairman, West Point Association of Graduates

"Scott Curran has written the rare book that takes the mystery out of doing good—and puts it within reach of anyone willing to start. The Better Good Framework is practical, generous, and grounded in decades of real-world experience at the highest levels of philanthropy. This is the playbook for turning everyday capacity into lasting impact."

—Michael Hyatt, *New York Times* bestselling author and business coach

"*Better Good* is the blueprint for leaders, organizations, and changemakers to become better at doing Good. Scott's clear perspective, sharp wit, and bighearted storytelling make the challenge of creating lasting impact more accessible, energizing, personal, and possible. *Better Good* is a timely, essential read for everyone who wants to pursue positive impact and shift their Good into high gear."

—Jana Babatunde-Bey, entrepreneur, film/TV executive producer, and social impact entertainment leader

"*Better Good* is the blueprint to create your unique impact. Scott Curran is who you go to when you're ready to uncover yours. In my work and life, he gave me a framework that I keep coming back to. I'm sure you will, too."

—Ameena Majid, impact and sustainability partner, Seyfarth Shaw LLP

BETTER GOOD

A Simple System for Creating Lasting Impact

SCOTT M. CURRAN

Simon Acumen
New York Amsterdam/Antwerp London
Toronto Sydney/Melbourne New Delhi

SIMON
ACUMEN

An Imprint of Simon & Schuster, LLC
1230 Avenue of the Americas
New York, NY 10020

First Simon Acumen hardcover edition August 2026

Interior design by Julia Jacintho

Manufactured in the United States of America

1 3 5 7 9 10 8 6 4 2

Library of Congress Control Number: 2026021401

ISBN 978-1-6680-9165-4
ISBN 978-1-6680-9166-1 (ebook)

To Ray and Asprey, their friends, and all future readers.
The world needs your Better Good.
I hope this helps you build it.

CONTENTS

INTRODUCTION

The Good Hiding in Plain Sight

Life is short. Do not forget about the most important things in our life, living for other people and doing good for them.

—Marcus Aurelius

It's hard not to feel overwhelmed today. The headlines keep coming—crisis after crisis, outrage after outrage. Civil unrest, wars, and humanitarian crises dominate our feeds. Climate disasters—floods, fires, tornados, and hurricanes—are accelerating with devastating consequences. Institutions that once seemed steady are wobbling, and trust in government, media, business, and even philanthropy is being tested like never before.

In the U.S. and around the world, agencies and institutions built to serve the public good are under strain or scrutiny, or being attacked outright. Nonprofits and universities are being drawn into culture wars they never asked for. The private sector is caught in the crossfire—rewarded one day for taking a stand as a good corporate citizen, punished the next for the same act of conscience. On social media people argue bitterly about whose cause is just.

It's a confusing time to care.

Sometimes it feels like the whole world is on fire, and we're standing there with a garden hose. You care. You want to help. But where do you even begin? Maybe you've asked yourself:

Am I doing enough?

Does anything I do actually matter?

Is it even possible to make a real difference anymore—especially without burning out or selling out?

If you've had these thoughts, you're not alone. And you're not wrong to feel this way. The ground is shifting beneath all of us and we feel unsteady. The systems that were designed to serve the common good are being reshaped in real time. But buried inside that disruption is an opening—an opportunity for each of us, and the organizations we belong to, to rethink what doing good really means and how we can do it better.

Here's what I've learned from decades of working alongside the world's leading doers, givers, bridge-builders, and changemakers—some household names, others invisible heroes: *There's a way forward. And it's hiding in plain sight.*

Doing good today isn't about being a saint or a savior. It's not about being rich or famous. It's about learning to spot the patterns—the hidden framework that successful do-gooders follow, whether they realize it or not—and using it to leave the world better than we found it.

This book gives you a simple, repeatable, and reliable framework to focus your effort and multiply your impact. It's the same one that's consistently powered great changemakers in our time—and, in truth, throughout all time.

GIVING IT ALL AWAY

It was one of those blurry days between Christmas and New Year's at the very end of 2014. My wife, Amy, and I had just finished the bedtime routines of our six-year-old son and four-year-old daughter. We were settling into an evening of catching up on work emails on our laptops, sitting on opposite-facing family room couches. It was a completely normal evening, but one that would turn out to be among the most consequential of my life.

At this time, I was general counsel of what would soon become one of the most scrutinized nonprofits in human history: the Clinton Foundation.

While Hillary Clinton had not yet declared her presidential candidacy, it was a foregone conclusion that she would announce in early 2015, run, and the prevailing wisdom suggested she would win. Nonetheless, I was preparing to leave the Clinton Foundation well in advance of the 2016 presidential election. Not having come from "the Clinton world" and with no plan to remain part of it, I suspected that the Foundation would likely become a shadow of its former self; many in the Clinton orbit would soon be angling for next-step opportunities within Hillary's administration. I wanted to move on as well, but outside of it.

I was facing a bit of a conundrum. I knew that I likely wouldn't work at an organization as high-profile as the Clinton Foundation again, given its unique position in the world. The foundation was extremely well known and highly regarded in the world of philanthropy and beyond. And with the heightened scrutiny and news coverage of our work in the lead-up to the election, it was becoming a household name outside of philanthropy. With each rapidly passing day, I watched as the cadence of news coverage accelerated, and rumor and innuendo turned our otherwise esteemed nonprofit into a political flashpoint.

Regardless, with its portfolio of initiatives and partners spanning global health, international development, climate change, women and girls' empowerment, and a dozen other extraordinary needle-moving initiatives, the Clinton Foundation—often in partnership with a vast array of other global partners—had pioneered a new model both for post-presidential service and philanthropy. It had been a wild ride that I'd stumbled into a decade earlier, following a mid-career return to graduate school, and I had learned so, so much.

While many friends and colleagues suggested I was a fool *not* to stay close and seek a prime government appointment or a cushy Clinton-friendly private sector gig, those weren't my goals. I felt there had to be a way to have a bigger and more meaningful impact. So, while I was still doing my increasingly chaotic and scrutinized work amid a flurry of executive leadership changes already underway, I began quietly but deliberately planning my exit. As I considered what could come next—another general counsel position? A move to a big-law law firm? Full-time teaching?—it felt like an impossible decision.

So, I did what any smart person in my position should do: I asked my wife.

I closed my laptop, looked up, and didn't say a word. For those unfamiliar with the unspoken language of the North American two-career household, a closing laptop followed by a silent stare is the universal spouse signal that it's time to have a talk at the next convenient breaking point for *their* work. As Amy looked up from her laptop, I asked a now-familiar question: "What should I *do* next?" She understood this wasn't about that evening's task list, and that we were picking up on the conversation about my career next steps, which had been evolving over recent months.

Because Amy is brilliant, she used this opportunity to turn the tables on me, using one of my favorite mechanisms for discovering what motivates people most. She asked me the same question I had asked hundreds of others who sought out "informational interviews" with me over the years. In order to quickly discover someone's truest, most deeply rooted motivation, I always asked a disarmingly simple question, requesting a quick reply without too much contemplation: "What would you be most excited to do tomorrow if time and money were no limitation?"

Over the years, I noticed a universal theme in the answers: with the constraints of time and money removed, pretty much everyone wants to do good in some form. They want to have an impact on the world. They want to change lives. This is at once highly encouraging (go, humanity!) and also daunting—because time and money *are* constraints in the real world. Without an effective strategy for how to overcome or work within those constraints, far too many people become disheartened and discouraged, and let their dreams of doing good get pushed aside by the more pressing needs of daily life and work. But that dream, for most of us, is still there.

Now, on the other side of my own question, I discovered the same impulse in myself. But I didn't just want to do good. Having been on the do-good journey in philanthropy for a decade, I wanted to do *more* good, *better* good—at scale.

I answered Amy instantly and with complete certainty. "I want to give it all away," I said. "It is all right here on my hard drive and in my head. It's too important, too valuable, and too helpful to just disappear."

What was "it"?

"It" was a framework for designing, building, and growing social impact initiatives for any individual and any type of organization—nonprofit, for-profit, social enterprise, cross-sector initiatives—that can transform lives, communities, and the world.

"It" was a relentlessly refined and user-friendly tool kit that resulted from our team's curation of the best advice, guidance, and tools shared with us by subject matter experts, lawyers, financial whizzes, top-tier consulting firms, and other professionals who supported—along with the hard-earned lessons from trial and error—the impactful work of the Clinton Foundation during a decade of stratospheric growth and impact.

"It" was every piece of advice, all the collective guidance, and all the resulting resources fine-tuned over time to become universally simplified and even more easily used by our colleagues who worked on more than a dozen large initiatives.

"It" was all right there on my laptop, along with the ability to apply this incredible tool kit easily. I wanted "it" to become available to anyone who wanted to quickly, efficiently, and effectively make a positive impact on the world. And in that moment of clarity, I really did mean *anyone*. I didn't want to gatekeep this tool kit just for globe-trotting leaders, data-crunching social scientists, executive directors of nonprofits, program leaders of major philanthropic initiatives, former heads of state, or Ivy League lawyers.

My moment of clarity prompted me to explore a path I'd previously (vehemently) refused to ever even consider . . . *consulting*. Ugh. I was allergic to it because over the prior decade, I'd watched consultants come and go with, at best, mixed results. Too many consulting engagements ended with my legal team untangling disputes or negotiating unexpected partings. After enough of those, consulting sat near dead last on my list. Then I realized that consulting might just be the fastest way to "give it all away"—to put the tools in more hands. In the fall of 2015, I launched Beyond Advisers, a social impact consulting firm that helps people and organizations that are burning to change the world. So much for "vehemently."

Since our launch, my team has used a streamlined and simplified approach that makes doing good easier for our clients, partners, and collaborators. I've worked with leaders in organizations like Starbucks, Chobani, the United Nations Foundation, and with the teams supporting the social impact work of former Presidents Clinton, Bush, and Obama, as well as celebrities like Will Smith and Sean Penn, to organize, amplify, and systematize their social impact efforts. And beyond the big names that attract outsized attention are hundreds of other nonprofit, corporate, and cross-sector social impact leaders who aren't famous but whose work should be. You'll read about several of them in the pages ahead.

What I have learned is that literally everyone who is doing Better Good at any and every scale shares a common approach that aligns with this framework. With it, organizations new and old, big and small, with limited resources or loads of resources, can achieve social impact success. Those without this framework struggle unnecessarily, wasting precious time, money, and opportunities in their efforts to do good on urgent challenges. Not to mention that individuals and organizations can rarely afford much trial and error, lest they burn out or run out of resources.

After more than a decade of running Beyond Advisers, I've seen this approach and tool kit really work—for everyone, every time. It's both highly effective and implementable in the limited time and spaces of our individual lives, yet also infinitely scalable to the full-time, collaborative work of building and running huge, impact-driven nonprofits, social enterprises, and businesses.

Although Beyond Advisers has helped so many incredible people do incredible things, a few years ago I also found myself faced with a dilemma we'll address later in the book: scale. I wanted to share this framework and the lessons learned with the countless people in the world who weren't my clients but wanted to have an impact. Yet how could I do this? We either had to turn our boutique consulting firm into a social impact superagency or find some other way to advance the mission of wanting to "give it all away."

Luckily, the answer came to me in the form of a book. *This* book.

WHAT EXACTLY IS "GOOD," ANYWAY?

For the purposes of this book, good is *all* good. And *all* good is good.

It's everything you might consider a means to improving the world or even just one tiny corner of it. It's *way more* than the official acts of government agencies, nonprofit organizations, and corporate social impact efforts. It includes every positive act we might consider doing in our lives and in our work, every day in every way, no matter who we are, where we live, or what we do for a living. More specifically, it includes:

- *Every* volunteer role you've ever held, whether for a one-day fundraiser or a long-term affiliation.
- *Every* donation you've ever made to a worthy cause, whether $10 or $10 million.
- *Every* social impact, environmental social governance (ESG), or corporate social responsibility (CSR) activity by a for-profit company.
- *Every* public-private partnership that combines the strengths of governments, NGOs, nonprofits, and private sector businesses.
- *Every* cross-sector social impact initiative that involves partnerships of purpose that transcend multiple organizations.
- *Every* social enterprise that leverages new models for doing good, such as B Corps, L3Cs, etc.
- *Every* impact investing vehicle or innovative approach to social finance that business leaders and markets increasingly use and measure for good.

- *Every* "1 for 1" sales model, pioneered by TOMS Shoes (a pair gets donated for each pair purchased) and adopted by many others since.
- *Every* cause marketing and commercial co-venture in which "A portion of the proceeds will go to benefit X."
- *Every* role you play with any of these programs—whether as a leader, a volunteer, a consumer, or simply as a fan interested in learning and doing more in your own life and work.
- *Every* small action you take each day in your life because you're motivated to do good, from holding the door to picking up a piece of trash on a walk.

The list goes on and on. What matters is not that you become an expert on all these types of good—merely that you're aware that they're *all* good! And more importantly, they're all needed. Especially now.

WHY *BETTER* GOOD?

This book isn't called *Most Good*, or *New Good*, or *Different Good*. Because new isn't always better. More isn't always better. Different isn't always better. Better is better.

We get so tangled up in either chasing or assuming the arrival of the next big thing—more time, more money, more influence, a new job, a different cause—that we overlook the power we already have and the good we already do in the present. The world doesn't need you to have or do more; it needs you to *use what you already have to do better.*

Better is accessible and personal.

You don't need a new career, a foundation, a million-dollar grant, or a Fortune 500 business to start doing Better Good (though any of those can be awesome, too). You just need awareness, intention, and a willingness to act from where you are with what you have and what's immediately possible next.

Better gives us agency in every moment when so much feels outside our control. You can't always make *more* time, but you can use your time *better.* You can't instantly find *new* resources, but you can apply your resources *better.* You can't always change the *world,* but you can change your *corner* of it in a way that makes it better—and that's how the world changes.

WHAT THIS BOOK IS (AND ISN'T)

I've spent over twenty-five years as a corporate lawyer, nonprofit general counsel, and now adviser helping people and organizations design, grow, pivot, and even—wisely—shut down efforts across philanthropy, business, social enterprises, and cross-sector partnerships. I could go deep into the weeds on organizational structures, 501(c)(3) tax rules, and legal compliance for philanthropies and businesses, but you won't find any of that here. (You're welcome.)

Instead, this book focuses on the *through lines* that cut across our efforts to do good: the common strengths that make any good endeavor work, the pitfalls that weaken them, and the human motives that drive them. The "perfect" model doesn't exist; the "right" model is the one that works for *you.* What matters most is awareness and intent—put to work through a simple, reliable framework you can use at any scale.

That's the Better Good Framework you'll discover in this book. And because knowledge without implementation is useless, you'll also get a tool you can use to put the framework into action in your life and work—a simple downloadable worksheet that brings the framework to life.

THERE'S AN INFINITE (AND GROWING) DEMAND FOR GOOD

It's easy to get despondent when thinking about the size, scope, and stubbornness of the world's problems. Though I'm upbeat and optimistic by nature, I won't sugarcoat reality. Despite decades and record levels of do-gooding, the world's most pressing problems endure, and in some cases are worsening . . . rapidly.

Longtime challenges like hunger, homelessness, illiteracy, preventable illnesses, and poverty persist despite decades of focused efforts to eradicate them. And compounding challenges of climate change, geopolitical conflict, and growing income inequality sometimes make it feel like we're moving backward. Organizations dedicated to these issues (large and small, old and new, from the Red Cross and Greenpeace to José Andrés's World Central Kitchen) haven't yet "worked themselves out of a job"—which is ultimately the goal of each one. Anyone who follows the news knows that the demand for doing good is infinite and always growing.

But this seemingly endless need is no reason to give up on any of those challenges. In fact, it's quite the opposite—we need to rethink *how* we confront them. We have to find new and better ways to do Better Good. Fortunately, there are examples of success and models we can both learn from and apply to our own lives, work, and the organizations we serve and lead. And if we are individually, collectively, and organizationally committed to doing Better Good using shared frameworks, we just might move old needles in new ways and actually solve some of these long-term challenges.

Part of this opportunity lies in the supply side of the equation. What's the total supply of good in the world, and how much of that supply is still untapped? Hint: a *lot* is untapped.

Of course, we all know certain institutions and professions that are always doing good, such as schools, hospitals, religious groups, and philanthropic endeavors. But those represent just a fraction of the potential supply of good. By far the most overlooked, underappreciated, and undermanaged source of good is *our individual lives.*

THE SURPRISING GOOD NEWS

Every tick of the clock of every day we are alive is full of the potential to make an impact. An extraordinary, even mind-boggling amount of collective time and corresponding opportunity is available to each of us, and it refreshes with each day we're fortunate to awake into. And each of us is more equipped and empowered than ever before to make an impact. We're more instantly and infinitely connected, with access to information, resources, and opportunity to deploy our assets and resources for good.

When it comes to doing Better Good, here are three powerful, wonderful, yet little-known truths:

- Doing good is easier than most people realize.
- Opportunities to do good are widely available to each of us in our lives and work, every day—no matter who we are, where we live, or what we do. (And you're probably already doing more than you think you are.)
- There's an established, proven, and universally applicable pattern that humanity has followed to make a positive impact time and again, hiding in plain sight. Once you learn it, you can start putting it to work right away and see immediate results.

You may be wondering, in a world where we increasingly associate doing good with the biggest billionaires, big organizations, big brands with deep pockets, and big brains with world-changing ideas, does this book apply to you?

YES! Doing good is not reserved to a few, it's available to literally every single one of us. It doesn't matter if you are . . .

- A student who feels you have no spare time or resources to dedicate to doing good.
- A stay-at-home-parent with a craving to do more in and for your community.
- A professional who'd love to use your skills or network to do Better Good but doesn't know how or where to begin.

- A volunteer for one or more organizations that already do good (locally, nationally, or globally) but could be doing more, and/or doing the good you do better.
- A retiree finally enjoying enough free time to "give back."
- A millionaire or billionaire who wants to emulate the likes of Melinda Gates, Oprah, MacKenzie Scott, or Dolly Parton in leaving a powerful legacy of impact.

If *any* of these descriptions apply to you, you are reading the right book. In fact, just about the only group who won't benefit are hardcore skeptics who don't believe doing good is important, possible, or relevant to their lives or work. And even if you fall into that group, I hope you'll stay with us, too! I have every intention of winning you over.

THE PEOPLE YOU'LL SOON MEET

The entire book is heavily grounded by stories, bringing these tools and concepts to life across a broad range of experiences and passions. You'll meet:

- A suburban mom of five boys who accompanied her husband on a work trip to the Philippines, experienced a life-changing introduction to a pressing need, and founded a global nonprofit out of her home by leveraging the community and resources she discovered in her own backyard.
- A pioneering career woman who turned her passion for rescue dogs into a national network of like-minded people who transport shelter animals to adopting families all over the country.
- A movie star who set up and eventually shut down his family foundation, but who I still regard as a social impact success (because of, not in spite of, his decision) despite later public controversy.

- A billionaire who one day casually asked me to help him give away a *billion dollars*.
- Several former presidents, other politicians, and public servants of every stripe whose relentless efforts to continue their service after elected office have created new models for doing good that may just continue to inspire the next generation of world leaders to put aside partisanship and elevate public service.

The only common threads among these stories are that 1) all of these people were determined to leave the world better than they found it, 2) they all found ways to apply their unique resources, and 3) they all overcame the limitations of only having twenty-four hours per day, conflicting priorities, and, self-doubts (yes, even the billionaire and the movie star).

If you've ever felt like you should be doing Better Good in your life and your work, this book is for you. It's for you if you've quietly longed for purpose or feared you'd missed your moment. It's for you if you want to do good—but without losing your mind, your margins, or your meaning.

It's been over a decade since I closed my laptop where I sat on the couch and was fortunate enough to have my wife ask me precisely the question I needed to be asked. A lot has changed in my life and the world in the intervening years, but I'm happy to report the patterns of success for making a difference in the world haven't. This unflappability stems from the one unrelenting force that underlies all the strategies, tools, and habits that lead to effective social impact and are all driven by a uniquely human force: vision.

That's what I want to help you find over the chapters ahead: *your* vision.

Let's get you unstuck. Let's get you equipped. Let's unleash your highest and best purpose. Let's get you moving forward.

As the old saying goes, "The best time to plant a tree was twenty years ago; the next best time is today." Today is here.

PART I

THE SURPRISING TRUTH ABOUT GOOD

What if doing good isn't something you start from scratch—but something already built into who you are?

This part of the book reveals three foundational truths that will reframe how you see yourself and the world around you. Together, they show that your capacity for doing good is not limited by your job title, bank account, or zip code—it's hard-wired, human, and already in motion. You'll discover that:

- You're already doing more good than you realize.
- Humans are wired for good—it's a natural impulse that can be explained by science and drives our behavior in every society.
- Good gets built through the three sectors that shape modern life: government, nonprofits, and business.

Governments and nonprofits are designed to do good by definition. Business, driven by profit, often faces more scrutiny—but it's also the arena where some of the most meaningful and measurable good happens today. As long as humans demand good, business will keep evolving to meet that demand.

As you read these chapters, watch how your perspective shifts—how patterns appear, how possibilities multiply, and how the work of doing good starts to feel closer, clearer, and more attainable than ever. By the end, you'll see that the capacity for good isn't rare or reserved. It's already within you, and all around you.

CHAPTER 1

The Good You're *Already* Doing

Each one of us matters, has a role to play, and makes a difference.

—Jane Goodall

It was 2001 and I was twenty-four, a first-year corporate lawyer, with a head full of three years of law school but feeling like I actually knew nothing.

When you begin practicing law, you quickly realize that it's called "practicing" for a reason—that law school taught you to think, write, research, and to a certain extent, act like a lawyer. But like most professions, once you're in the "real world," you realize that you're really just getting started, and the learning and improving never ends. Most of the documents I'd draft for partners at my firm came back with more ink from their handwritten edits than from the printer, and then I'd start again. My sense of achievement after scaling the twin peaks of graduating law school and passing the bar exam was quickly replaced by the reality that I was now back at the base of a new, much larger mountain as a first-year associate.

Outside of work, I had a new condo in Chicago's newly revitalized West Loop neighborhood, yet I barely had any furniture to fill it. Not only was I strapped for cash, paying down my law school loans every month on top of living expenses, but I was also strapped for time. I had to scrounge for an hour here or there to see my very smart, very wonderful girlfriend, who was also in her first year of practice and lived just a few blocks away. Having been together since our first days of law school, we knew that marriage was in the cards, but I couldn't even begin saving for a ring. It was overwhelming.

Yet in my youthful exuberance I wanted to do it all, and I especially wanted to help make the world a better place by contributing to my communities and the causes that I cared about. I wanted to make a difference beyond my seemingly inept redrafting of language for simple memos, to say nothing of more complex merger and acquisition deals. But it didn't seem like I would ever find the time or means. I actually feared this might be the recipe for decades of do-gooding dreams deferred that could easily result in a midlife crisis. It wasn't hard to see how that could come to pass.

Then something unexpected happened. My first professional opportunity for doing good appeared in my inbox—and it had been hiding in plain sight all along: ferrets.

Yep, ferrets. You know, those surprisingly cute weasel-like animals that some (usually eccentric) people keep as pets. I had first gotten one, a little ferret named Aspen, in college. Unlike many ill-advised college pet acquisitions, I was delighted by and committed to ferret ownership. I had even read a book called *Ferrets for Dummies*. Like I said, huge nerd. Aspen was a joyful little soul whose sweet, goofy antics made her a perfect pet for our seven years together. And as a well-informed, conscientious ferret owner, I of course joined the Greater Chicago Ferret Association (GCFA). As one does. Its annual fee entitled me to its newsletter and other "benefits of membership," such as an annual gala (let your imagination run as wild as a ferret on that one!). I mostly just felt good supporting the cause of ferrets in need. Little did I know, this was the beginning of my own Better Good journey in animal rescue.

One day I received an email from Norman, the head of the GCFA, just as I was stressing about my law school loans, not having enough time with the person I loved, and not finding much personal fulfillment outside of work. Norman was a kind soul, like a tall, skinny Santa Claus with an even gentler disposition. "Hey Scott," he wrote. "I don't want to impose, but I know that you're a lawyer and was hoping you might be able to help."

GCFA had a problem with a volunteer who had effectively turned against them. The reasons were, from an outside perspective, minor and typical of sincerely held differences of opinion about running an animal rescue and engaging volunteers. The recourse in such situations is generally straightforward. If you're a volunteer and don't like something about the organization with which you're volunteering, you should probably just move on and redirect your efforts elsewhere. The volunteer in this case, however, was charged by emotion and had dug in for war: sending email blasts to other volunteers deriding the work of GCFA, making unfounded accusations driven by boiling emotions, and baselessly suggesting that donor dollars were being misspent and that future donations should be directed elsewhere. In other words, she got mad, had gone too far, and had crossed some significant legal lines.

Interesting, I thought. I called Norm, who got me up to speed on the conflict and asked if I could help them sort it out. I replied that I'd give it some thought and see what was possible. I liked feeling needed. I liked the sound of helping. And I was energized by the possibility of doing so.

Truth is, I was unsure about the process for leveraging firm resources for pro bono clients (much less ferret-related clients), and I knew I didn't yet have enough relevant legal expertise to help resolve the situation alone. So, I walked down the hall to chat with Sheryl, an employment lawyer at my firm. To my pleasant surprise, she agreed to join me for a foray into the world of ferret rescues and their volunteers.

After a few fact-gathering calls, we had the information necessary to gently explain the organization's perspective to the volunteer, lay out the increasingly serious damage she was posing for GCFA, and make a clear request that she move on from the organization . . . or else. This was the nicest version of what is commonly known as a "cease and desist" letter. It had to be written with firm clarity about the facts and the consequences, but also enough delicacy to be absorbed by its recipient, de-escalate a sensitive situation, and not appear unnecessarily heavy-handed if it was made public.

It worked! The volunteer realized she had taken things a bit too far, offered an unexpected apology, and agreed to move on. Ultimately, as is often the case for many of us when we're aggrieved, she simply wanted to be heard. And this process gave her that assurance and a new perspective. All was well again in the land of ferrets.

Meanwhile, I felt good. No, I felt *amazing*. I had actually helped—as a lawyer, with a firm at my back! It wasn't heavy or hostile. It was constructive, considerate, and kind to all involved. It was awesome. And I now had a vision for the future of what was possible with my new professional credential and the resources it could marshal. I was no longer just a stressed-out young lawyer running on the unyielding treadmill of adult life, with no space to help my community. I had done something good. And I did it with time that was already baked into my workday.

I was hooked.

HIDING IN PLAIN SIGHT

This episode from early in my career is really about "finding your ferret"—which is to say, how hard it can be to see the opportunities for doing good hiding in plain sight, and how easy it is to feel so busy and limited in our resources, that we're blinded to the many ways in which we can, fairly easily, make a positive impact in the world.

We all struggle to keep up with the hustle of daily life, which makes it hard to launch ourselves into new missions that we care about. Or we let limiting beliefs about what is possible hold us back. Sometimes those beliefs are about our own ability to make an impact or about the willingness of others, including our employers and colleagues, to help us in the effort.

The poet William Wordsworth wrote, "To begin, begin." Easier said than done, Wordsworth! How can we possibly make an impact when at every turn it appears we have nothing extra to spare—no extra time, extra money, extra energy . . . when it takes almost everything just to show up and get through the day?

On top of this, even if we do find the emotional wherewithal to throw ourselves into one of these causes, we face overwhelm. There is SO MUCH happening around the world that it can be paralyzing to even figure out what to focus on and where to start. How could I ever help combat climate change, reduce systemic violence, or clean up that pesky ocean plastic when I live in freaking Illinois!?

Even those of us who know we have a role to play can find it hard to know where to start, how to keep going, and what to do over time. Should I donate money? *To whom?* Should I join an organization? *Which one?* Should I volunteer my time? *When/where/how/for how long?* Should I just help my friend or my employer with their thing? *And will that be meaningful to me?* Are any (or all) of these tasks "one and done," or should I keep going indefinitely? *And how do I know?* Should I ask my employer for time or money to help? *Is that even a thing?*

This is why we often give up before we even start. We let the litany of questions—or worse, limiting beliefs about our own ability—win. Or we shrug and say that "they"—some indefinite group of more qualified do-gooders—should do something about some or all of those problems. Psychologists call this "the diffusion of responsibility" or "the bystander effect." Facing the stress of stepping out of our comfort zones, we put our hopes in the vague, impersonal "someone"—not realizing that each of us is as much "someone" as anyone else.

The first step to overcoming confusion, overwhelm, and passivity is to shift from a scarcity mindset ("I can't") to an abundance mindset ("I can") and turn "shoulds" into "musts."

YOUR SMALL, MEDIUM, AND LARGE ACTS OF IMPACT

As we shed those limiting beliefs, prime the abundance mindset, and turn shoulds into musts, let me explain one of the core principles of this book. You are *already* doing good—likely way more than you even realize. In fact, I bet *you are doing great* good. Each of us has an existing social impact footprint, driven by the small, medium, and large choices we make every day. And the good you're already doing will become the foundation for doing *Better* Good. So let's start by identifying these small, medium, and large acts of impact, so you can more intentionally *grow* that impact.

Small acts of impact are everywhere throughout our daily lives, often and easily overlooked, but abundant when we take a fresh look. These include picking up trash in public when you see it, recycling, and using reusable bags at the grocery store. They include rounding up for charity at the supermarket checkout and dropping a few bucks into a church collection plate or supporting the school fundraiser. They include donating used clothing or household items to a local shelter or some canned goods to a local food drive. They include those muffins you baked for that PTA bake sale, and that time you ran a 5K to raise money for cancer research. At the time, these small actions might have seemed minor and easy to dismiss as "no big deal"—but they absolutely add up and provide fuel for your Better Good engine. From the collective impact of each of our individual acts of kindness, to the example we set and the inspiration it spurs in others, the force multiplier effect of small acts should not be underestimated.

Medium acts of impact take more ongoing time and effort than small ones, but they're still part of your day-to-day. Medium acts include serving on a board or committee of your local PTA or church, joining a civic organization, or leading a Scout troop. They include volunteering for regular shifts at a local food kitchen, homeless shelter, or humane society, supporting vendors at your local farmer's market, and teaching your kids to prioritize volunteer and service opportunities.

In your workplace, they include implementing or taking advantage of a donation matching program or raising your hand when they need a new coordinator to run the service project, rallying your colleagues to join you, and doing it all again the following year.

Large acts of impact are meaningful steps that can change your life in significant ways, inspire others, and become pivot points for your entire future. These include an ever-widening array of opportunities such as buying an electric vehicle, running for office, converting your house to solar energy, serving in a branch of the military, or joining the Peace Corps, AmeriCorps, or City Year. They include committing to a multi-year board leadership term for a nonprofit or going back to school for a graduate degree in public service (been there!). They might even include leaving the private sector for a new career in government service or philanthropy (been there, too!).

The above examples aren't exhaustive, but will hopefully help you recognize all the good you and those around you are already doing. It's worth noting that what constitutes small, medium, and large will of course differ for everyone depending on their circumstances. What's a big act for some could be a small act for others, and vice versa.

Each of our lives include a unique blend of small, medium, and large impact we're already making, even if we don't recognize that impact as impact. Your journey of doing Better Good is already well underway, with important momentum to build on. After all, momentum begets momentum!

EXPLORING MY OWN IMPACT FOOTPRINT

If you inventory the things you're already doing, both big and small and in between, you'll uncover patterns. Those patterns reveal our (sometimes hidden) priorities. Let me start with my own experience as an example of discovering the good hiding in plain sight in my own life and work.

Let's pick up where we left off with the ferret shelter. When I was a young professional, I was, among other things, a lawyer, a ferret owner, and a member of the GCFA. Those pieces of my profile dovetailed when the organization needed specialized help that I could provide as an associate at a law firm committed to pro bono work. As a young adult, I was just beginning to pull the thread of my potential to do good. When I took the time to stop and further inventory my own impact footprint and uncover opportunities for expanding it in service of Better Good, I started seeing even more opportunities unfolding all around me.

For example, in my Chicago neighborhood, which had previously been a forgotten stretch of vacant brick and timber warehouses and parking lots, there were many needs and corresponding ways to be a positive part of its growth and transformation. There were community social events, planning sessions, and a brand-new community association that new residents like me could join to support and get involved in our soon to be thriving neighborhood.

At my law school—conveniently located near the same neighborhood where I lived and worked—there were alumni opportunities galore for recent grads that I had never thought about, until I realized they were just waiting for alumni like me to participate. For example, I could volunteer to mentor for student orientation sessions, résumé writing, interview practice, moot court judging, new student receptions, and career counseling. And they only required an hour here or there during the year and were conveniently located in the few blocks between my condo and my office.

On the street corner in those same few blocks I could buy a *Street-Wise* newspaper, a publication written and sold by Chicago's homeless population. More than just a handout of spare change to someone in need, this was a "hand-up" exchange of value. The stories in the paper provided readers with greater awareness of and connection to the plight of homelessness in Chicago.

Spurred by that eye-opening pro-bono experience in an office where I thought I had no "extra" anything, and in the communities of which I was a part (heck, in the three blocks between home and work alone), I started to see increasing opportunities to do Better Good everywhere I turned. It was like that first peek inside Willy Wonka's chocolate factory, when you realize that everything you see at every turn is sweet, sweet goodness.

This discovery process led me to explore other small- and medium-size opportunities, each leading me to the next. Those ultimately resulted in an unexpectedly big life detour to leave corporate law and pursue a masters of public service degree in Arkansas (of all places!). That experience then led me to an eye-opening field service project, a life-changing internship, a consequential capstone project, a post-graduation fellowship, and then a full-time position at the Clinton Foundation, where I would quickly, if unexpectedly, add a legal title onto my initial program work, and eventually become general counsel, all within ten years that flew by. Then *that* experience, in turn, opened the door to a subsequent consulting, counseling, coaching, and teaching career. The one "big" decision to pursue a master's degree for eighteen months led to a seismic shift in my career and life over the ensuing twenty years that continues unfolding into new adventures. Because these types of opportunities are hiding in plain sight all around us all, the same is possible for you. I'll just help you connect some dots.

As Wayne Dyer put it, "When you change the way you look at things, the things you look at change." Once you start looking *with* purpose for opportunities *of* purpose, you'll find them.

THE ELEMENTS OF THE SOCIAL IMPACT FRAMEWORK

We can start systematically identifying the good we're already doing—our social impact footprint—by better understanding the elements beneath every impact footprint, which are found in what I call the Better Good Framework.

In my experience, this framework underlies the social impact footprint of every individual, organization, and initiative working toward Better Good. And this approach has been highly effective for not only identifying the impact we're already having but also zeroing in on where we can leverage our resources to do more. It is used successfully by everyone from former U.S. presidents to A-list celebrities, from corporate titans to philanthropic superstars, to my neighbors.

The Better Good Framework consists of your PPP + TTT + SSS. Your PPP are your Profile, Platform, and Passion—who you are in the world. Your TTT are your Time, Talent, and Treasure—the resources you bring to making an impact. SSS elevates your existing social impact footprint by incorporating Scale, Sustainability, and Storytelling—how you go from good to great in making a long-term impact. And yes, every person and organization has all nine, to varying degrees, making for an individually unique and collectively dynamic experience for each of us in our lives and in our work.

Your *Profile* is comprised of your personal credentials and your network, whether that means an educational degree or your book club friends.

Your *Platform* is the stage you stand on in this world and from which you can impact the communities, organizations, and causes you care about. Your platform might include a social media following or a professional organization.

Your *Passion* encompasses the varying degrees of care and concern in your life. We all have a mix of passing concerns and crawl-through-glass causes we care about deeply, but for business, this might mean the culture they want to create, the stakeholders they serve, or the communities they support.

Your *Time* can be deployed in three categories. Some actions require literally "No Extra Time" and can be performed by anyone, no matter how busy. Some require "Found Extra Time," which is time out of your day, still relatively small, when you can have some impact. And some require "Transformative Time," a significant life change dedicated to a big commitment.

Your *Talents* are your skills and expertise, professional or otherwise. For example, I have talents as an attorney, a social impact consultant, a husband, a father, and a dog rescue volunteer.

Your *Treasure* includes financial or physical assets—and you're probably already giving more than you realize, whether you're maximizing employer matching benefits as part of an annual giving initiative, "buy one, give one" promotions, or even buying Girl Scout Cookies.

Then there's the three-part advance concept part of the social impact framework. These may be less familiar to those earlier in their journey of doing good but are helping any endeavor for good—big or small—go from good to great.

Scale is how you approach growing what already works so that you can further expand your impact toward even greater heights.

Sustainability is how you maximize efforts to keep going, even when the going gets tough, so that your impact lasts over time.

Finally, *Storytelling* is how we send a message to the world around us about how we make an impact so that we can engage with and attract the support of others who are similarly aligned.

By looking at your life and work through the lens of your current impact footprint and the Better Good Framework, which helps you envision the future of your impact, you'll see that you're not only already doing a great deal, but you can do even more good despite all of your busyness. Change the lens and the landscape shifts. You'll start spotting opportunities you used to overlook.

THE SOCIAL IMPACT FOOTPRINT FOR ORGANIZATIONS

"Enjoy dinner at City Barbeque and support the West Suburban Humane Society." As soon as I saw the first sentence of that promotional email, promising a 25 percent donation on every order on a specific night, I was sold.

As much as I wish my family cooked the same number of homemade dinners as my mom did, the truth is that we order in or eat out fairly often. As two working parents juggling careers with clients in diverse time zones who have unpredictable scheduling demands—

to say nothing of having two kids involved in cross-country, band, and soccer—time to cook remains elusive. And so, several times a week, we grab something on the way home. But I often feel a nagging guilt about it.

That's why I always feel the sweet relief of assuaged guilt when I see a promo like that one for City Barbeque. If I encounter an opportunity to combine the convenience of takeout with a fundraiser to benefit a local band, team, church, or humane society, I pretty much *have* to support the cause, right? The band, team, church, or puppies are counting on us!

And from the perspective of a business, this model is far more valuable than just making busy parents feel a little less guilty about falling short of the Martha Stewart home cooking ideal. It's a smart business strategy to build community engagement right into your marketing and advertising. It's a classic win-win example of doing well by doing good.

This strategy isn't limited to local community shops or restaurants. Some examples from big business that you'll learn more about as we go: Patagonia's famous "don't buy this jacket" tag on a jacket for sale encourages sustainable consumption. Walmart's move in the early 2000s to only carry concentrated laundry detergent reduced water use, plastic packaging, and shipping fuel consumption while increasing customer value *and* corporate profit; it also gave other retailers a rock-solid example of how to consciously and profitably create impact around the world.

Similarly, Bank of America's Better Money Habits program helps customers make their home ownership dreams a reality. Chase's online Financial Education Center advances financial literacy for their customers. The "1 for 1" model pioneered by TOMS has spread like wildfire, regularly influencing our purchasing decisions. Nike's Flyknit shoes aren't just among their highest performing; they use recycled polyester. And consumer products giant Unilever reports that their brands with a strong sustainability focus, such as Dove, Ben & Jerry's, and Hellmann's, consistently outperform others, driving 70 percent of the company's growth.

From the convenience of a dinner out that makes us feel full in more ways than one, to previously simple decisions about laundry detergent that we didn't even know could be part of a social impact initiative or our own social impact footprint, doing good has become interwoven into our everyday lives. There's no escaping such options—and not a moment too soon.

As political movements shift and the role of government in social impact ebbs more than it flows, there's a greater opportunity than ever for each of us individually, and all of us collectively, to step up and step into our greatest social impact potential. As consumers, we'll see later that one of the ways we can do Better Good is by using our *Treasure* to further social impact. Where we spend our dollars matters, and if we can learn to recognize the social impact of the business all around us, we can support it more intentionally. Shift the vantage point and new options come into view.

Can you see the opportunities? They're everywhere. And we're just getting started!

INTO THE GOLDILOCKS ZONE

A quick confession: starting in sixth grade, I went to Space Camp—four times. I wanted to be an astronaut. Badly. (I know, huge nerd. And proud of it.) I haven't made it to space (yet), but I've never lost the sense of wonder that comes from looking up. And occasionally, that perspective helps clarify things here on Earth.

Astronomers use the term *Goldilocks Zone* to describe the narrow band around a star where conditions are *just right* for life to thrive. Too close and a planet burns. Too far and it freezes. But in the Goldilocks Zone, things grow, evolve, and endure.

The same principle applies to how we live and work for Better Good. When your passion (what fuels you) aligns with your proficiency (what you're good at), you enter your own Goldilocks Zone—the place where energy and ability meet. It's where effort feels natural, results compound, and you're most likely to keep going when things get hard. My overriding passion as an adult turned out not to be space, or even ferrets, as cute and whimsical as they are. And my proficiencies certainly weren't as an astronaut (and while I have loved caring for several types of animals, this just isn't a skill I can do much with beyond treating my pets really well). I discovered that my Goldilocks Zone is precisely what this book is all about—helping people discover where joy and impact meet so they can do Better Good.

You'll see The Goldilocks Zone Principle appear again throughout the Better Good Framework. It helps clarify your Profile, powers your Platform, and comes into fuller focus in Passion. It also shapes how you'll think about your Time, Talent, and Treasure, guiding you toward the kinds of good that last.

So consider this your first launch sequence—a mindset that will keep you centered, balanced, and ready to launch into your own Goldilocks Zone of impact.

KEY TAKEAWAYS AND ACTION ITEMS

Key Takeaways

- **Every person and organization already has an Impact Footprint**—a base of good that's already happening, whether or not you've noticed it.
- **"Finding your ferret"** means spotting the opportunities hiding in plain sight, starting where you are, with what you have, and what you can do now.
- **Small acts add up.** When you build on what you're already doing, momentum grows naturally.
- **An abundance mindset** ("I can") opens doors that a scarcity mindset ("I can't") keeps closed.
- The Better Good Framework—your **Profile, Platform, Passion, Time, Talent, and Treasure** (PPP + TTT)—shows you where and how to grow your impact next.
- **Scale, Sustainability, and Storytelling** (SSS) complete the Better Good Framework for maximum impact over time.
- **Identify your Goldilocks Zone.** Pay attention to where your *passion* overlaps with what you're best at (proficiency). This overlap is your "Goldilocks Zone" where effort feels natural, results compound, and your greatest opportunities for Better Good are found.

Action Items

For Individuals

- **Start with what's already good.** Make a list of the small, medium, and large ways you already contribute to your community or help others.
- **Find your "ferret."** Pick one thing you care about and one skill or resource you can offer—it doesn't have to be big or perfect.
- **Check the Goldilocks Zone.** Identify causes you already care about *and* you're already good (or getting good) at contributing to—those are early Goldilocks Zone candidates for Better Good.
- **Act close to home.** Choose one simple action you can take this week where you already live, work, or spend time.
- **Engage others.** Tell one person what you're doing and invite them to join or share an idea.
- **Keep it going.** Repeat the action next week. Momentum builds through consistent action.

Action Items

For Organizations

- **Map your Impact Footprint.** List the ways your organization or team already helps others or strengthens community—even in small ways.
- **Build on what works.** Choose one small or medium action to expand or repeat this quarter.
- **Goldilocks fit (quick scan).** Identify efforts that align a core organizational passion (mission/vision/values) with core team skills and abilities (what you do best).
- **Make it accessible.** Create one opportunity for your team or your customers to do good that takes little or no extra time for them.
- **Celebrate and share.** Tell the story of one small impact you made together in internal communications or in external marketing and communications networks (e.g., newsletters, social media, impact reports, etc.). These stories will create momentum that inspires the next round of action.

CHAPTER 2

Humans Are Wired for Good

People will forget what you said, people will forget what you did, but people will never forget how you made them feel.

—Maya Angelou

Let's talk about the F-word. No, not *that* one. *Feel* is the most important "F word" in this book, and perhaps in our lives. As we set out to explore opportunities to do Better Good, here's an important fact you must keep in mind: *humans are biologically, emotionally, and socially wired for good because feeling good is addictive.* This has been true across all of human history, across every geographic region, system of government, religion, and culture. The average person's attraction to goodness runs deeper than any fad—hard science backs it up.

What if you want to do good, but you don't know where to start—so you don't? Or what if you sprint for a few weeks and flame out? That's not a character flaw; it's biology misfiring. And it feels bad.

Want to know the antidote to feeling bad? It's feeling good. Our bodies are ancient hardware, still processing modern stresses the same way they do the stress of being chased by a bear—same fight-or-flight cascade, same side effects. The good news: the same body that floods us with stress-inducing cortisol also offers a counterbalancing system of feel-good chemicals we can recruit on purpose. If we're going to step into Better Good, remember two truths: 1) we're wired for it, and 2) feeling good about doing good is a secret weapon you can summon when you need it most.

If you've ever lost a few minutes or even an hour to a social media rabbit hole of feel-good videos, you've felt this phenomenon in real-time.

A hearing-impaired toddler has just been fitted with a cochlear implant and is sitting on his mother's lap. The doctor turns on the hearing aid for the first time. The eager mother gently asks, "Can you hear Mommy's voice?" The child turns his head, nods, and smiles the biggest smile you've ever seen in pure delight. The child cries, the mother cries, the doctor and nurse cry—and you start to cry, too.

A dog sits in a barren, concrete kennel at a crowded shelter, where the caption tells us that she's been stuck for months. As some humans approach, her head is sunk low, her ears are back, and her eyes stare straight ahead with what appears to be sadness and anxiety. Then a leash appears, voices rise, and the pup's tail starts wagging cautiously, then frantically. She is suddenly alert and excited as she realizes that she's finally being adopted. As she leaves with her new family, we can see that freedom has turned her into an exuberant, transformed state, with the promise of a happy life ahead of her. Is someone chopping onions in here?

These videos aren't just appealing; they're addictive. What's going on when we watch them, along with countless movies, TV episodes, and even commercials that elicit similar emotions? (Is that Sarah McLachlan singing "*In the arms of an angel*" I hear?) Why do we feel good when we *do* good, when we *see* others doing good, and even when we just *think* about—or read these examples of—good?

THE BRAIN CHEMISTRY OF GOOD

Our brains contain a sophisticated reward system that constantly reinforces a wide range of positive behaviors, from our pumped-up feelings after workouts to the warm and fuzzies that follow gestures of romantic love, to tearjerking acts of familial support, to the beautiful buzz that follows random acts of kindness—given *or* received (same science on both sides).

Each time we do something that triggers this neurochemical reward system, we automatically get an incentive to do it again . . . and again . . . and again. We want that feeling everywhere, all the time, and there's no limit to the amount of good we crave. It's similar to the addictive appeal of a giant bucket of popcorn or a bag of chips and even mirrors the addictive behaviors of drug use—just a lot healthier for us and more beneficial for the world. Win-win. Yay for healthier addictions!

The most important neurochemicals driving this process are dopamine, serotonin, oxytocin, and endorphins. In his book *Leaders Eat Last*, leadership expert Simon Sinek describes these as "happy chemicals." They are the same ones released when we receive a compliment, win a game, finish a race, fall in love, or experience other deep connections or tender moments. But even more important: these brain chemicals have been absolutely essential to the survival of our species. It's useful to know a bit about how they work, so we can unlock their potential to inspire even Better Good. Here's a quick, non-scientist's overview:

Dopamine is the "reward chemical." It is released when we achieve something meaningful, motivating us to repeat behaviors that bring joy. Acts of kindness, generosity, or witnessing good deeds trigger dopamine, reinforcing the satisfaction we feel and encouraging us to do more good. Research shows that even anticipating doing something kind can release dopamine, giving us a boost before the act is completed. Dopamine is the brain's way of saying "Do that again!" Each success triggers a rush that motivates us to keep going, creating a built-in feedback loop for perseverance.

Serotonin is the brain's mood stabilizer. It creates a sense of well-being when we connect with others and contribute positively. It's the chemical equivalent of a deep breath and a good night's sleep. Helping others or observing acts of compassion boosts serotonin levels, fostering a calm sense of purpose and contentment. Studies suggest that serotonin release is closely tied to feelings of respect, pride, and recognition in social settings, meaning that when our good deeds are acknowledged or we see others benefit, serotonin strengthens the positive feedback loop.

Oxytocin is nicknamed "the love hormone" or "the bonding chemical." It's released during acts of kindness or connection, fostering trust and empathy. When we engage in or witness acts of care and kindness, oxytocin deepens our sense of connection with others, building stronger social bonds. It's your brain's version of a group hug—and why you want to call someone to be sure they got home safe. Psychologists also call it the "moral molecule" because oxytocin not only encourages trust and generosity but also makes us more likely to act selflessly, creating ripple effects of good in our communities. This neurochemical makes people feel safe and more inclined to work together toward shared goals. Sinek notes that oxytocin's effects are cumulative; the more we experience positive interactions, the more trust and cooperation grow. Oxytocin is essential for sustainable, people-focused leadership that prioritizes the well-being of others over short-term gains. It builds love for our romantic partner, our family, friends, colleagues, and community.

Endorphins are known as "the natural painkiller." They reduce discomfort and stress, creating feelings of euphoria and relaxation during activities like exercise, laughter, or acts of kindness. They're the reason a long run, a big laugh, or a perfectly timed fist bump can make the world feel right again. When we do good or see others doing good, endorphins are released that enhance our feelings of joy and help us feel emotionally uplifted. Interestingly, endorphins are also triggered by what researchers call "helper's euphoria," the unique rush of satisfaction we feel after brightening someone else's day.

When we feel good after doing or seeing good, we're awash in some combination of these chemicals working together to prime us for more. And while this science may be new to you, it has been part of our biology and the communities we humans have created since we first arrived on the planet. These chemicals impact our behavior in our homes, communities, and the organizations we serve, every day.

THE HAPPY CHEMICALS IN ACTION

Human beings have survived since our hunter-gatherer days by working together, whether in clans, tribes, villages, cities, or larger organizations. Anthropologists agree that cooperation is essential for survival, so our brains evolved to produce these feel-good chemicals whenever we worked together toward shared goals. From the cavemen onward, those who helped provide food, care for kids, and build resources for the common good were rewarded with both the happy chemicals in their brains and the mutual support of their communities. Their altruism made them more likely to live long enough to pass down their genes to the next generation.

Good deeds foster stronger social bonds and more happy chemicals, leading people to do even more good deeds, thereby enhancing the survival of communities through tough times. Repeat over and over for 200,000 years or so.

We continue to experience this same phenomenon today, whether in small moments like dropping some quarters into a Salvation Army bucket or grand gestures like saving a community center through a breakdancing competition (the plot of *Breakin' 2: Electric Boogaloo*, a rad '80s breakdancing movie with a social impact message before its time). It's why you hold your head a bit higher, pull your shoulders back, and feel just a bit more awesome when you hold the door for a stranger, help a struggling mother get her stroller up some stairs, or undertake just about any other act of kindness. Research shows that the activation of the brain's reward centers is the same for all such moments, consistent across ages, genders, countries, and cultures.

Even small acts of kindness or moments of empathy trigger this reward system, which makes us want to repeat and perpetuate good deeds. Whether you're volunteering, helping a neighbor, receiving a compliment from (or giving one to) a colleague at work, or simply watching a heartwarming video, your brain rewards you with these chemicals the same way it rewarded our ancestors, around the world and throughout history. In his book *Good to Great*, Jim Collins coined the phrase "flywheel of momentum" to describe how small actions, consistently repeated, lead to exponentially greater impact and create lasting change and sustained long-term growth. This flywheel of momentum has driven human evolution for millennia, fueled by the happy chemicals coursing through our brains and driving us to higher levels of Better Good as a species surviving on a fragile blue marble spinning through space.

Keep this in mind whenever you hear skeptics disparage doing good because they think it doesn't belong in one industry or sector, or that human nature is ruthlessly competitive. That's simply not true. It *is* "feel good mumbo jumbo" if mumbo jumbo is shorthand for the analysis of the interplay of chemicals. But it isn't unserious or unscientific. The fact remains that doing good for others is a fundamental, undeniable part of human biology and psychology, and benefits every aspect of life and work.

This doesn't mean, of course, that there aren't exceptions or fair arguments about limitations, boundaries, and balance. It also doesn't mean that *everyone* is equally wired for good. But throughout the broad sweep of human history, those who completely reject empathy and benevolence, or believe it should be sequestered only to certain parts of life, have been a very small minority—and are sorely mistaken. Betting against good is betting against the best parts of human nature.

Then there is the "moment" in which we find ourselves of late. The prolonged noise of politics and culture wars can make it feel like we're facing a crisis of confidence in human kindness itself. Many people are asking questions they've never had to ask before: Is it still okay to care about doing good? How much is safe to do—

or talk about—publicly? Will I be shouted down for being "woke" (and is that good or bad)? Sound familiar?

The loudest voices often reward outrage over empathy and conflict over care, leaving individuals and organizations unsure whether they can help without being misread or do good without triggering political tripwires that increasingly seem set to catch us in the act of doing good. That uncertainty has a chilling effect. It breeds self-doubt, slows action, and, in some cases, leads to paralysis or outright retreat—especially inside institutions where the fear of division or becoming a target can outweigh the instinct to serve or just be a good citizen (or corporate citizen). But this is an illusion of the moment, not a change in our nature. And it's an opportunity to reaffirm who we really are—as people, communities, organizations, societies, and even nations—and the kindness that glows at the core of 99.9 percent of us humans.

The noise may be loud and intentionally divisive, but it hasn't altered the reality that humans are wired for good—and always have been. In fact, the very conditions that make doing good feel harder are the ones that make it more necessary. The pendulum may be swinging, but it doesn't redefine who we are. It can't. Instead, it clarifies the stakes—and underscores the importance of having a clear, steady framework to help individuals and organizations move forward with confidence, intention, and resolve. Never forget for a moment, or in any moment: this is who we are, and how we've always been.

THE RIPPLE EFFECT OF THE HAPPY CHEMICALS

These biological facts also help explain why we're inclined to "pay it forward" when we benefit from someone else's efforts to do good on our behalf, especially when we most need it or least expect it. We get a jolt of happy chemicals from receiving their good, and then we subconsciously crave more rewards by doing more good. Those chemical responses can trigger a chain reaction of kind words and deeds.

Have you ever brought donuts to work for no reason, put them in the break room, and then shared the news with others? Or maybe you discovered that someone else had brought them and enthusiastically spread the word. It wasn't just the sugar rush impacting your desire to tell everyone; it was the happy chemicals prompting you to share your joy and excitement as a path to building community, even if only over a glazed donut. The same applies to those volunteer days when you showed up with surprising enthusiasm for wearing matching T-shirts and spending the day doing something good, together, for your community. It wasn't about the T-shirt.

The brain has specific "mirror neurons" that help us empathize and feel joy when we do good or even when we just see others being kind or generous.

The longer you dwell on such moments or content, real or fictional, the happier you'll feel and the more likely you'll subconsciously want to pay it forward by doing something good for others. It's like nourishment for our brain, emotions, and hardwired desire to feel good. It reinforces itself, drawing us toward Better Good.

NEXT LEVEL GOOD

We can't be what we can't see. That's why practices like mindfulness, meditation, visualization, and even manifestation are like special Jedi techniques for nurturing happy chemicals. These aren't escapes from reality, but ways to shape how we see and shape it. These practices help us train our attention toward possibility instead of paralysis. They help rewire our perception of what's possible within the sometimes brutal realities of the world's problems.

Science also backs these next-level practices. Our human bodies are still pretty primitive, and therefore subject to simple hacking by our own brains. Just as it's true that thinking negative thoughts—or envisioning something sad or tragic, real or imagined, past, present or future—can bring us down and put us in a funk, positive transformation can happen by simply thinking about, visualizing, or anticipating positive experiences. Doing so activates the same happy chemical pathways that light up when we actually experience them. Ever taken a stroll down memory lane with some old family photos or scroll through Instagram videos that whisked you back to a simpler time, flooding you with feelings of warmth and nostalgia? That's your brain and body reinforcing those good feelings. In other words, imagining good primes us to *notice* good, to *feel* good, and to *create* more good. Momentum begets momentum.

Consider the Baader-Meinhof phenomenon—also called the "frequency illusion"—that kicks in when heightened awareness makes you notice more of what was already there. This is the phenomenon of test-driving a red car and then seeing red cars everywhere. The number of red cars didn't change; your attention did. When you aim that same lens at the good we see in the world, you'll see more of it, too. The perception shift doesn't pretend things are better than they are or that the problems of the world aren't present—it simply helps you see the good that *is* there, more vividly and more often, so you can build on it.

When we practice mindfulness or meditation, we quiet the noise long enough to notice what's working, who's helping, and where goodness and hope still exist. When we visualize a better world—or even a better next step we can take within it—we start to believe it's possible. That belief shifts behavior, and behavior compounds into impact. Better Good begins in our minds long before it manifests in our actions.

Let me be clear, this isn't blind optimism or toxic positivity. It's conscious awareness—choosing to see the good that's already around us so we can build upon it. The more we train our brains to look for progress, generosity, and connection, the more capable we become of creating those moments ourselves. We can literally "become the change we wish to see in the world."

On many occasions in my work with clients, I'm asked what Kool-Aid I'm drinking. They want to know how I arrive with a perhaps psychopathic level of enthusiasm to some pretty challenging circumstances, conditions, and conundrums that clients—and the world—are facing or seeking to address. I wish I could tell you I was a Zen master. I'm not . . . my monkey brain runs wild. But I am exceedingly intentional about seeing the good around us, even if it is only found in the opportunity to try to take the next right step to "be the change."

That's the real next level of good: not just reacting to what is, but intentionally envisioning what could be—and then acting on it.

WHY HAPPY CHEMICALS MATTER NOW MORE THAN EVER

As I write, we're living through one of the most turbulent periods in modern history. The headlines alone can send our cortisol levels soaring before breakfast. The amount of division, outrage, and uncertainty is enough to make anyone feel like the world is running low on hope and high on despair. There are more than enough bad chemicals and bad feelings to go around.

But the same biology that powers our stress response gives us the antidote in the form of the happy chemicals, our body's built-in system for continuous renewal, resilience, and connection. When we intentionally engage them—through kindness, connection, contribution, gratitude, or purpose—we're giving ourselves the biological capacity to face and counteract the pain we see in the world.

These same pathways don't stay at home when we head to work or into other organizations we serve, support, or lead. They shape how teams connect, how customers respond, and how institutional cultures endure and evolve. Leaders who design for small wins, recognition, and real connection aren't being "soft"—they're being intentional about leveraging biology to drive performance and retention, as we'll see in the next chapter.

This isn't unrealistic optimism. It's about agency. We can't always control the problems that surround us, but we *can* control the chemistry we cultivate within us. The more we nurture practices that release and reinforce these positive feedback loops—doing good, witnessing good, celebrating good—the stronger and more unflappable we become. We literally build the internal infrastructure to keep showing up for others and for ourselves.

This is why awareness of our happy chemicals matters so much right now. They remind us that our capacity for hope and goodness isn't a naive view of the world, but rather, a natural way of coping with it. It's how humanity has always adapted and advanced, from the first communities that gathered around campfires to the global networks of changemakers working to heal and rebuild today—including you.

This is where the science and the soul of Better Good meet. When we recognize that our biology rewards us for helping others, we start to see the path toward our passions more clearly. The components of good that make us light up—the causes that move us, the people who energize us, the moments that leave us inspired—are all clues from our biology pointing us toward purpose. When we follow those signals, we align what feels good with what *does* good. That's where momentum begins. That's where the Better Good flywheel starts to spin.

So in this hard moment and the many to come in the future—even amid times of noise, negativity, and exhaustion—remember that your body already holds the chemistry of Better Good. Your job is to use it. To lean into what lifts you. To notice the good, do the good, share the good, and repeat—all in service of more of those happy chemicals coursing through your veins. Because the more we nurture the science of feeling good, the more equipped and motivated we are to create a future full of Better Good.

KEY TAKEAWAYS AND ACTION ITEMS

Key Takeaways

- **The F-word.** The most important F word to our biology and collective human experience is the word *feel.*
- **Humans are wired for good.** We feel good when doing good because that's how we've been wired since the beginning of humankind.
- **This wiring serves important functions.** Our innate happy-chemical "engine" prevents two common failures: paralysis before you start and burnout after you do. Learning to activate your happy chemicals is key to sustained Better Good.
- **Greater understanding = greater impact.** Understanding this wiring, and leveraging it at home, in our communities, and at work, helps us do good more often and more effectively.
- **It keeps us going when the going gets tough.** By recognizing that the imperative to do good isn't just moral but biological, we can harness that energy in our lives and work to keep doing Better Good.

Action Items

For Individuals

- **Embrace your biology!** Write down what experiences make you smile, sigh, and feel a little flutter in your life and in your work.
- **Heighten the experience:** Deliberately pay attention to your body whenever you do something good for others or see others do so. What happened to your posture, breathing, sense of anxiety, or calmness in that moment? How long did those changes last? Do you find that the more you pay attention, the more you see (you should)?
- **Curate your scroll:** Intentionally curate your social media ecosystem to prioritize the motivational quotes, clips, or other content that you find especially inspiring. Bulk up your social media diet with a heaping dose of goodness and turn this pastime into a purpose-driven practice.
- **Crank the flywheel by engaging others:** Share your growing awareness that feeling good about doing good is a natural part of our wiring and makes our everyday experiences better. Compare notes with others and explore how this shared discovery amplifies your individual and collective efforts.

- **Inventory your efforts:** Think about the work you do that brings you joy—at home, at work, and in other organizations you serve and support. Which efforts are most emotionally fulfilling? Begin an intentional "happiness inventory" that will help you focus further efforts going forward.

Action Items

For Organizations

- **Design for small wins (dopamine).** Break big initiatives into visible micro-milestones and celebrate each one publicly (e.g., #WinOfTheWeek in Slack or all-hands).
- **Institutionalize gratitude (serotonin).** Add a 90-second "shout-outs and thanks" segment to every meeting; rotate who leads it so recognition is peer-to-peer, not just top-down.
- **Create connection rituals (oxytocin).** Start meetings with a brief "human check-in" or a prompt like "one good thing you noticed this week." Keep it short but constant; consistency beats length.
- **Model the chemistry.** Leaders who show empathy, celebrate progress, and express human emotions like joy and excitement create the best kind of contagious energy.

- **Build connection.** Create simple rituals—a team lunch, a volunteer day, or a quick check-in—to boost oxytocin and trust.
- **Share stories of impact.** Regularly highlight real examples of your work making a difference to fuel serotonin and pride in newsletters, customer and stakeholder communications, and on social media.
- **Inject fun.** Laughter, movement, or shared service projects release endorphins—and strengthen culture.

CHAPTER 3

Doing Good in Groups: Government, Nonprofits, and Business

Out of clutter, find simplicity.
From discord, find harmony.
In the middle of difficulty lies opportunity.
—Albert Einstein

Hamdi Ulukaya almost threw the mailer away.

It was 2005, and the thirty-two-year-old Turkish immigrant was standing over a stack of junk mail in his small apartment in upstate New York. When he had arrived months earlier, his biggest dream was to learn English and maybe go to business school someday. But when he saw a notice about a shuttered Kraft yogurt plant for sale in South Edmeston, something about it caught his attention. The facility had been closed for more than a year, the equipment was rusting, and the town around it was fading. But for Hamdi, it looked like possibility.

Maybe it was curiosity. Maybe it was instinct. Maybe it was that stubbornly optimistic and inspiring belief shared by so many first-generation immigrants and Americans—that anything, given enough care and purpose, could be rebuilt.

So, instead of tossing it, Hamdi called the real estate agent and made an appointment to check it out. He walked through the silent factory floors, heard the echo of his footsteps, and saw what others didn't: potential. Not just for bringing a yogurt factory back to life, but for helping other people like him achieve their own dreams.

Everything was stacked against him. He didn't have money or access to investors. He didn't have a business plan that would impress a Wall Street boardroom. But what he did have (along with his vision of what was possible) was access to something America has long-offered its boldest dreamers: a loan through the U.S. Small Business Administration (SBA).

That loan—made possible by a partnership between government and private lenders—was the spark.

Hamdi bought the plant, hired four of its laid-off workers, and began making yogurt the way he remembered it from his childhood in eastern Turkey. He named his company Chobani, the Turkish word for *shepherd*. Within a few years it would go from a start-up in a forgotten, declining town to the top-selling Greek yogurt brand in America, employing thousands, revitalizing communities, and reshaping an industry.

The SBA, a government institution, made that life-changing loan. Local dairies provided the milk, giving them a stable new market. State officials helped Hamdi expand operations and navigate regulations across multiple states. Community colleges trained new employees. Local families found jobs, purpose, and connection. And as the business grew, so did Hamdi's commitment to pay it forward—through profit sharing with employees, inclusive hiring of refugees, and ultimately the creation of the Tent Partnership for Refugees, which now engages hundreds of companies worldwide to help displaced people rebuild their lives through work.

Hamdi Ulukaya's story is bigger than a product or industry. And it's so much more than just a feel-good headline or a retrospective on a business origin story. It's about our interconnectedness, our shared humanity, and the potential for doing good in our lives and work that can be unleashed when individuals, organizations, and institutions operate together toward their highest and best purpose in pursuit of Better Good—in and across government, the private sector, and civil society. It's a love letter to true American greatness. It's proof of a truth we too often forget: that doing good is rarely the work of a single actor or institution. In reality, it's the result of diverse interconnected forces working in harmony to make our world a better place.

THE ROLE OF INSTITUTIONS

In the last chapter, we explored how our brains reward kindness, connection, and contribution—traits that have fueled human survival since the beginning of time. But the modern world no longer runs on campfires and tribes. Today, in societies like the United States and other developed nations, the gears of human progress are powered by institutions: government, nonprofits, and business. Over generations, we've built these systems to advance our shared pursuit of making life better for everyone. Each gear is distinct, yet interdependent—turning in relation to the others to keep society moving forward.

Nearly everything we do, every day, happens in relationship to and with these three institutions, including our pursuit of Better Good. We live in a society built, maintained, and managed by the functions of government. We learn in nonprofit schools, get health care in nonprofit hospitals, and serve, and are served by, our fellow humans through nonprofit institutions ranging from philanthropy to churches to associated charities. We go to work and buy or sell products and services in private sector businesses. These are the interrelated, overlapping, and dynamic systems where we show up and engage with one another in the increasingly complex societies in which we live and work.

For the most part, it all works . . . at least historically. Government provides for common defense through expansive military and defense systems; our general daily health and welfare are enhanced through the work of institutions like the Centers for Disease Control (CDC) and the Food and Drug Administration (FDA) that track disease, monitor quality and safety of crops, food, and medications; we have infrastructure that helps us go about our lives, in the form of safe roads, bridges, and aviation systems that allow most of us to strap into an airplane seat without even thinking about the Federal Aviation Administration (FAA) facilitating safe travel. All of this requires no extra effort from us beyond paying our taxes, voting, and generally being decent citizens. "Good government" does much more than meets the eye.

Like the government, nonprofits do good by definition, too. I'm using the literal definition of nonprofits, meaning any institution that does not involve a profit-seeking return. In practice, this includes philanthropy that funds good causes and the charities that deliver them—housing the homeless, feeding the hungry, rescuing animals, and advancing thousands of efforts that fall outside what government and business can't or won't do. Speaking in tax code (humor the lawyer in me for a second, please), these include everything from charitable organizations (the classic 501(c)(3)s) to advocacy groups (501(c)(4)s), professional associations (501(c)(6)s), labor unions (501(c)(5)s), social clubs (501(c)(7)s), and veterans' groups (501(c)(19)s). Together, they represent every corner of civic life that puts mission before money.

Then there is the private sector. Unlike government and nonprofits, businesses are not designed for social return—they're designed for profit. For this reason, companies face sharper pressures and scrutiny than governments or nonprofits for the Better Good work they do. Market demands, stakeholder expectations, and cultural scrutiny require a different set of considerations for businesses to justify their efforts to wade into social good. And yet, from early American company towns and fair-trade roots, to modern supply chains and commitments beyond shareholders alone, businesses have long acted as corporate citizens within the same ecosystem that sustains them. In layman's terms it benefits them to do good by society and to serve a wider array of stakeholders, a term that applies to everyone a business touches across the value chain beyond shareholders alone, including employees, customers, suppliers, neighbors/communities, investors, shareholders, and the environment.

Today the role of business as a corporate citizen is under intense pressure: customers and employees increasingly expect products and practices that do less harm and more good, while some investors and commentators urge stricter focus exclusively on financial returns. Underlying realities and a sensible discussion about appropriate roles and boundaries are too often reduced to political attack, partisan debate, and culture-war slogans like "go woke, go broke."

But there's a bigger, undeniable market reality at play. Markets serve humans, and humans are wired for good. So demand for credible corporate good is durable—even as backlash rises and falls with political tides. That tension—profit engine versus public expectation, speed and scale versus trust and guardrails—is precisely why we'll unpack the private sector more deeply, and explore how businesses can meet their core mandate *and* their civic responsibilities in ways that are practical, measurable, and built to last.

In short, these are the three gears of our civic architecture. When the gears mesh and move well together, the ecosystem underlying Better Good runs smoothly: government sets standards and supports shared infrastructure, business supplies the torque that carries ideas into daily life in demand-driven markets, and nonprofits turn values into service at the edges where the other two leave off. If one gear slips, the others can take up slack. When they engage together, progress moves and compounds, as we saw with the inspiring growth of Chobani. If one of them seizes up, the others are profoundly impacted, and ripple effects extend throughout society.

With this interdependent mechanism in mind, let's look at each gear in turn—focusing most deeply on business, where there's a more delicate balance between human, market, shareholder, and stakeholder mandates, and where much of today's friction, acceleration, and opportunity for serving greater good now lie.

GOVERNMENT: OUR ORIGINAL ENGINE OF COLLECTIVE BETTER GOOD

At its best, government is humanity's grand experiment in shared progress: we pool resources, elect representatives, and build systems that serve everyone. From public schools and clean water to National Parks and NASA, the infrastructure of modern life exists because we organized for Better Good.

When you think about it, the SBA loan that launched Chobani was the essence of a government institution doing exactly what it was designed to do: empower its citizens to create opportunity and community value. Some might call it bureaucracy. I call it Better Good at scale. It is an example of government operating at its best.

Government builds bridges, literally and figuratively. It created Social Security, the GI Bill, the CDC, and the countless grants and protections that allow businesses, nonprofits, and individuals to innovate, learn, and thrive. But the government also faces headwinds: political polarization, gridlock, and eroding trust. When confidence drops, public systems strain and outcomes suffer. When entire institutions of government are fundamentally recalibrated or altogether eliminated, seismic events shock the entire ecosystem.

Yet, as Einstein's third rule of work reminds us: "In the middle of difficulty lies opportunity." So even in this turbulence, there's an opportunity for other balancing institutions of our society—philanthropy and the private sector—to step in and address the disruption to the extent they can.

And that's exactly what's happening now. Across the globe, as governments wrestle with these shifts, competing demands, and growing constraints, a wave of other organizations are stepping in to both remind government of its obligations for Better Good and to also reimagine what recalibrated good can look like in practice.

There's no replacing government, only complementing it. Given its scale and mandate, it remains the largest gear for good. Highways, air traffic control, public health, food and drug standards—these baseline functions are the invisible good we rely on every day. At our best, that service also reaches beyond our borders—disaster response, global health, and development partnerships (long led by USAID) that signal a reliable neighbor to the world—even as recent reorganizations and funding cuts have tested that leadership.

The partnership between Hamdi Ulukaya and the SBA is one story among millions. Every community development grant, every local infrastructure partnership, every public-private or public-philanthropic partnership carries the same approach of people and institutions working together—demonstrating how the gears mesh to make life better.

The work now is to renew and reinforce the government's promise by keeping the gears aligned, clear on roles, and accountable to the people they serve. Easier said than done, but essential if government is to remain the central gear that keeps the rest aligned for Better Good.

NONPROFIT INSTITUTIONS: THE MOMENTUM FOR BETTER GOOD

When most people think of "doing good," their minds first jump to the philanthropic sector—the foundations, operating nonprofits, and community organizations that exist to serve without profit motive.

It's an understandable instinct. From the Red Cross and Habitat for Humanity to local food pantries, animal rescues, and after-school programs, these are the institutions most visibly and directly associated with helping and found throughout most communities. They fill the spaces the government can't reach and business can't justify. But to see philanthropy only as charity is to miss its full power.

Philanthropy is the catalyst of good. It allows the other gears—government and business—to turn more smoothly, to partner more effectively, and to achieve Better Good more robustly. It funds the experiments, the safety nets, the bold ideas that might never otherwise even get off the ground.

The nonprofit ecosystem is far broader than most realize. Beyond headline-grabbing foundations and global NGOs, it comprises local hospitals and universities; churches, synagogues, mosques, and temples; museums, community theaters, and research centers. It's the third-largest sector in the U.S. economy and arguably its most underappreciated engine of innovation and trust.

When Hamdi launched the Tent Partnership for Refugees, he joined a long line of leaders who recognized that philanthropy is more strategy than side project. Tent is a wonderful example of an operating nonprofit. It isn't a traditional foundation that gives away money, but undertakes its own direct work to engage and mobilize its partners—especially businesses—to hire and train refugees. This work turns empathy into employment and purpose into progress. Yes, it serves a bottom line. And it's an undeniable path to Better Good that crosses sectors. All originally made possible by a government-backed SBA loan program. If that isn't the Better Good ecosystem at work, I don't know what is.

The Tent Partnership for Refugees is also representative of the new face of philanthropy that is increasingly dynamic, entrepreneurial, and interdependent.

This leads us to the third gear—the one undergoing the most rapid evolution and facing the most scrutiny in recent decades, and perhaps the one with the greatest potential to redefine Better Good in our time.

THE PRIVATE SECTOR: A GROWING ENGINE OF BETTER GOOD

The private sector shapes how we live, what we buy, how we communicate, and even how we define success. And increasingly, it's also shaping how we do Better Good.

Business as a force for good isn't a new concept. Quaker merchants in the 1700s built companies grounded in fair trade and honest labor, not as a branding or marketing campaign, but to do business in line with their values. Milton Hershey built an entire Pennsylvania town to house, educate, and care for the workers who made Hershey chocolate. It wasn't what some today might dismiss as a performative corporate PR move, but was instead driven by real corporate need and a belief that business success should be shared by the people who helped create it. Some might call Milton and the Quakers the pioneers of Better Good business. I'd suggest they weren't outliers or exceptions forging unknown paths alone. Rather, they were decent human beings and principled business leaders who saw the opportunity for rising business tides to lift all stakeholder boats. And they were in the company of numerous other forward-thinking business leaders and innovators at the time—folks like George Cadbury, the Guinness family, and Andrew Carnegie, who saw the growing imperative of integrating worker well-being, community stability, and long-term social investment into the architecture of how successful businesses scaled and endured.

For much of the twentieth century, the same spirit and belief in business as a force for good quietly and consistently persisted in businesses and communities large and small. But as global capitalism expanded, quarterly earnings reports became the more dominant benchmark of success. The concept of "shareholder primacy"—that a company's sole purpose was to maximize profits for investors—took hold, reshaping business education and culture for decades. To be fair, many companies and founders still supported charitable causes or local initiatives, but those efforts were usually separate from the core business. For most businesses, profit remained the organizing purpose. In effect, it was as if the business gear had been pulled out of the Better Good engine.

As the twenty-first century unfolded, the world became more connected—and more transparent—than ever before. Consumers began asking harder questions about impact and purpose—often in the "public square" of social media—and then voting with their wallets. Employees started doing the same, flexing their agency in the job market and carefully choosing where to work . . . or not. We all became more immediately and comprehensively connected to the consequences of our purchasing actions, from the supply chain side of corporate choices to purchases on the consumer side. As consumers and markets began demanding businesses act like true corporate citizens, corporations increasingly discovered opportunities to meet that demand by doing good while at the same time doing well financially.

As this consumer and employee pressure mounted, the shift didn't stop at the market—it reached investors, too. Increasingly, they realized that ignoring environmental, social, and governance (ESG) risks could be bad for returns. And as a new generation of consumers began demanding it, leaders began redefining success. The modern era of ESG began taking shape in the early 2000s. Building on decades of socially responsible investing and corporate responsibility, the 2004 UN report *Who Cares Wins* formally introduced the term, and by the mid-2000s, global investors were embedding ESG principles into financial decisions. Leaders like Paul Polman at Unilever, Larry Fink at BlackRock, and Ray Anderson at Interface helped shift the narrative about "doing good" from a side project to a core strategy.

In 2019, the Business Roundtable—representing CEOs of America's largest companies—formally rejected shareholder primacy alone, declaring that corporations should serve *all* stakeholders: customers, employees, suppliers, communities, and shareholders alike. The CEOs of the Business Roundtable didn't invent stakeholder capitalism—they simply recognized where the market was already moving. The Roundtable finally said the quiet part out loud.

The result: doing good is no longer an afterthought, it's a competitive advantage and a business imperative . . . a shift that brings a different analysis of what "success" looks like. This shift applies a new set of metrics to determine how well businesses serve society, and whether the good they were saying they do is real at all.

There's another friction point worth naming: because business is built for profit, even sincere social impact efforts are often viewed as suspect—tainted by the self-interested motives of business leaders. That purity test is understandable—but incomplete. Motive purity does not equal impact quality. What matters is whether intent, methods, and measured outcomes align with real needs, operate within clear guardrails, and stand up to independent scrutiny. By those standards, some efforts will fail the test. But many, if not most, will pass. Instead of focusing on deifying or demonizing business, we should instead demand evidence, transparency, and improvement over time.

THE ECONOMICS OF GOOD

As Richard Branson famously put it, "Doing good is good for business." He's right—and we now have the data to prove it.

A 2020 Deloitte study found that purpose-driven companies grow at *three times* the rate of their peers. Meanwhile, Accenture reports that such companies enjoy higher employee retention, stronger customer loyalty, and greater brand equity. And Edelman found that 64 percent of consumers choose, switch, avoid, or boycott brands based on their values and social impact.

The same biology that releases dopamine, serotonin, oxytocin, and endorphins when we do good as individuals also fires inside our bodies when we buy and work—if, that is, we feel we are contributing to the greater good. Teams thrive on purpose. Customers reward companies that make them feel part of something larger than themselves. And when businesses design products, policies, and partnerships that activate this wiring and meet this innately human demand, both the economic and social impact results multiply. We need only look at what's happened across industries:

- Patagonia built an empire by selling both jackets and conviction—famously running a "Don't Buy This Jacket" ad to reduce waste and still seeing sales soar 30 percent the next year.
- TOMS popularized the "buy one, give one" model, which inspired brands like Bombas (donating an item for every purchase) and Warby Parker ("Buy a Pair, Give a Pair" through global partners), among others. Over time, many of these companies have evolved the approach away from strict one-for-one

models toward more flexible, pooled, or programmatic impact funding that deploys a portion of profits across issue areas while maintaining a clear purchase-to-impact link.

- Seventh Generation, founded on a Native American principle that every decision should serve the next seven generations, was acquired by Unilever for $700 million—and kept its mission intact.
- Starbucks reimagined itself not as a coffee company, but as "a people company serving coffee." Its foundation, supply chain ethics, and refugee hiring commitments reach far beyond the venti latte.
- Microsoft committed to become carbon negative by 2050—removing more carbon than it has emitted in its history—tying climate goals to procurement, product design, and a dedicated carbon-fee fund.
- Amazon's Climate Pledge and Walmart's Project Gigaton harness supply chains at scale, cutting emissions and waste far beyond their own four walls.
- Walmart, for all its critics, used its supply chain power to incentivize detergent makers toward concentrated formulas, reducing 125 million pounds of plastic waste and saving hundreds of millions of gallons of water, transportation fuel, and storage space annually.
- American Express launched *Small Business Saturday* in 2010, turning a recession-era idea into a durable civic habit. What began as a corporate initiative to boost local merchants is now a national ritual that's driven well over $200 billion in additional small-business spending since launch—an example of big enterprise catalyzing hometown economies.
- Newman's Own turned salad dressing sales into social enterprise, giving away 100 percent of net profits (rather than distributing them to shareholders) to the Newman's Own

Foundation, which has granted more than $600 million to community organizations to date, proving that a business built on generosity can far outlast its founder.

These are just a few examples among millions that illustrate how doing good is a feasible, lucrative business strategy that can be both principled and profitable, serving shareholders and stakeholders alike.

CAPITAL WITH A CONSCIENCE: IMPACT INVESTING

Any discussion of Better Good in the private sector requires mention of how capital increasingly moves with a conscience. Impact investing—the practice of directing capital toward ventures that generate both financial returns and measurable social or environmental benefits—has exploded in recent years. The Global Impact Investing Network (GIIN) estimates the sector has surpassed $1.16 trillion in assets under management.

Investors are funding affordable housing projects, education initiatives, and healthcare solutions—not despite their profitability, but *because* of it. As returns materialize, so does impact. It's the financial version of the flywheel effect we explored earlier: the more good these investments do, the more money they generate, and then investors can do even *more* good with that money, and so on. The flywheel gets bigger and stronger with more and more impact.

And this doesn't just happen at institutional scale. Everyday investors can now participate through sustainable index funds, ESG portfolios, or microfinance platforms like Kiva, Grameen, and Opportunity International—giving individuals the chance to turn small investments into global ripples of Better Good.

In 2015 I got a call from a friend at a prominent investment firm in Chicago asking if I knew anyone who could help his company segue into the emerging field of impact investing. I introduced him to a friend, former colleague, and frequent collaborator who was leading the Social

Impact, Innovation, and Investment program at NYU's Wagner Graduate School of Public Service. Within a few years, the home page of the firm read (and still reads today—turbulent times and all) as a private investment firm that seeks to deliver both financial returns and social impact, combining the pursuit of profit alongside purpose.

Money moves when purpose pays.

PURPOSE AS POLICY, NOT PR

When purpose is policy—not packaging—it performs. As Chobani's Hamdi Ulukaya says, "If you are right with your people, if you are right with your community, if you are right with your product, you will be more profitable, you will be more innovative, you will have more passionate people working for you and a community that supports you." Far more than a slogan, this reflects a principled operating choice—local sourcing, rural reinvestment, profit-sharing for employees, refugee hiring—that improves the company's bottom line and people's lives.

Businesses and brands that embed purpose deeply into their DNA are the ones thriving, now and over time, despite headwinds they may face from one direction or another. Chobani's introduction of a profit-sharing program called Chobani Shares signaled a belief that everyone who helps build the company should share in its success. When Salesforce created their 1-1-1 model for the 1% Pledge—through which they pledged 1 percent of equity, 1 percent of product, and 1 percent of employee time to philanthropy (and have since encouraged others to do the same)—they also built a corporate and marketplace culture that can both sustain trends and withstand scrutiny. Our task isn't to worship or condemn business, but to require evidence, transparency, and steady improvement—and then reward what works.

The choice to embed purpose throughout businesses has ripple effects in making employees feel seen, customers feel connected, communities feel valued, and investors feel confident. Political winds may shift and forces may apply pressure against such commitments and correlated campaigns, but nothing changes the innate consumer demand for Better Good.

That doesn't mean every company gets it right. Some overpromise. Some underdeliver. Some go too far, others not far enough (all in the eyes of beholders with different points of view). And yes, some do wrap a thin layer of achievement in equally thin green paint (aka "greenwashing"—using the appearance of wins as proof of real impact, even if it isn't). Just as there are some bad humans in the world and some bad nonprofits that squander their promise, there are also businesses that fail to meet their full potential of Better Good. But we shouldn't undercut the efforts of those that are at least trying by painting all corporate impact efforts with a single brush just because some come up short, get it wrong, or aren't as sincerely intended as others.

Imperfect progress (which exists in every sector) is still progress. The private sector players that win in the long run are the ones that keep learning, improving, pivot when necessary, and persist in their pursuit of Better Good. The key is transparency and accountability through measurement and metrics that validate and verify.

MEASURING WHAT MATTERS

A famous business saying teaches us, "What gets measured gets managed." In the world of social impact, the corollary is: "What gets measured gets believed." To separate genuine Better Good from performative PR, new frameworks have emerged to validate impact.

- B Corp Certification now serves as a global gold standard for balancing profit with purpose.
- LEED (Leadership in Energy and Environmental Design) certification sets benchmarks for sustainable building and energy efficiency.
- Fair Trade labels guarantee ethical sourcing and fair wages.
- The Dow Jones Sustainability Index tracks corporate performance on ESG metrics.

- The Global Impact Investing Network (GIIN) measures the financial and social returns of capital deployed for good.

These aren't just (but certainly can be used as) virtue-signaling badges. They're actual accountability systems with verifiable metrics beneath them. They tell—and reassure—investors and consumers that "This is real."

And the market rewards it all. LEED-certified buildings command 20 percent rent premiums. Certified B Corps like Athleta, Bombas, and Ben & Jerry's report higher employee satisfaction and customer retention. Investors pour trillions into ESG funds.

Evidence, effort, and endurance are the real currency of impact.

NAVIGATING THE BACKLASH

Of course, there are always people looking for ways to criticize and punish good work—especially in the current climate. As "woke capitalism" became a political buzzword and culture war battle cry, some companies that had championed social causes faced fierce backlash. Campaigns that once earned applause were suddenly labeled as divisive and executives found themselves caught in the crossfire. For instance, Target's once-routine gay pride merchandising shifted from inclusive celebration to political flashpoint, drawing boycotts, threats, and headline scrutiny.

But history suggests these storms are temporary. Better Good work deeply rooted in corporate culture will withstand the shifting—and even intensifying—winds. Less sincere or deeply rooted work may not. But consumer demand for ethical, sustainable, and socially responsible products isn't going away. In fact, it's rising—especially among younger generations who will soon make up the majority of the workforce and marketplace. Skeptics might continue to argue that some of this is simple PR. And that may be true at times. But if trees (actual or metaphorical) still get planted, motive matters less than measurable outcome.

Markets swing. Pendulums swing back. Political winds shift. But human wiring doesn't change. When given the choice, we still buy the yogurt that supports farmers, the shoes that support kids, the coffee that supports fair wages, and the product or service that costs less, provides more, and happens to also do Better Good. The companies that remember this—and stay the course—are the ones that will endure.

THE WORK OF DOING BETTER GOOD

None of this is easy. Some initiatives fail. Others backfire. But that's never a reason to stop trying and there are always reasons to keep trying and evolving.

Every company, nonprofit, and government agency can start where it is. Build trust. Measure progress. Partner widely. Adjust often. Lead with humility and transparency.

And for every one of us—whether you're a CEO, a mid-level manager, frontline worker, a student, or someone figuring out your next step—you don't have to wait for a new job title or a bigger budget to start doing this work. You're already inside the systems that shape the world. You have agency every day through how you spend, work, invest, and lead.

Better Good ecosystems are ones where every effort, every decision, and every dollar and day's work contribute to something larger than ourselves. Government builds bridges. Philanthropy lights the way. Business provides paths for purpose in the products and services we consume. Together, they carry us forward. We all have a voice and a vote in how oriented toward Better Good the institutions, organizations, and businesses in which we invest our time, talent, and treasure really are.

As you learn the Better Good Framework in the chapters ahead, you'll see how it can be put to work in and across all kinds of industries and organizations to keep the gears of Better Good in our society turning. Because when they slow, real people feel it, and when they move, real lives and communities are positively impacted.

KEY TAKEAWAYS AND ACTION ITEMS

Key Takeaways

- **Humans do good in groups.** We achieve Better Good through organizations found in three primary institutions: government, nonprofits, and business.
- **All good is good, regardless of sector.** Government good, nonprofit good, and business good—often imperfect, always consequential—each plays a role in our interrelated ecosystem of progress toward Better Good. Profit does not disqualify private-sector good. Dysfunctional leadership does not negate government's potential. Bad apples in the sector do not invalidate all nonprofits.
- **Private sector skepticism is natural but not disqualifying.** Unlike government and nonprofits—which are both built without a profit mandate—business is profit-driven, so its version of good draws harsher scrutiny and skepticism. This scrutiny is surmountable when companies set clear guardrails, measure real outcomes, and open them to independent verification.
- **Purpose pays.** Businesses that align mission with meaning outperform peers and retain their people.
- **Transparency builds trust.** Metrics and certifications turn goodwill into proof of impact.

- **Momentum begets momentum.** Small acts of Better Good—multiplied across millions of choices—create exponential impact.

Action Items

For Individuals

- **Use your vote and your voice.** Back public leaders who prioritize Better Good over partisanship and private gain, and who protect the baseline functions (infrastructure, health, safety) that make the whole system work.
- **Back high-performing nonprofits.** Support mission-driven institutions that fill gaps government and business can't or don't; look for clear missions and proven results.
- **Spend with intention.** Favor companies that publish verifiable impact metrics (and third-party validations) and show year-over-year improvement—not just slogans, PR, or greenwashing.
- **Advocate at work.** Rally colleagues and leaders to adopt or expand purpose-driven practices; propose one concrete initiative you can help deliver this quarter.
- **Invest with intention.** Align part of your portfolio to impact vehicles (e.g., ESG/impact funds or community finance) and review holdings annually against measurable outcomes.

- **Remain vigilant.** Learn to spot greenwashing; reward evidence, transparency, and credible course-corrections over perfection or PR.

Action Items

For Organizations

- **Start with systems, not slogans.** Map your role in the three-gear ecosystem (government, nonprofits, business). Clarify where you create value, where you create risk, and where partners are best suited to support your efforts for Better Good.
- **Define purpose with materiality.** Tie your "why" to a short list of material issues for your business and society; publish the trade-offs you're choosing and why.
- **Make a theory of change operational.** Link inputs, activities, outcomes, and evidence. Fund, staff, and engage with your impact initiative as a core business strategy, not a side project.
- **Build a portfolio, not one-offs.** Run a mix of pilots, proven plays, and moonshots. Use counterfactuals (what would have happened without our effort?) to judge real impact.
- **Align governance and incentives.** Put purpose on the board agenda; tie leadership reviews and comp to a few financial and impact Key Performance

Indicators (KPIs) reviewed at the same cadence as "regular" performance (with the goal of making Better Good part of that mix and cadence).

- **Measure what matters.** Use credible, widely recognized standards (such as B Corp, LEED, Fair Trade) and independent validators. Report misses alongside wins to enhance credibility.
- **Amplify approach to stakeholder capitalism.** Reflect environmental and social costs in reporting, sourcing, and product design; reward teams for total value creation, not just financial margin.
- **Partner where others are stronger.** Pair with public agencies for scale and nonprofits for first- and last-mile trust; agree on roles, data sharing, storytelling and exit criteria to create credible cross-sector partnerships.
- **Anticipate scrutiny before it arrives.** Run premortems, scenario plans, and a response playbook for high-prominence issues; prioritize evidence, consistency, and course correction as necessary.
- **Invest in culture as infrastructure.** Train managers on ethical decision-making, equip employees to spot greenwashing risks, and celebrate measurable progress over performative gestures.

PART II

WHO YOU ARE: PPP

Now that you've seen how good works in the world, it's time to turn the lens inward.

Over the next three chapters, you'll begin building your Better Good Framework by exploring the qualities that make you—and only you—uniquely equipped to make an impact that lasts. These are your Profile, Platform, and Passion—together, your personal foundation for doing Better Good.

Every person and organization already has a Profile, whether or not they've ever named it. Sometimes it's intentional, sometimes accidental. Chapter 4 helps you uncover it—taking stock of your experiences, credentials, relationships, and personality to see how they already position you for good.

Your Platform is where that profile meets the world. Shakespeare said that all the world's a stage, and each of us stands on it daily in different ways. Chapter 5 helps you identify the stages you already stand on—and those within reach—so you can use your influence with purpose.

Your Passion is the rocket fuel that keeps you moving. When you know which causes matter most, you'll find the energy and clarity to keep showing up. Chapter 6 helps you chart that course—connecting the dots between what you love, what you're good at, and where you can make the biggest difference.

By the end of this section, you'll see that doing Better Good doesn't start somewhere else—it starts with who you already are.

CHAPTER 4

Your Profile

Knowing yourself is the beginning of all wisdom.

—Aristotle

In 2009, Nancy Economou was in many ways the quintessential suburban mom, with a life that felt like a carefully balanced juggling act. She had five sons at home (yes, *five*) which meant that her days were a relentless stream of pickups, drop-offs, sports practices, extracurriculars, and everything else that goes with maintaining a busy homelife. Weekends weren't much different, filled with more sports, social gatherings, and her steadfast involvement in the church that grounded her family.

Her calendar was so packed that it felt like the classic jar-of-rocks science demonstrations—already full, yet still fitting pebbles, sand, and water to prove just how much more could fit. Nancy's jar already felt full to the brim. But after accompanying her husband on a work trip to the Philippines, she discovered there was room for more. Much more.

During a volunteer opportunity while on the trip, Nancy visited a village where she met a young Filipino girl whose face was burned and scarred by a fire from a kerosene lamp. Wanting to learn more about the use of kerosene in the village, she sought out and met scores of other families. Many, it turned out, lived in darkness at night to avoid the expense of burning kerosene, their only source of light after the sun went down.

The people she met were stuck in a poverty-inducing cycle, relying on dirty, dangerous, unhealthy, and expensive kerosene. For the neediest families, the kerosene budget can consume up to 30 percent of the meager household budget. But without access to reliable electrical grids, they needed kerosene for lighting, cooking, and heat. They had to work hard to conserve it to save money, limiting productive hours to daytime, which made it difficult, if not impossible, for adults to work or kids to learn after the sun went down. When they did use kerosene, it emitted carcinogens in poorly ventilated homes. On top of those long-term hazards, kerosene fires were both common and devastating. Homes were destroyed, precious possessions lost, and people suffered severe, often fatal burns. Kerosene was more than a fuel source; it was a trap, chaining families to poverty, illness, and loss.

When Nancy returned home, these stories stayed with her. They followed her like pieces of an unfinished puzzle. Her continued curiosity led her to further research that revealed these crushing cycles weren't unique to the Philippines. Similar stories could be found in developing countries the world over. Nancy knew she had to do *something*. But she struggled to figure out how she could do *anything*. After all, she was just a busy suburban mom with a completely full life. Wasn't she?

Fast-forward fifteen years.

If you meet Nancy today, you'll find a polished, sophisticated leader of a world-class nonprofit, someone you'd assume has been doing this all her life. The organization she founded, Watts of Love, has distributed more than 100,000 solar lights across fifty-five countries, impacting over 700,000 lives by providing more safety and security, and by extending the productive hours of the day past sunset. Both the lights and the educational resources that Watts of Love distributes alongside them allow recipient families (and entire villages) to use their newfound productivity to drive transformational economic growth and increases in educational attainment. Their work has increased median household incomes by an average of 15 percent in the villages where it has deployed this growing model of individual, family, and community empowerment.

Many more of us are likely to identify with 2009 Nancy than with nonprofit powerhouse Nancy. We have full lives, and we want to do good. But as Uber drivers and office workers and stay-at-home parents, we can't always see how to do the good we want to do. When we look at what Nancy was able to accomplish with Watts of Love, many of us think that there's no way *we* could get there. So we default to our everyday patterns, putting off our pursuit of Better Good for some future "someday" with some eventual set of circumstances, assuming we don't have what we need today.

That "someday" narrative sells you short. You have more layers and leverage than you realize. You're working with way more than you think you are. Just like Nancy, you have qualifications, skills, and passions that are the exact gifts you need to do more Better Good. So how do you begin uncovering those gifts? By evaluating the person you present to the world in every moment of every interaction—the you that is full of opportunity, even if you don't fully see it yet. In other words, we'll start with your Profile.

WHAT IS YOUR PROFILE?

Your profile is the unique mix of qualities that shape who you are, how you move through the world, and how you do Better Good. It's more than what's on your résumé. Your profile is dynamic, multifaceted, and ever-evolving, which can seem complicated but doesn't need to be.

Here's a quick overview of the elements of your profile, which we'll unpack further as we go.

- **Credentials.** These are the formal and informal qualifications you've gathered through education, training, and experience—degrees, certifications, hard-won lessons, and even failures that taught you something essential. Your capabilities are amplified by—but aren't limited to—what appears on your résumé or LinkedIn. They also include every skill you've built from life itself. Maybe you're a master negotiator because you grew up in a big family, or a logistics wizard from years of running school carpools or community events. All of it counts. Credentials are what you've earned *and* what you've learned.

- **Connections.** Your relationships with the people and networks intertwined with your journey: friends, mentors, colleagues, clients, classmates, neighbors, and the stranger who opened a door that changed your life. Whether through work, school, faith, hobbies, or happenstance, every relationship adds a thread to the web of influence and opportunity around you. And that web is often wider than you think. Many of the world's greatest impact stories start not with capital, but with connection—with one person introducing another who shares a mission to do good.

- **Character.** Character is the personality, spirit, and presence you bring into every interaction—the blend of temperament, values, and traits that shapes how you engage with the world. Your character determines how your capabilities and connections come to life. It's the heartbeat of your Profile and the lens through which others experience your work.

Some elements of your profile—especially your core credentials and character—form the bedrock of who you are. Once you establish those elements, they remain relatively stable whether you're twenty-five or sixty-five, and no matter how your career evolves.

Other elements, like your connections, job title, affiliations with organizations or causes, and expertise you become known for, all shift, expand, grow, and evolve over time. The key is to remain aware of how each evolves, because together, they form the foundation from which you'll do Better Good.

And here's another twist: the way you see yourself often isn't the way the world sees you. Had Nancy merely seen herself as a busy mother of five, she may have limited her potential for evolving into the leader of a powerhouse nonprofit she is today. Sometimes, you have to shift your perspective and look at your own life through a different lens to open the path for becoming your best self. You may find that you're already equipped to do Better Good using your profile in ways that may be hiding in plain sight.

You've likely seen this play out in your own life.

When asked, "What do you do?" most people respond with their job. To this day, I almost always immediately respond with "I'm a lawyer." It's a quick and convenient primary identifier, though it is far from an accurate descriptor of my professional life, let alone my *entire* life (where husband, dad, rescue dog dad, optimist, Space Camper, improviser, ukulele player, Jimmy Buffett superfan (aka Parrothead), runner, dreamer, youngest of six, and lots of other roles factor into my profile).

I'm not alone here. I've met kings, queens, presidents, and prime ministers who, after various types of introductions—usually in highly professional situations—always delight by saying something to the effect of "but of course, my best title is . . ." and fill in the blank here with something endearing like mom, dad, spouse, grandparent, godparent, dog parent, etc. I love the dog parent royalty. They're my favorite.

The older we get, the more diverse our profiles become. But we rarely share the entirety of it in a single conversation. No one wants to sound like a braggy jerk, and we don't necessarily need to share everything about ourselves when first meeting someone. That could get a touch awkward. But it's important to start expanding the way you think about your profile—even if it's only for your own thinking and your own sense of self—so you see yourself as much more than any single identifier.

Being fully aware of your profile is critical for doing Better Good because when you bring the fullness of your profile to the world, you can connect more authentically to your own purpose and your potential for good. Because the opportunity to do good exists in every part of our lives and work, it's important to have as clear a view as possible of *all* aspects of who we are and how we show up in those various aspects.

Let's unpack each of these aspects a little further.

CREDENTIALS

Credentials are the formal and informal qualifications, experiences, and skills that you've gained. This includes *every* indicator of credibility and expertise—not merely the major, LinkedIn-friendly credentials bestowed by colleges and universities, professional associations, and job titles. It also includes easily overlooked credentials that result from lived experiences that give you undeniable credibility in less obvious spheres. Together, these formal and informal credentials form your core competencies—the signals that tell others they can trust you to deliver.

To get your gears turning, consider the following informal credentials:

Maybe you're a CPA, but you're also thrilled to serve as the unofficial CFO of your household, stretching every dollar with an expertise no spreadsheet could capture.

Maybe you never studied marketing, but your ability to sell 500 boxes of Girl Scout cookies every season suggests otherwise.

Maybe (like me) you get as much enjoyment from planning trips as from taking them, and you *love* helping others plan a trip to one of your favorite spots by sharing well-researched recommendations. (If you ever need help planning a Disney cruise, I'm your guy!)

In other words, credentials aren't *just* about what's framed on your wall—they're about what you know and what you've done, even if you don't fully realize how valuable those experiences are. As you expand your thinking and map your own credentials, consider the following categories that you might sort them into:

- **Macro-credentials** are the "official" ones. These include degrees, professional certifications, and significant career or life experiences that everyone includes on a typical résumé. Beyond degrees and certifications, you may have macro-credentials like having served in the military, Peace Corps, leadership programs, or in elected office. For me, my macro-credentials are my undergrad degree in speech communications, my law degree, and my masters in public service.

- **Micro-credentials** are more focused skill sets—like CPR certification, Photoshop skills, or having been a camp counselor. One of my own favorite micro-credentials is being a graduate of the Second City Improv training center, which sounds "funny" (need more terrible puns? I'm your guy) at first, but absolutely gave me transferable skills that come in handy in many professional situations. "Yes, and" isn't just the cardinal rule of improv, it's a life skill!

- **Informal credentials** are those that no one hands you a diploma or certificate for, but that might matter just as much. Think of managing a household, organizing family reunions, planning trips, coaching a youth sports team, or launching a side hustle. These are very real credentials in their own right.

- **School-of-Life credentials** are often seismic events that change who we are, such as a serious medical diagnosis and ensuing fight, raising a child with special needs, a life-changing car accident, or a shooting that turns your greatest title into one of survivor. Think about accidental activists like Malala Yousafzai, the families who lost their kids at Sandy Hook, or some of the then-teenagers who survived the Parkland school shooting and went on to become advocates and activists. All have turned tragedy into triumph as activists for important causes.

All of these credentials have value, but the key next step is identifying which ones matter *most* to us in our lives and work, and especially what "core credentials" we rely on most in presenting ourselves and our work for Better Good in the world.

Michael Hyatt, one of my favorite experts on productivity, talks about the powerful intersection of passion and proficiency: "If you design your life so that you spend most of your time working on things you are passionate about and proficient at, the discipline to do those things comes easily." In Chapter 1 we dubbed this the Goldilocks Zone—the sweet spot where what motivates you and what you're good at align. When you look at your credentials through this lens, you can see which ones sit at the intersection of passion and proficiency—and which ones drift outside it. Those in the zone represent your greatest opportunities for contribution.

In the chapters ahead, we'll see how this same alignment powers your Platform, deepens your Passion, and ultimately fuels your ability to scale and sustain Better Good. For now, think of your Goldilocks Zone as an internal compass—helping you zero in on the credentials that are *just right* for the good you want to do.

If you have a credential you no longer feel passion for, it's unlikely to serve you well. For instance, I had to take classes in statistics, finance, and tax law, but I'm allergic to spreadsheets and often have to shut down and reboot my brain if I open up Excel on my computer or see too many numbers on any page. So when a nonprofit I serve seeks volunteers for their audit and finance committee, I won't raise my hand. In fact, I sink slowly into my seat, hoping to disappear. I'm neither passionate nor proficient in those areas.

While the world may see your credentials differently than you do, don't let others' perceptions drive you to commit to something that isn't in your zone of passion and proficiency. Keep your focus on those credentials that fire you up and harness your skills, even if they aren't as prestigious as some of your other credentials. That's the best way to contribute at your highest and best level for the long haul.

CONNECTIONS

The company we keep is a big part of who we are and what we're capable of achieving. One of the original motivational and life coaching gurus, Jim Rohn, famously said, "You are the average of the five people you spend the most time with." His protege Tony Robbins expanded on that concept: "The quality of your life is the quality of your relationships." This is your *access story*—who can open doors, amplify, or accelerate your idea.

Your connections and relationships aren't just the people you see every day, or on major family holidays, or even on your holiday card list. They include an entire network of diverse connections that can be activated for good, such as all the individuals and networks you're connected to through work, school, family, faith communities, hobbies, or sheer happenstance. When you add them all up, your connections probably extend much further than you think (Kevin Bacon included).

Remember that high school friend you haven't seen in a few years who's now an executive? That colleague who volunteers at an organization you admire? The neighbor you always chat with at the dog park or at a kid's soccer practice? You may not feel close enough to any of them to consider them connections, but they absolutely fit this definition: anyone who might open doors, provide support, and amplify your efforts to do Better Good.

Think of your network as three broad categories of connections, which you can leverage in different ways.

- **Close connections** include your immediate family, close friends, and trusted colleagues. These are people you feel comfortable calling on for a favor at any time, and who will always help you if circumstances allow.

- **Middle-tier connections** include casual friends, more distant relatives, former classmates, and colleagues you chat with regularly but not quite intimately. Imagine anyone who cares about you even if you only spend quality time with them a few times a year.

- **Extended connections** can include friends of friends, alumni groups, fellow members of religious or community organizations, social media connections, former colleagues, and that LinkedIn contact you messaged once and never followed up with.

Don't overlook dormant connections—the people you haven't contacted in years but who may still be glad to hear from you. These are the ones you haven't engaged with for a long time but can still be extremely valuable. That old coworker who started a nonprofit? They might be the bridge to your next opportunity and might be thrilled to hear from you, especially if your current efforts overlap with their interests.

While I was writing this book, one of my old friends from my early days in Arkansas was appointed CEO of a new *billion-dollar* start-up established by five high-profile, ultra-wealthy founders. We've seen each other a few times in the past couple of decades and always pick up where we left off. Upon seeing his name all over the press and LinkedIn, I dropped him a personal note simply to say congratulations. Where his new adventure may go or how our future might overlap from that point forward is anyone's guess. But the dormant relationship isn't invaluable because it's dormant; it can always come out of hibernation, full of potential and personal delight.

I've learned time and time again that the greatest ideas result from the most unexpected conversations and brainstorms. And the next great idea or opportunity is often in the mind of someone who's engaged on the topic in a new and different way.

One of my good friends and frequent collaborators—a former general counsel of a social media giant—first introduced himself while we were both waiting in line for coffee at a conference. Though it began with just two guys having some pleasant small talk, that chance encounter sparked a friendship and collaborative partnership that has influenced key pivot points in my life. One such serendipitous moment occurred during my transition from the Clinton Foundation to what would become my consulting firm, Beyond Advisers, when it was little more than an idea I was incubating. As I was waffling with self-doubt, his confident encouragement that it was a smart model worth pursuing was crucial reinforcement at an important time—something I never could have imagined when we were joking about our caffeine addictions years earlier. And beyond Beyond, we regularly compare notes about our shared love of—yep—Disney Cruises. Never underestimate the power of a moment, or the serendipity of a single conversation.

CHARACTER

The third main element of your profile is your character. Driven primarily by your personality and values, your character shapes the unique way you engage with the world. Some of us are natural connectors, others are deep thinkers. Some thrive in big, energetic settings, while others do their best work in focused, one-on-one conversations. This is your *presence story*—the energy and values people experience when they work with you.

Your character traits—including your energy, curiosity, optimism, enthusiasm, humor, leadership, or ability to connect with others—are just as much a part of your profile as your credentials and connections. These are the qualities that shape how you approach doing good, and they're often the reason people rally around your efforts.

Let's use two of my former colleagues as an example. Bill Clinton's natural outgoingness (charm, charisma, storytelling ability—whatever you want to call it) has served him well, separate from his impressive credentials and extensive connections. In contrast, Hillary Clinton is widely viewed as more introverted, but equally smart, serious, and accomplished. Her humor and charisma are less fully on display at all times but often surprise people who are delighted to discover her biting wit and uproarious laugh in small group settings. She is a lot more than the serious leader we tend to see under the bright public spotlight. You've likely seen glimpses of this in her appearances on *Saturday Night Live*, late night talk shows, and occasional quips during public appearances. In fact, she's legit hilarious.

Let's be clear: there's nothing inherently better or worse about either of their personalities, or yours or mine. We all show up in different ways at different times, sometimes quite intentionally, and there are many effective ways to show up and engage with the world. What people appreciate, enjoy, or are attracted to in our efforts to engage with them varies from person to person. And it is this tapestry of personalities that creates dynamic connections that ultimately lead to new insights and breakthroughs. There is no right or wrong, just different.

Consider how character shapes contribution. Hillary Clinton's steady seriousness and deep preparation have defined her public leadership, but her warmth, humor, and curiosity—traits that emerge most in smaller settings—help her connect and mentor behind the scenes in powerful, personal ways. And Bill Clinton's easy charisma bridges divides, energizes rooms, and makes people feel seen, enabling extraordinary high-stakes convenings. Each personality amplifies impact in a different way, showing there's no single "right" way to show up—only the importance of showing up as yourself. I don't offer these examples because they are big names, I offer them as great examples from which we can all learn. There are countless others like them from which to draw inspiration and important lessons.

Which mode feels most like you—connector or quiet strategist, visionary or detail-driven executor, front of room energizer or behind the scenes builder? Name it. Then use it.

When it comes to assessing your own character as a component of your profile, don't be shy about elevating your strengths and honestly assessing your perceived weaknesses. Shed any modesty or self-doubt. Ask a trusted friend or colleague what they think your superpowers are. Then listen, take notes, and draw lines between the common threads of their feedback. You'll likely gain some keen and surprising insights about how others see you.

It's also important to remember that because our personalities are dynamic and unique, they will come across differently at different times for different audiences. So it makes sense to consider how your character differs from situation to situation. Are you more effective in front of a crowded room or in a small group meeting? How do you show up one-on-one? With a stranger versus with a longtime friend?

Keep in mind that our perceived greatest strengths can also be our greatest weaknesses, and vice versa, depending on the context. My gift of gab (a "D1 yapper," as my kids say) means I'm great in many conversations but also sometimes a bit too loquacious in other situations. It's natural to feel insecure about some of your character traits and wonder what is truly a strength or a weakness. We can all be a little myopic or insecure about our personalities. The key for our purposes is to inventory it all (especially the parts where passion and proficiency overlap), accepting that who you are and how you are wired can contribute greatly to your profile, as a core part of how you can do Better Good.

HOW NANCY USED HER PROFILE TO CHANGE THE WORLD

All of which brings us back to Nancy. As you'll recall, she returned home from the Philippines consumed by the widespread problem she witnessed there and determined to do something about it. But what could she do?

One obvious path would have been to make an impact by finding and financially supporting a nonprofit that was doing something to help those villagers living in darkness. To be clear, there's absolutely nothing wrong with this approach; financial support (aka "checkbook charity") is a critical component of social-impact success. But donations and fundraising aren't *all* we are capable of, and that wasn't how Nancy wanted to direct her impact. She felt the gravity of the issue and the opportunity, and felt compelled to do more.

It turned out that upon closer inspection, Nancy's profile was much more powerful than she had ever imagined. Her self-assessment and inventory of her profile revealed tremendous resources in all three categories:

Credentials

- Ninja-level management and coordination experience as a mother of five.
- The leadership skills of a key figure in her local and church communities.
- Sales experience and skills that came from previously working for Cartier jewelry.

Connections

- Her husband worked in industrial lighting.
- Her brother was a professional photographer.
- She had a strong network of supporters who would certainly help—friends, fellow church members, local business leaders.
- She had a wider group of more casual friends and acquaintances who could help support her cause.
- The town next door happened to be the headquarters of Molex, an industrial lighting company whose executives she could approach.
- A neighbor who was an expert in global philanthropy happened to introduce himself one day. (That was me!)

Character

- Extroversion, which made sharing her experiences and ideas easy for her.
- Tremendous enthusiasm and passion, which gave her a knack for engaging and inspiring others.
- Persistence, which always kept her moving forward in tough situations and during the challenging logistics of the work.

With all of these resources at her disposal, Nancy founded her nonprofit, Watts of Love. Among her key steps:

- She asked her husband (the industrial lighting expert) to sketch out the kind of solar lighting that would be both cost-effective and durable for long-term, sustainable use in poor villages.
- She used her infectious enthusiasm to recruit her network of friends, family, and church colleagues to donate, fundraise, and spread the word. Some even volunteered to join her on her next trip back to the Philippines.
- She got her brother (the photographer) to donate his creative skills and illustrate their website and fundraising materials.
- She successfully engaged executives at Molex, a global electronics manufacturer based in a neighboring suburb to contribute their design and manufacturing capacity to develop and distribute a second, even more durable version of their solar light.
- She engaged with commercial airlines (like American) to transport both lights and teams of volunteers around the world, so they could show recipients how to use the lights as educational and economic development tools.
- She developed a replicable and scalable model for Watts of Love, applying lessons learned in initial locations such as that first village in the Philippines. The organization built on those test cases to grow their work in communities in need around the world.

Watts of Love now has its own strong organizational profile that inspires other nonprofit leaders—all because one "busy mom with a full schedule" didn't stop at that part of her profile. It's an extraordinary success story, but what's really inspiring is that Nancy doesn't see herself as extraordinary. She merely inventoried, analyzed, and expanded the profile she already had. She found that despite her already full days, she had both the passion and the proficiency to pursue this cause to its full potential.

At some point, most of us feel the call to meet a need, right a wrong, address an ill we see in the world, or at least become part of the solution in our own corner of it. But like Nancy, we often question our individual ability to make a difference or whether our full lives have room to add one more thing. We may think, "Somebody should do something about that." But we're each just as much somebody as anybody else! We all have the potential to do good because we all—already—have a *profile* that unlocks this potential.

What's also worth noticing is how well positioned Nancy was to help once she allowed herself to engage the problem fully. The need she encountered intersected with skills, relationships, and resources already within her reach—experience organizing people, access to design and manufacturing expertise, proximity to global distribution, and a network willing to show up. When those elements came together, action became possible, or even almost inevitable, in a very concrete way.

This kind of alignment is easy to miss if we're not paying attention. But when you begin to look at the world through the Better Good Framework, situations like this start to stand out more clearly. Not because the world has suddenly changed, but because your awareness has. Instead of asking, "Who am I to do something about this?" the better question becomes, "Where do my capabilities and relationships already overlap with a real need?" That's often where the most effective and sustainable impact begins—and where opportunities that once felt distant reveal themselves as closer and more actionable than we ever imagined.

PUTTING YOUR PROFILE TO WORK

One of the coolest aspects of working for the Clinton Foundation was the opportunity to meet some of my personal heroes, often at unexpected times and in unexpected ways. While some of my colleagues got giddy about heads of state or movie stars, as a four-time Space Camper I was most starstruck (pun intended) by folks like world-renowned astrophysicist Neil deGrasse Tyson. Neil has become iconic for his many books, articles, television appearances, and social media content that make the mystery and majesty of the universe simpler to understand for mainstream audiences. During a 2012 Clinton Global Initiative meeting in Chicago, he participated in a "Future of Global Impact" panel. At one point in between sessions, as I found myself in a hallway with him, we said hello. As we shook hands he said, "Hi, I'm Neil." For me, it was like meeting Michael Jordan.

I offered my usual introduction, explaining who I was and what I did at the foundation, and thanked him for being there. "And if you don't mind my sharing," I added. "I am a four-time Space Camper, so I'm particularly delighted for this opportunity to say hello."

Typically, these interactions end here for busy celebrities like Neil. But he's not typical. "Thank you so much," he said. "I'm honored to be here. And it's a pleasure to meet you. If you don't mind, I have one note for you. Next time, no matter who you meet, lead with Space Camp. It's the best part!"

I never forgot that advice. I elevate it often in introductions whenever (even remotely) relevant, and if nothing else it gets a laugh and makes my intro memorable. And in a similar cosmic connection over a decade later, I didn't miss a beat when I was introduced by a mutual friend to another nerd icon: Bill Nye the Science Guy.

"Pleasure to meet you, Bill, I'm Scott . . . four-time Space Camper, and a big fan."

Mr. the Science Guy was just as delighted as Neil had been, and this quick bonding led easily to a conversation about my current work, which of course had nothing (directly) to do with Space Camp.

Lead with the best part of your profile—the part that is most authentic to who you are and how you show up in the world. It opens doors a job title alone can't.

To begin mapping your own profile with greater clarity and confidence than ever, consider these questions:

General

- What's your primary identifier—the shorthand way you define yourself when asked "Who are you?" or "What do you do?"
- Given your new knowledge and framework for understanding your profile, how does that primary identifier fit for you? Too big, too small, just right?
- Now think about your secondary identifiers—the roles you play and the identities that shape how you show up in the world. Parent? Mentor? Artist? Teammate? Community volunteer? These aren't credentials or skills, but the parts of your life that influence your perspective and priorities. List as many as you can think of.
- What are the less obvious *credentials or skills* you've gained along the way—things that might not appear on a résumé or on LinkedIn but could come in handy in certain situations?

Credentials

- What are your macro- and micro-credentials, such as degrees, certifications, and job titles past and present?
- What are the informal credentials that you might leave off of LinkedIn but might come in very handy in certain situations?
- Which credentials are you less enthusiastic about now than when you got them, and should therefore take a back seat when thinking about leveraging your profile to do good?
- Which of your credentials hit the sweet spot where your passion and proficiency overlap?

Connections

- Who are your closest, most important connections—the ones you nurture frequently and who will certainly be there for you when you need them?
- Who are your middle-tier connections, the ones who might offer hidden potential and extraordinary value if you develop them?
- Who are your casual or dormant connections, the kind who might still respond enthusiastically if you offer them a chance to do Better Good?
- What organizations and associations do you participate in, whether based in your profession, your local community, your religious affiliation, your hobbies, or your alumni status?
- Are there ways you can be more active in those groups and bring more of their members into your mid-tier or extended connections categories?

Character

- Are you mostly an extrovert or an introvert? Practice pointer: after two hours at a professional networking event, do you feel energized or drained?
- Are you a more effective communicator when talking to a single person, a small group of peers, or a big audience, when you're up front and under the spotlight? Or, are you most effective away from the spotlight or stage, and prefer to use your voice by writing, blogging, or posting on social media?
- Do you feel inspired or discouraged when facing a big challenge?
- Do you have better ideas during vibrant team brainstorming sessions or during quiet periods of isolated deep thinking?

Most of us underestimate our profiles—until someone holds up a mirror.

It's really important that you know precisely who you are, what you stand for, and how you work for Better Good.

ORGANIZATIONS HAVE PROFILES, TOO

Think about businesses and brands that you absolutely love—the ones to which you're completely loyal. Organizations have profiles, too: credentials (what they make or do), connections (stakeholders across the value chain), and character (the brand and behavior people experience).

Some profiles are decades deep. McDonald's still epitomizes fast, convenient, affordable food, even as their business model evolves. Apple's culture-shaping innovation identity outlived Steve Jobs because it's embedded in how the company ships products, not just how it markets them. Ben & Jerry's kept its quirky, values-driven character after selling to Unilever. And Disney's storytelling magic now spans far beyond parks, films, and streaming—proof that a durable profile can scale and sustain without losing its soul.

Organizational profiles include more than private sector brands. The Mayo Clinic, for example, is one of the most recognized names in healthcare worldwide, known for cutting-edge innovation, world-class treatment, and patient-centered care of the highest quality. Its reputation as a leader in medical research and treatment is so well established that the name itself is synonymous with trust in healthcare.

Similarly, major universities have some of the most distinct and enduring profiles in the world. Harvard, MIT, and Oxford, for example, each represent a different brand of excellence. Even smaller or more specialized academic institutions have well-defined profiles that set them apart, in fields such as business, engineering, the arts, or even social impact.

Global nonprofits also build distinct, durable profiles: the Red Cross (disaster relief), World Wildlife Fund (conservation), and Doctors

Without Borders (independent medical aid in crises). Their brands are the visible signals—names, symbols, stories—that people recognize. Their profiles are the fuller operating identities—mission, methods, relationships, and behavior over time. When a brand expresses its profile faithfully, trust compounds.

Even government agencies have profiles that transcend leadership changes and shifting policies. NASA, for instance, is more than just a space agency—it's a symbol of human ambition, exploration, and scientific advancement. The NASA brand is so strong that it inspires everything from space exploration to pop culture. Similarly, entities like the National Park Service, the Smithsonian Institution, and the Centers for Disease Control and Prevention (CDC) all have distinct profiles that guide public perception, funding, and long-term mission continuity, even as individual leaders come and go.

Most important: a profile isn't what an organization says in any particular quarter, in an impact newsletter or annual report—it's how it shows up through consistent action over years. The clearer the profile, the stronger the connections, the better the results. Just as individuals can unlock new opportunities by recognizing the full scope of their credentials, connections, and character, organizations can do the same.

FIND YOUR PROFILE GOLDILOCKS ZONE

Exploring your profile is a balancing act. It's easy to either oversimplify who you are or overcomplicate what makes you unique. The key is knowing which parts matter most for doing Better Good.

Every profile has a Goldilocks Zone all its own—the point where who you are and what you do best come into balance. It's where your contributions feel natural, your energy multiplies, and your impact sustains. Stay close to this core.

For instance, if you're *passionate* about organizing your neighborhood's book club, and are *good at it*, that should absolutely be part of your profile. Those skills will come in handy as you continue down this path to doing Better Good.

The same applies to organizations. Impact sticks when it aligns with who you really are and what you already do well. That alignment becomes the foundation of your organizational profile for Better Good. For example, a law firm might lean into pro bono in ways that expand the reach and depth of their work to communities around the world, as the law firm DLA Piper has done with its boundary-busting work to expand beyond traditional pro bono into a dynamic global nonprofit called New Perimeter. More examples exist across industries. A bank might back microloans for small businesses. And a publisher might donate books, time, and expertise to promote literacy. When companies chase causes *outside* their Goldilocks Zone, the work struggles in headwinds. When they anchor to core strengths, they set themselves up for success to scale and sustain.

KEY TAKEAWAYS AND ACTIONS ITEMS

Key Takeaways

- **Profile anchors the Better Good Framework.** This chapter is the first "P" in PPP + TTT + SSS = The Better Good Framework—the part that makes you more aware of your potential for Better Good and more intentional about spotting opportunities and setting priorities. We start with Profile because knowing who you are is the key that unlocks everything that comes next.
- **Profile is more expansive than we often first think.** When we take a minute to truly assess ourselves, we discover that we have gloriously diverse and impactful profiles.
- **Everybody is somebody.** And each of us can make a difference—even if your profile for doing so isn't perfectly obvious at first glance.
- **Your profile is dynamic.** It contains multitudes, comprised of the unique blend of credentials, connections, and character that shapes how you do Better Good.
- **Your Goldilocks Zone sharpens focus.** The strongest profiles—individual or organizational—stay rooted in their Goldilocks Zone, where passion and proficiency overlap.

- **Discovery and expansion await.** The hidden truths you uncover about yourself can supercharge both your enthusiasm and your effectiveness.

Action Items

For Individuals

- **Map the elements of your Profile.** Summarize your Credentials / Connections / Character on a single page.
- **Target your Profile Goldilocks Zone.** Circle the elements of your Profile that sit at the intersection of passion and proficiency.
- **Take action.** Identify one way to use your profile this month to do Better Good at work, at home, or in your community.
- **Revisit quarterly.** Profiles grow and shift—so should your awareness.

Action Items

For Organizations

- **Assess your organization's Profile.** Audit your organization's profile using the same framework.

  Credentials: What do you uniquely make, offer, or deliver?

Connections: Who do you serve and collaborate with?

Character: How do people experience your culture and brand?

Check alignment. Does your external brand reflect your internal reality?

- **Activate engagement where it matters most.** Anchor future social-impact initiatives in your core strengths—your organizational Goldilocks Zone.

CHAPTER 5

Your Platform

All the world's a stage,
And all the men and women merely players;
They have their exits and their entrances;
And one man in his time plays many parts . . .
—from Shakespeare's *As You Like It*

David Fajgenbaum was only twenty-five years old the first time he heard what no patient wants to hear from a doctor: "We've tried everything. There's nothing else we can do."

As he lay in his hospital bed with tubes running in and out of his body, he struggled to comprehend this devastating news through the unbearable pain. His organs had begun to shut down and his family filed into his hospital room to say their final goodbyes, while a priest arrived to read him his last rites.

But David wasn't done yet. In a last-ditch effort to save his life, doctors backtracked on their "nothing else we can do" pronouncement and tried a combination of seven different chemotherapies. Somehow, he survived.

It was all still so hard to believe. The previous six months had been a nightmare made real. He had been a healthy college quarterback turned medical student, training to become an oncologist. He had chosen to specialize in cancer in memory of his mom, who had died of a glioblastoma when he was a college freshman. But David himself then became critically ill with a rare and deadly illness called Castleman Disease, which led him to that moment of crisis in the hospital.

Later, he would relapse and nearly die four more times in the next three years. By the time the doctors said those fateful words for the fifth time—*there's nothing else we can do*—he knew he likely wouldn't survive another relapse. Yet desperation, grit, and a medical background led David to take matters into his own hands.

He knew his only hope would be to find an existing drug that could be repurposed for him. From all those years of medical school he also knew this was possible because many diseases share the same underlying mechanism that can be treated by the same drugs. He began studying his own samples in the lab and found a medication, sirolimus, that emerged from the data as a contender. It had been sitting on the pharmacy shelf all along, used to treat other diseases but never tried for Castleman Disease. David began testing it on himself, and it worked.

He has now been in remission for more than a decade. He married the love of his life, had two children, and wrote a book about his journey, *Chasing My Cure*. And he joined the faculty at the University of Pennsylvania to continue chasing cures for other diseases, saving countless lives.

David spoke on the main stage of the Clinton Global Initiative (CGI) in 2022 to share his story and announce the launch of his nonprofit, Every Cure. I was lucky enough to be there, and listening to David tell his story gave me goose bumps.

Every Cure uses data, technology, and AI to discover the hidden potential of every approved drug to treat every disease possible. Of the 18,000+ known human diseases, there are only treatments for about 4,000 of them. What this means for you and me is that one in ten of the individuals we know and love will be diagnosed with a rare disease for which there is no known treatment. Every Cure, in just its first three years of operation, has already discovered dozens of new drug-disease pairs that hold the potential for life-saving and life-improving treatments hiding in plain sight. It has also attracted more than $100 million in grant and government funding, giving it the resources to save potentially millions of additional lives in the years ahead.

All because David stood on the stage—the platform—he was uniquely positioned to stand on, by virtue of experiences he hadn't anticipated or wanted, but which resulted from life happening for him, not just to him.

David has since shared this story—and the unfolding story of Every Cure and the lives it has saved and improved—on stages all over the world. In 2025 he gave a TED Talk, returned to the CGI stage to share Every Cure's progress, and sold the film rights for a movie based on his book, *Chasing My Cure*. Each appearance widened the platform that carries his work—and its impact.

David's story reminds us: "We've tried everything" doesn't have to be the end. In fact, sometimes it's the moment a platform for Better Good begins to expand.

From the moment he saved his own life, David's platform widened: in places (from Penn medical research labs to CGI and TED), industries (medicine and pharma lanes that conferred trust), organizations (Every Cure plus academic and hospital partners that "borrowed the halo" of his story), and online (media, podcasts, LinkedIn, and a book—all of which turned one talk into durable, shareable assets). The core message stayed mostly the same, but the stages multiplied.

That's the pattern you'll use in this chapter to think about your own platform: map your existing stages, then extend the ones that compound your impact the fastest—starting with stages that align with your Goldilocks Zone.

WHY FINDING A STAGE MATTERS

Shakespeare was right. All the world *is* a stage, and yours is likely bigger, bolder, and broader than you think. Your platform is the constellation of places and spaces where your work, your story, and your relationships reach, move, and engage people. When you see it clearly and use it deliberately, three things happen: attention concentrates, allies find you faster, and your effort compounds into bigger results. When you don't leverage your platform to its greatest potential, your efforts fragment and you stay busy, but your impact stays small, your message drifts, and you're more vulnerable to burnout.

We all stand on platforms larger than we first realize, with room to expand farther than we imagine. It's an ongoing process. Some of us are just recognizing that the rooms, relationships, and routines of our lives already form a stage for impact. Others, with wider public reach, still have to focus energy where it matters most to avoid dilution.

The same is true for organizations: their platforms are powerful assets that too often go underused, misdirected, or left unattended. Recognizing, refining, and reinforcing these platforms—personal or collective—is the shift from doing good to doing Better Good.

Platforms are no longer reserved for celebrities and CEOs. In fact, they never were when it comes to making a difference. We all have platforms, and we've had them since before this metaphor came to dominate social media. Your everyday circles—colleagues, neighbors, customers, classmates, congregations—are already platforms that move real people to real action. That said, the larger and clearer your platform, the greater your ability to create, lead, and attract others to Better Good. Leveraging yours matters now more than ever, when standing out in increasingly noisy and crowded spaces (both in real life and online) is harder than ever.

My goal in this chapter is simple: help you see your platform more clearly, expand it more intentionally, and use it more deliberately. Clarity compounds effort. The clearer your platform, the farther your Better Good work travels—and the more you can maximize and optimize your time, attention, and credibility.

DISCOVER YOUR PLATFORMS

It can be easy to mix up profile and platform. So, what's the difference?

Your profile is *who* appears on stages—your connections, credentials, and character. Your platform is *where* you can be heard—the rooms, roles, channels, and communities available to you. David's profile (survivor-physician-nonprofit founder) gave him the credibility to speak his Better Good story; his platforms (research lab, UPenn, CGI, TED, media) enabled the right people to hear him and take action to support him.

To maximize impact, start by mapping your current platform—where you *already* are, in life and in work. Here is a simple four-part framework for understanding your platform: places, industries, organizations, and online spaces. This framework isn't exhaustive, but it's a great starting point to establish a clearer and more confident view of when, where, and how you show up in the world.

Places

The places you physically inhabit provide the first and often most important platforms for doing good. Human nature leads most of us to "give where we live and do what we know"—to focus effort on the needs of the places where we spend the most time. Consider where you live and work, and other places with which you have a close connection. These are your *connected communities.*

As we move and travel, our circles expand. Causes we connect to even on brief visits become ones we connect and commit to all our lives. This is why people in landlocked states care deeply about the health of our oceans, and why I follow dog rescues in Hawaii and sweet potato farmers in Arkansas (long story). The diversity of our lived experiences and connections to places reveal opportunities to expand our platforms.

Nancy's connection to our shared home community in Illinois, where Watts of Love is headquartered, is strong. So is her connection to other communities Watts has served around the world. The village in the Philippines where she first identified the need for sustainable, reliable light holds a special place in her heart. And more than 150,000 homes in more than fifty-five countries have each created a connection to her cause and the teams that have joined her on trips to deliver light, love, and hope to these places. Nancy's deep feelings of connection and care are similar to the feelings that military veterans and Peace Corps, AmeriCorps, and Teach For America members feel for the places where they lived and served.

Take a moment to consider the most meaningful places in your life—your childhood or current hometown, the sites of core family memories, or other locations of deep personal connection. All are foundational to your platform and make up your connected communities.

Industries

What we do for work shapes where we spend our waking hours and who trusts us. This makes industry a ready-made platform. We often develop lifetime relationships with some of our colleagues, who become deeply integrated into our existence outside of the work we do together.

Whether you work in business, law, manufacturing, agriculture, transportation, hospitality, or a hundred other areas, what you do for a living (in addition to being a primary identifier of your profile) provides a platform to engage with colleagues, customers, and other contacts to deliver value to the communities you serve.

Our neighbors know Amy and me as lawyers. So when a neighbor has a legal question, we get a call. When I was growing up as the son of a doctor and a nurse, "Doc and Lois Curran" got a call whenever a neighbor kid was injured. Mechanics help with car troubles. Teachers help entire neighborhoods navigate educational issues and challenges. David, as a rare disease survivor and expert, gets calls from people the world over following a rare disease diagnosis, seeking the kinds of miracles that Every Cure's work seeks to make possible. The industries we serve in professional capacities become platforms for serving others.

Start here: treat your workplace and resulting networks as stages you already have and prioritize the ones closest to your Goldilocks Zone.

- Ask a mentor for guidance on leveraging the organizational platform for Better Good—and then mentor someone yourself in their own efforts to do good when the time is right.
- Volunteer your expertise to an industry organization.
- Champion an ethical practice or cause in your field; write and post about it.
- Propose a service project or spotlight a partner doing meaningful work.

Every meeting, email, and conversation inside your industry is a stage you can step onto to champion and attract others to Better Good.

Associations, Clubs, and Other Organizations

From the spaces immediately adjacent to our work to the communities in which we live, there's an array of other organizations that expand our platform for pursuing Better Good. National professional associations, specialty associations, your local PTA, and civic and social clubs from Soho Houses to Junior Leagues and Young President Organizations to Moose Lodges (yes, Moose Lodges still exist!) are ready-made platform extensions within a few miles of most of us. Add church roles, library or school boards, city councils, and local foundations. Then layer on national organizations and associations and the list keeps growing.

These entities support and enhance the good work we do and unite us with others who share a similar focus. You and I may be strangers to each other, but when we both show up at an association or club event, we know why we're there and have an immediate connection with others.

Think of this category as stage extensions that let your work reach farther without rebuilding the stage. Associations, clubs, and other organizations are your planks that lengthen the stage. Use them to reach deeper and wider without starting from zero. These organizations may require relatively little extra time for a chance to extend your reach and impact. Some examples to get your mind turning on this category's vast potential:

- Professional Associations: American Bar Association, American Medical Association, American Dental Association, American Marketing Association, American [Anything] Association, National Education Association, Society for Human Resource Management, trade unions, etc. In the nonprofit industry, organizations like the Nonprofit Leadership Lab, the We Are For Good community, and Board Source all provide platform-expanding resources, community, and engagement opportunities.
- Clubs: PTAs, YMCAs, Scouting Troops, Soho Houses, Young Presidents Organization, the Moose, the Masons.
- Alumni associations: If they gave you a degree (or a certificate), they probably have an alumni association. Beyond degrees and certificates from colleges and universities, *their* associated organizations—like fraternities and sororities or sports teams—have alumni associations. Many large employers do, too.
- Leadership Programs: From community leadership programs to the Presidential Leadership Scholars Program, and from peer leadership programs in school to Aspen Fellowships, there's an entire ecosystem of programs built to identify, connect, and develop exceptional leaders across fields. Whether academic, civic, or creative, these communities offer powerful networks and lifelong opportunities to learn, lead, and contribute.
- Don't overlook niche groups: Space Camp (by the way, did you know that I'm a four-time space camper?), Second City Training Center, Disney Institute, conferences, and online programs like MasterClass.

These affiliations all expand your platform without requiring you to reinvent yourself or start from scratch. Engage them intentionally to connect, influence, and contribute in meaningful ways.

I've seen this firsthand in my own field in some unexpected ways. Even the most established associations can suddenly find themselves called to step more boldly onto the stage they already occupy when the moment demands it.

Consider what happened in 2025, when the American Bar Association—long seen by many as a steady but unremarkable professional association—found itself reinvigorated and on the front lines of national debate. As political pressure and lawsuits mounted against major law firms for defending constitutional principles, the ABA stepped forward as a voice for the rule of law itself. It spoke up. It convened leaders across the legal profession to defend access to justice, professional independence, and the integrity of the legal system as the foundation of democracy. In doing so, the ABA became a robust platform for Better Good: protecting the institutions that protect us all. I dug out my expired ABA membership card, proudly renewed my membership, and started seeking ways to explore that stage, beginning by following their social media and lending my likes to the cause.

It's easy to see organizations like the ABA as monolithic, but they're made up of people like you and me who leverage their individual platforms to harness a collective one. This matters, especially now. Consider the ones you are part of and how you can leverage your platforms for maximum impact.

Start here: take an inventory. What organizations, associations, or clubs are already part of your world? Which ones align with your passion, profession, or purpose and sit nearest your Goldilocks Zone? And how can you activate these platforms to do Better Good?

Unexpected Platforms

You might be thinking, *Sure, Scott—platforms sound great for lawyers, executives, founders, or those working in the trades with unions and other built-in platforms. But what if I'm a hair stylist? A rideshare driver? Or a solo-preneur?*

Good question. Most of us picture microphones and big audiences. The fuller picture includes everyday spaces already within reach. When you widen your aperture, what first appears ordinary becomes extraordinary. A chair in a salon. The front seat of a car. A classroom, a kitchen, a checkout counter. Each is actually a powerfully intimate stage where lives intersect and stories unfold. With greater awareness and intentionality, these everyday spaces are full of potential to become pivotal platforms for Better Good.

Take Lorenzo Lewis, for example. I first encountered Lorenzo while in the audience at the same Clinton Global Initiative where David Fajgenbaum launched Every Cure. Lorenzo took the stage for one of those five-minute lightning talks that unexpectedly delight and inspire a room. He isn't a billionaire or statesman or movie star. He's a barber from Little Rock, Arkansas, with an incredible personal story, including having been born in a prison. Through The Confess Project, which he founded, he's turned barbershops into safe spaces for mental-health conversations—training barbers to listen, validate, and guide their clients toward care.

Today, The Confess Project supports more than 1,000 barbers in over forty cities, reaching well over a million clients each year. No big budgets. No celebrity endorsements. Just awareness, empathy, and the simple power of showing up for others where you already stand and work. It's a genius model, and a powerful platform, hiding in plain sight.

If your work involves hands, faces, or human contact—if you connect with people every day—you already have a platform that can change lives. Use it for Better Good. Sometimes, all it takes to turn work into purpose is paying closer attention to the conversations you're already having in the spaces where you already are.

I'll never forget the DoorDash driver who delivered an order to my brother and me in the parking lot of the hospital where our father was in his final days. She looked at us and said, "Whatever your reason for being here, I hope it's a blessed day for you." When I thanked her and noted we were, in fact, saying goodbye, she nodded and replied,

"Then I'll be praying for your peace and comfort on the road ahead." In a moment between strangers, she poignantly harnessed a simple platform for good in a way that has stayed with me.

Lorenzo's work with barbers, and a few words from a DoorDash driver arriving at a vulnerable moment, can be about much more than hair or hunger. The world's most powerful platforms for Better Good aren't always the biggest stages.

Online Spaces: Your Digital Stage

If all the world's a stage, then the internet is an infinite arena—always on and globally accessible, and with vast, instantaneous reach. Unlike traditional platforms that require being in a specific place at a specific time, online spaces allow your profile, expertise, and influence to grow, evolve, and impact others—often *far* beyond your immediate surroundings.

Your personal online presence, whether actively curated or passively maintained, includes how you present yourself, the conversations you engage in, the content you post, and the way you interact with others. Whether through Facebook, Instagram, TikTok, Twitter, YouTube, personal webpage, a blog, private groups, public forums, or even Goodreads, your personal online presence can be a massive platform for good.

Use it to inform, inspire, and invite action. Share causes that align with your passions (more on that in the next chapter). Celebrate others doing meaningful work. Offer helpful insights from your field or your lived experience that may serve others. Support campaigns or fundraisers that reflect your values. Comment thoughtfully, thank generously, and highlight solutions instead of just problems. Even a small, consistent signal of positivity and purpose builds trust and momentum within your circles. I get notes every week in response to my newsletter that readers are grateful for the positivity alone.

You don't have to have a large audience. Credibility and consistency matter more than follower counts. Put out the right signal, and the platform will grow with the right audience at the right time. As the saying goes, your vibe attracts your tribe. Build authentically, and your platform—and followers—will expand.

For many of us, LinkedIn is the default platform for our professional lives, but our professional platform doesn't stop there. It also includes other places you contribute your expertise. For example, your bio on your company or firm's website could reference your social impact work, or that you lead its volunteer work, or an affinity group, your status as a military veteran, your service on your city council, or any other service in your community. If *all* of your colleagues use their online bios the same way, your workplace begins to seem like the home of social impact superheroes. Powerful.

Or, if you're a business owner or executive, perhaps you have a blog, newsletter, Medium, Substack, or similar outlet associated with your work. If you do (or if you can create one), feature the ways in which you and your organization show up as a force for Better Good. Highlight your social impact initiatives, your service days, the organizations your corporate foundation supports, the portfolio of contributions you make either through direct donations or via matching contributions you make for employees. You never know when a thoughtful work-related social post, an insightful conversation on a webinar or podcast, or a quote you contribute to an article might result in a new connection or advance your standing as a credible thought leader to whom others may reach out to engage.

Better yet, feature your customers' or clients' work doing the same . . . this is a client relationship turbocharger. Good is contagious, so share it whenever possible. The specifics of these strategies aside, simply featuring them in the assets you already maintain online sends a signal of your commitments and contributions as a corporate citizen. And they matter to your team, customers, and stakeholders alike.

Always think: "portfolio, not posts." With each post, article, newsletter, or podcast appearance that you share, you're investing your desire for Better Good into the greater market of do-gooders.

STEP FURTHER ONTO THE STAGE

Platforms are more accessible and expandable than ever. We live in a world where a real estate developer turned reality TV show host persistently leveraged his platform to reach the highest elected office in the United States. Twice. Proof positive of the compounding power of consistent, intentional use of platform to achieve unimaginable reach.

The U.S. presidency isn't the only example. So many others have leveraged initially modest platforms to reach extraordinary heights unrelated to their initial notoriety. From Kim Kardashian advocating for the rights of the incarcerated to David Hogg, a Parkland High School shooting survivor, emerging as a national voice for gun control and broader political engagement, examples abound of unlikely and unexpected ascension to bigger stages. And these are merely a few high-profile cases. Many people leverage their existing platforms to create bigger ones that continuously expand their reach and their mission, even without becoming household names.

Most of us, however, wonder whether adjacent platforms are truly ours. For instance, David Fajgenbaum was unsure how he could share his story on the CGI stage in a way that would impact the audience and help him rally support for his new nonprofit, especially within a five-minute time limit. Such insecurities can afflict *anyone*, even brilliant doctors like David. And, believe it or not, even movie stars.

I once stood at the back of a darkened room at a CGI breakout session that had just gotten started, when the insecure whisper of another late arrival next to me distracted me from the voices of the experts on the well-lit stage. Impressed by the illustrious panelists onstage, he said to the person next to him "What the f*** am *I* doing in this room?" I instantly recognized a familiar voice but couldn't immediately identify it. I looked to my right, squinting through the darkness, to see a four-time Academy Award nominee standing next to me. He had clearly arrived early for his own panel and had popped into this breakout session to watch from the back wall . . . only to find himself feeling like he might not measure up to others. It proves the point that we *all* feel insecure in certain rooms, whether on stage or quietly standing along the back wall. It doesn't mean we aren't on the right stage or in the right room. As I often tell people: if you're in the room, you belong, so act like it and make your contribution.

The point is this: ordinary people with purposeful stories and intentional use of their platform can reach extraordinary audiences and foster seismic impact. Shed any limiting beliefs, say yes to rooms that feel "too big," and invite others onto your stages, from the smallest to the biggest.

Courage is a platform expander. The moment you act like you belong, others respond and buy into your mission. In a world where it seems any voice matters, those speaking about their efforts to do good should be heard loud and clear.

YOUR ORGANIZATION'S PLATFORM

Every organization has its own platform, too—stages from which they can lead, serve, and scale their impact. Whether a global brand, nonprofit, local business, or public institution, organizations hold great influence. And just as with individuals, their platforms are bigger—and more powerful—than many probably see at first glance.

At this moment in history, many of the institutions that once served our shared social safety net are retreating from their roles. Government's willingness to act as a force for common good is diminishing, leaving widening gaps in social, environmental, and economic support. Those gaps fall to others to fill, to the extent they can. Which is why it's more important than ever for organizations across every sector—and especially for influential brands—to step forward with clarity and conviction. The private and nonprofit sectors are faced with an outsized responsibility to model what responsible leadership looks like—using their platforms to signal what they stand for, where they stand, and inviting others, including their customers and teams, to stand with them for the principles and people that matter most.

Organizational platforms are also increasingly shaped by how and where they show up online, how they communicate with the world, and how they empower their employees, customers, supporters, and stakeholders to pursue Better Good. As we established in Chapter 3, we now live in a world where customers and talent intentionally affiliate with organizations that reflect their values. They vote with their time, talent, and treasure to support and serve organizations that reflect their values.

So if you're leading—or you have a leadership role in—a public or private company, big or small law firm, a school, nonprofit, or other organization, how are you using your platform? How are you empowering your people and showing up in your industry and community in ways that activate your values? Maybe your organization doesn't need a new stage—it just needs to step further onto the one it already has to do Better Good.

ACTIVATING YOUR PLATFORM

Recognizing the scope of your platform is step one. Leveraging and expanding it comes next. The key is to take inventory, assess where you're most engaged, and identify where you have room to grow. Start with platforms you already have and then expand deliberately.

Map where you already have attention (rooms you're in, roles you hold, channels you control), choose one cause or message that sits at your Goldilocks Zone, and undertake one repeatable action each month. Pick the stage that, if strengthened, lifts the others most. If you're in the room, you belong—so act like it. Invite others onto your stage, step onto theirs, and let small, steady signals stack into outsized outcomes.

KEY TAKEAWAYS AND ACTION ITEMS

Key Takeaways

- **Your platform is your stage.** It's where your work is seen and trusted—across places, industries, organizations, and online spaces.
- **It's bigger than you think.** Clear eyes and intentional use mean more reach, more allies, more compounding impact.
- **Platforms compound impact.** Small, steady signals (posts, talks, convenings) stack into larger outcomes over time.
- **Borrowed stages extend reach.** Affiliations (employer, alma mater, boards, associations) extend your reach without starting from zero.
- **If you're in the room, you belong.** Courage and consistency expand your platform.

Action Items

For Individuals

- **Inventory your current platforms.** Where you live and work, your industry and professional networks, associations/clubs, and your digital footprint.
- **Quick self-check.** Where do people already listen to you? Where can you invite others? Where do you show up repeatedly?
- **Start simple.** Prioritize one message plus one stage. Choose the message that aligns with your Goldilocks Zone and the single stage that, if strengthened, lifts the others.
- **Take action every month.** At work or with organizations you serve, accept one meeting or speaking invite or add a recurring 3-minute "impact note" to a team meeting. Publish a monthly LinkedIn post or newsletter. Host a small panel/webinar by "borrowing the halo" of your company, alma mater, or board.
- **Re-inventory quarterly.** Keep what compounds. Drop what drains. Double down on what invites collaboration, reach, and growth.

Action Items

For Organizations

- **Audit the organizational platform.** Map physical, professional, and digital stages. Identify where you are known vs. where you want to be known.
- **Align message and values.** Name the few causes/ issues you'll consistently show up for. Clarify who you serve and what you stand for.
- **Equip your people.** Provide simple tool kits: messaging guardrails, social guidelines, speaker decks. Recognize and reward employees who activate aligned platforms.
- **Set a cadence.** Establish a quarterly platform plan for thought leadership, convenings, service days, and campaigns. Pair internal moments (all-hands, launches) with external signals (posts, op-eds, partner spotlights).
- **Partner to multiply.** Mesh gears with business, government, and nonprofit counterparts. Co-host events. Cross-post and co-brand where appropriate.
- **Measure and govern.** Track action, impact, and measurable results (sign-ups, donations, volunteer hours). Establish brand-safety and growth paths so courage and consistency can coexist.

CHAPTER 6

Your Passion

When we know WHY we do what we do, everything falls into place. When we don't, we have to push things into place.

—Simon Sinek

We were the only two people in the hallway. It was September 2023, just past 8:00 on the second morning of the second year of a rebooted Clinton Global Initiative. Only a small number of attendees were already in early morning sessions before the main program was set to begin. I had rounded the corner from one corridor to the next when I saw him: world-renowned chef and humanitarian José Andrés, standing surprisingly alone as he finished a chat with a fan who was hurrying away with excitement following a selfie.

José is best known as the founder of World Central Kitchen (WCK), an extraordinary nonprofit that provides fresh, nourishing meals to communities in crisis. Whether after natural disasters or in active war zones, his team shows up where traditional aid often can't, delivering the comfort and dignity of hot meals when it matters most. For instance, WCK served over 3.6 million meals to the people of Puerto Rico following Hurricane Maria in 2017, and they partnered with hundreds of Ukrainian restaurants to serve hundreds of millions of meals to civilians after the Russian invasion in 2022. His many accolades include the U.S. Presidential Medal of Freedom, and his kinetic speeches—equal parts rallying cry and moral lightning bolts—draw crowds around the world.

But now there was no crowd or line of other selfie-seekers. Just José and me.

We made eye contact and he smiled an inviting smile.

"Good morning, José! So nice to see you. Quick question?"

He nodded instantly and intensely. "Yes!"

Reminding myself that this CGI event space was a platform on which I now stood (this was my first year attending as a guest and not as staff—so chin up and shoulders back, Curran), I resisted the inclination to overthink or shy away from the moment. I just asked the question that always lingered in my mind when I thought about José Andrés and WCK's work: "How do you scale?"

He walked toward me quickly. His hand landed firmly on my shoulder to pull me close.

"Well, you see . . ." he began. And then he *went.* For the next three minutes, I was a congregation of one for a sermon about his life's work.

He spoke about the urgency of feeding people in moments of crisis—about how in the midst of disaster, when infrastructure crumbles and leaders fail, a warm meal becomes the most intimate and important act of humanity. He spoke of the sacredness of preparing food and the universal dignity in sharing it. He spoke about nourishment—not just of bodies, but of spirit, of community, of hope. He spoke not with his head, but with every fiber of his being. Whoa.

And yet—he didn't answer my question, at least not directly. Not at all, really. At least not in my nerdy sense of what I was expecting to hear about scaling global operations (it takes a lot of people, resources, and coordination to feed millions) and meeting the ultimately unmeetable demand of the world's hungry. But somehow, it didn't matter. I left that conversation inspired . . . and strangely full.

The scale question is still important, of course, and we'll talk about it in later chapters. World Central Kitchen can't be everywhere hunger exists. No one can respond to every war zone, every earthquake, every broken supply chain. But José's response made one thing incredibly clear: this man isn't powered by a strategic plan or burdened by the challenge of considering scale. He is powered by pure, unadulterated passion. He hasn't just discovered his Goldilocks Zone, he's living in it.

Feeding people isn't just what he does. It is his purpose. His mission. The passion for which he'll crawl through glass, and often worse.

WHY DOES THIS MATTER TO YOU?

That's the real question behind any attempt at doing good, isn't it?

Passion is another word for what Simon Sinek calls your "why." It's not what you do or how you do it, but the deeper reason that fuels you. The belief. The mission. The fire. For some people, that's strategy. For others, it's storytelling. For many of us, it's justice, compassion, creativity, or connection. For me, it's scale. I love helping people and organizations scale their ability to do good. But ask someone to name their "why" out loud, and they often freeze or stumble.

I remember sitting across from a friend over coffee and asking, "So what's your *why*?" He stared at me blankly for a moment, stared at his coffee, and finally shrugged. "I think I'm still figuring that out," he said. "But I *do* know what I'll crawl through glass for."

That was the moment I realized: for many of us, our passion *is* our why. It's not some perfectly polished mission statement. It's whatever keeps us up at night. It's what pulls us out of bed in the morning. It's what we care about so deeply that we can't *not* act. It's the thing (more likely a few things) we rarely get tired of doing, and keep doing even when we do.

That's what this chapter is about: not what you like, or even what you love. It's about what moves you to do something that matters, even—especially—when it's hard. It's about discovering, naming, and *organizing* your passion—so you can use it to do Better Good. With an infinite (and growing) demand for Better Good in the world—especially when political winds shift, governments scale back, and businesses are punished for some of the good they do—you have an infinite range of options to make a difference. Like José's passion for feeding the hungry in the hardest places, your passion can point you in the right direction. If you can identify it.

"WHAT'S YOUR PASSION?"

We've all heard this question—at a job interview, on a college application, over drinks with a friend, on a date, amid a career pivot, in a late-night scroll through motivational Instagram quotes. It's one of the most common questions we're asked about our lives. And one of the most confusing.

If you google "follow your passion," you'll discover dozens of contradictory opinions about passion. Ditto if you watch TED Talks, read career advice blogs, or ask people you admire.

"Follow your passion," say those who argue that it's the only way to build a meaningful life and career.

"Whatever you do, *don't* follow your passion," say others, who see passion as a trap that keeps many people in low-paying jobs when they should be developing marketable skills.

Cal Newport, in *So Good They Can't Ignore You*, is more nuanced, arguing that passion *follows* skill—not the other way around. Focus on what you're good at first, and passion will catch up later.

Scott Galloway, in *The Algebra of Happiness*, seeks a middle ground, warning that "follow your passion" is terrible advice if you're broke, but admirable if you've already built up a financial cushion and marketable skills (or if you're blessed with a trust fund).

Seth Godin and Elizabeth Gilbert offer a counterpoint that hits closer to home for our purposes of doing good. They describe passion as a *compass*: not something you blindly chase, but something that helps you navigate the world with purpose. They approach passion as a directional force that helps you choose wisely and keep going, especially when things get hard.

Here's where I land: they're all right . . . but only partially.

Passion isn't an either/or conversation. It's a both/and. When it comes to building a life and career (or organization) with impact, your passion is always relevant, and Newport and Galloway's guidance is helpful. Because skills are always relevant in our work and the organizations we lead and serve. But skills alone are not the only variable, and passion for what we do and the causes we serve is absolutely essential if you want to advance along the spectrum of doing Better Good. Your passion is the fuel that helps you sustain and scale the good you do in ways that are—and remain—meaningful to you.

Passion comes in all shapes and sizes. We use the word for just about everything—our careers, our hobbies, our families, our friends, our relationships, our hopes, our dreams, our favorite foods, our fantasy football teams. It's the catch-all term for what lights us up, and that's great. Life is better when we live it with passion.

But it also creates a problem: if everything is a passion, nothing stands out in a way that helps us focus on what truly matters most to our sustained focus and commitment. Even when we narrow our focus to "causes," the list can still get overwhelming fast.

You might say you care about the environment—but do you mean climate change, plastic pollution, coral reef preservation, sustainable agriculture, or all of the above?

You might say you're passionate about animal rescue—but is it dogs, cats, ferrets? Certain breeds? Specific shelters? Local rescues? Global advocacy? All the animals in all the places? Easy, Noah . . .

Suddenly, a simple conversation about your passion can start to feel like scrolling through a dropdown menu with 500 options. And that's before you even consider how your level of care or capacity for action might vary from cause to cause. So please keep in mind that we're talking specifically about *causes*—the issues you care most about in the world and the challenges you feel most drawn to help solve. We aren't solving for all the other kinds of passions—about careers, family, relationships, and personal growth. Those are important, too, but not our focus. Instead, we're focusing on the need for a better path for understanding, identifying, categorizing, and prioritizing the causes of concern for which we want to do Better Good.

INTO THE GOLDILOCKS ZONE

Given all of this conflicting advice, it's tempting to put the whole passion question aside. *I'll figure that out later,* we tell ourselves. But "later" often becomes "never." We default to what we've always done. And we get what we've always gotten.

There has to be a better way. There is.

As we defined in Chapter 1, your Goldilocks Zone is the overlap of passion and proficiency—the place where what fuels you meets what you do well, and where energy and ability meet. It's where effort feels natural, time disappears, and impact compounds. It's the sweet spot where joy and effectiveness reinforce each other, and where you're most likely to keep going when the going gets tough.

When you're in your Goldilocks Zone, showing up doesn't feel like work. You jump in without being asked. You don't have to force yourself to care, to focus, or to follow through. You *want* to. You understand the problem quickly, contribute meaningfully, and feel the satisfaction of seeing progress. And because you enjoy it, you come back. Again and again.

Too little passion for a cause means we flame out. Too much without grounding in skill or structure, and we burn out. But *just right*—when the things you care most about align with the things you do best—you find the zone where meaning meets momentum. Where doing good feels less like effort and more like flow.

This is especially important when times are tough, when vulnerable people are hurting, and when resources are tight. It's easy to fall into despair and throw up your hands because the world's needs are too great. Don't do that. Instead, focus on identifying and deploying your energy inside your Goldilocks Zone, by being honest about the fact that you don't care equally about every potential opportunity to do good. And that's okay! In fact, it's more than okay—it's good.

THREE TYPES OF PASSIONATE CAUSES

Our passions come in degrees. Not every cause pulls us out of bed in the morning. Not every issue keeps us up at night. We can't fix everything, and we shouldn't try. Our brains and our calendars don't have the capacity to care about everything all the time. We simply can't give our time, talent, and treasure equally to every issue that tugs at our hearts. We have to prioritize.

So let's stop treating all passions like they're the same. Instead, let's categorize them more purposefully so we can direct our energy where it matters most. Without this kind of clarity, we become like bottle rockets without a stick—flaring up randomly, launching into the air without direction, and fizzling out too quickly. But with the right categories and focused intention, we gain the clarity to chart a course with consistency, purpose, and staying power, exploding with energy in the *right* direction.

Here's a framework to take a meaningful inventory of your passions, so you can better focus, act, and maybe even scale your efforts.

Causes of Passing Concern

These are the causes that pop up on your radar now and then. You care—legitimately—whenever one of these crosses your radar. But not deeply and usually not on your own initiative. Maybe someone posts a link on social media, so you click. Maybe your grocery store invites you to "round up for charity" at the checkout line, so you do. Maybe a neighborhood kid knocks on your door, raising money for the Scouts, a club, or sports team.

These are the kinds of causes we support lightly when prompted, but they're not ones we actively seek out. They're like background music—the easy listening in your do-good soundtrack. And that's perfectly fine. These causes still matter. But they're not where your focus should go if you're trying to build a sustainable, purpose-driven approach to impact.

Some actions you might take for this type of passion:

- Sign a petition.
- Throw a couple of bucks in the bell-ringer's bucket at the holidays.
- Purchase wrapping paper, chocolate bars, or a magazine subscription from that nice kid soliciting door-to-door for their softball team.
- Send an email or show up to speak to your school board or town council to share your thoughts about an important issue of the day.

I love signing petitions for sincere friends and neighbors who are running for local office. I'll always support the local school fundraiser. And to this day, if you hit me up for Girl Scout Cookies or a fundraiser for the kids' soccer team trip, I will gladly overpay for some Thin Mints or caramel popcorn.

Causes of Consistent Care

These are the causes with a real and recurring presence in your life. They're often tied to people, places, or experiences you care about. Maybe it's the church in which you grew up; the animal shelter where you adopted your dog; your kid's school; the autism awareness nonprofit that a friend founded; or the 5K you run each year to fight a disease that has affected your family.

You show up for these causes. You donate enough to feel a bit of sting in your wallet. You volunteer, attend events, rally friends to join you. You know the mission, understand the challenges, and support the work over time. These causes are part of your identity—but not the center of it. You're a consistent contributor, a dependable advocate. When these organizations call, you answer. You've got skin in the game, and their presence in your impact footprint is visible. But if you had a million dollars to give away, you probably wouldn't give them more than, say, 20 percent. These aren't going into your will.

Some actions you might take for this type of passion:

- Join the planning committee for a local nonprofit's annual fundraiser, committing one night a week for a few months.
- Support your college's alumni association, not just via donations but also by serving as a mentor for students interested in your field.
- Show up for your local assisted living facility's volunteer corps, spending one afternoon a month hanging out with seniors who don't get many visitors.
- Instead of merely emailing your school board, go to the meeting where the new budget is being debated and raise your hand to speak up.

For me, this category captures my feelings about animal rescue in general. If you're working to save endangered species, I'm listening. If you're helping find homes for stray cats in the Midwest, I'm glad to help. But your cause still won't be one of my most urgent and essential, because for me, it's all about the dogs. I'd crawl through glass for them.

Crawl-Through-Glass Causes

This is your highest tier of passion—the kind that defines you. These are the causes that get you out of bed early, keep you up late, and rarely leave your mind. You wear the T-shirt. You have the bumper sticker. *And* you're the person your friends associate with this issue. *And* you might serve on a board of directors, lead a campaign, build a new organization, or even shape your career around this cause. These causes are woven into your life and values at a cellular level. If you're lucky enough to come to the end of your life with a nice lump of savings sitting in the bank, these causes will be in your will—they might even endow a fund for a scholarship or get your name on a building if you've got a higher-end estate plan.

But passion alone isn't enough to keep the fire burning, and this takes us back to the idea of the Goldilocks Zone: The real magic happens when you pair that deep devotion with what you're *good at.* Passion is the fuel; proficiency is the engine. One without the other sputters. Together, they hum. You've developed skills (or are developing them) precisely because you've gone all in on this cause—and that cycle keeps feeding itself. You care about the cause, you're good at contributing to it, and the better you get, the more you care.

Your crawl-through-glass causes—within your Goldilocks Zone—are where you'll do your most meaningful, sustainable, and scalable work in your growing social impact footprint. Not because it matters most in the world, but because it matters most *to you.* Other causes may come and go, but these remain constant. Think Nancy illuminating poor villages, David finding cures for "incurable" diseases, and José feeding people in desperate need.

Here are examples of some actions you might take for this type of passion:

- Publicly share your support for these causes on a regular basis. Wear the merch proudly.
- Promote these issues on your daily social media scroll when the opportunity arises.
- Bring them up in conversations with friends, colleagues, and strangers alike to raise awareness and rally support.
- Become not merely an occasional volunteer but a *dedicated, reliable* volunteer—the kind who becomes the glue of any organization.
- When you're ready, seek or accept a leadership role, such as committee chair, local chapter president, or board member.

- Depending on your life circumstances, consider taking a gap year to immerse yourself in an organization that works on your crawl-through-glass cause.
- If the stars align, perhaps even consider workplace efforts or even a career change that align with your most important causes.

Here's how this works for my own crawl-through-glass cause of dog rescue. Our family doesn't just adopt shelter dogs; we foster and adopt special needs dogs that almost no one else will take. I evangelize for nonprofit shelters (and against puppy mills) at every opportunity (#AdoptDon'tShop). I'm willing to give advice and support to *any* family that's considering adopting a rescue dog for the first time, if they reach out with questions. I join, support, and lead fundraisers. We've got provisions in our estate plan to support rescues when we're gone. And I don't see any of this work or expense as a burden—I see it as a privilege. It involves a lot of time and effort, but because of the pattern recognition and repetition involved, it's become second nature for our entire family. Moreover, due to decades of work on this front, we're connected to individuals and organizations nationwide that often prove helpful in various circumstances. So while it can involve lots of challenges, hard work, and occasionally a little heartache, because this work is at the center of my own Goldilocks Zone where passion and proficiency overlap, I don't perceive it as hard. Even though it actually sometimes is.

COMMON PASSION PITFALLS

Even with these categories in hand to more easily identify your passions, it's easy to veer off track. We all want to do good. But too often, we end up diffusing our energy in ways that leave us exhausted, unfulfilled, or wondering why our efforts don't seem to be adding up. Here are a few of the most common passion pitfalls that derail our ability to remain aligned with the causes that matter most.

Pursuing Someone Else's Passion

Sometimes, we end up chasing causes we've inherited through family expectations, social circles, or organizational culture. Maybe your parents were lifelong supporters of a particular charity, or your workplace has a default annual fundraiser that everyone joins. These aren't bad causes, but they may not be *your* cause. When we confuse obligation, projection, or peer pressure for passion, we risk missing the fire that comes from authentic alignment.

It's okay to say "no thank you" to the requests that come with these causes, to scale back, or make just a token contribution and note you're directing your focus to another cause about which you're excited—and maybe even share details about it to turn the tables in the best way possible. You never know if saying no to the wrong thing (for you) may help raise awareness or spur engagement from others about the cause about which you're more passionate.

If you receive an ask about a cause of passing concern requesting a level of commitment or time you don't feel inspired to give (whatever that may be, big or small), you've got my permission to delete or decline it. If it's a personal request, thank the requestor for thinking of you, for being committed to doing good, and just note that you've recently committed to another cause with which you're more aligned and engaged. Then use that pivot point as an opportunity to tell them about it. It's okay—actually, it's essential—to protect your focus. Be picky in whatever ways best serve your passions for Better Good. All causes eventually find their people, and it's essential that you concentrate on yours.

Getting Stuck in a Low-Alignment Zone

This one's especially tricky. You might be great at something—say, serving on a board, managing a budget, organizing logistics, or running a campaign—but dread every minute of it.

You're in the "proficient but passionless" zone, where well-intentioned people burn out while doing good work. We sometimes mistake activity for progress, which is great for staying busy, but doesn't work when it comes to sustainability of your vision and mission. Remember, your Goldilocks Zone lies where passion *and* proficiency intersect. If you're dragging your feet, if your heart isn't in it, or you're just not feeling it, it's a sign to reevaluate.

Here's how to do just that: "If it isn't a resounding yes, then it's a no." Try it. It works! And this makes sense when you think about it: for something to be a "resounding yes" you've really got to be into it. Whether it's the cause itself, or the opportunity to support or work with others you respect and admire in a way you know you can uniquely contribute. If you're ready to jump in and keep going for the long haul, that's a "resounding yes" and a green light. If not, proceed with extreme caution, apply the filter outlined above, and be selective—not to be stingy with your support, but to protect your focus and resources.

Your time, talent, and treasure are valuable and deserve to be devoted to the right causes for *you*. Just because you're good at something—and others see that—doesn't mean you have to do it for everyone. Of course, you should remain open to new things, listen for details and opportunities that may excite or engage you in new ways. That's how we discover new opportunities. But when it comes time to make a serious decision, apply the "resounding yes" test to the request, and be picky about your contributions to ensure strong alignment.

Right-Sizing Commitment

Amid the many potential opportunities—and good reasons—for supporting various causes in your life and work, it's essential that you right-size your commitment. Otherwise you risk one of the most common pitfalls of all: burnout. Maybe you care about *so* many things that you say yes to everything. Every volunteer opportunity. Every school event. Every donation request. But without a system for prioritizing, you end up scattered, stretched thin, and stuck in the shallow end of impact. You're doing a lot, but not necessarily doing much of it well. And if you try to inventory your social impact footprint in any given year, the scattered nature of your myriad contributions makes it nearly impossible. Some people love this and wrap their Better Good identity around this approach. If it's an intentional choice and the way you want to proceed in your work, great! But if being the one who says yes to everything all the time is running you ragged and burning you out, it isn't sustainable and doesn't serve the causes that need your full attention. Your "Not To Do" list is sometimes more important than your "To Do" list.

Let's be clear: none of this is about ignoring causes of passing concern or turning our noses up to the causes others care about. It's being intentional about *right-sizing* your focus and effort—about pouring *your* rocket-fueled energy (which isn't infinite) into what counts most and in the ways that keep you going. You can still sign the petition, share the post, and round up for charity at checkout. But the deep, intentional, enduring work? That belongs to the causes you're most connected to—the ones that live in your Goldilocks Zone. Those are the ones that deserve your best energy, your unique strengths, and your loudest voice. That's where your passion becomes power and your level of commitment feels just right.

Protect the core of your Goldilocks Zone by being judicious about your commitments. Say no to other opportunities—worthy though they may be—that aren't a "resounding yes," and use the resulting opportunities to share your passion for Better Good with others that may raise awareness or rally support for the crawl-through-glass causes you care about most.

A CAUTIONARY TALE

So what happens when you pursue a project that's out of alignment with your real passion? At best, you get a short-lived effort. At worst? A slow-motion energy drain with opportunity costs all around.

I was once invited to a call with a law firm representing an NBA star. He had just launched a new nonprofit, helmed by his mom and supported by other family members. Not unusual. Also, often perilous. These setups tend to combine good intentions with little experience—especially with 501(c)(3) rules about "private benefit," which can quickly turn heartfelt efforts into IRS headaches, or worse.

But this time, I was actually encouraged. The player had a solid legal team involved—smart folks making sure the foundation was legit from jump. So I joined the call, optimistic. But I quickly noticed a huge problem.

From the NBA star, his mother, and his legal team, I felt no passion. No vision. No energy. Zero. Zip. Zilch. We might as well have been making small talk about the weather. The kind of strategy meeting that's usually a rocket-fueled download of dreams, mission, and excitement was, instead, putting me to sleep.

But I held out hope. Maybe I could light a spark. When it was my turn, I brought the full caffeinated-with-Better-Good Scott: heartfelt praise, strategic clarity, a dose of CGI inspiration (including a reference to my decade of CGI hallway chats with the GOAT's mom, Deloris Jordan, about the Jordan family's foundation, which she led), and a roadmap to real impact. They politely appreciated my enthusiasm. Then . . . back to neutral. No liftoff. No follow-up. No forward motion. Sad trombone.

Months later, I checked in. Zero progress had been made. The new foundation was just a vessel of good intentions. Bummer. But, sadly, not uncommon. Too many well-intentioned, high-profile achievers feel that starting their own nonprofit or social impact initiative is part of a portfolio expected of their status and standing. Many simply feel compelled—but not driven—to develop this part of their portfolio along with their fame or success. But good intentions unsupported by a strong foundation, without a right-sized, tailored focus, and a vision for scale and sustainability as an interwoven part of their story, ultimately become side projects that fall by the wayside, especially if they were never in their true Goldilocks Zone to begin with.

If you're not driven by passion for a particular cause or opportunity and are just going through the motions of what you think is expected of you given your position in life, think hard before launching a "passion project" that may be entirely lacking in, ya know, actual passion.

Even with the right people in the room and smart guidance on paper, the fire still matters. Without it, you won't make the kind of progress that comes with digging deep when the going gets tough, as it almost always does. And if the fire's not there at all? That's okay—you can use that as an opportunity to pivot to something else that actually lights you up and keeps you going for the long haul. We'll talk more about scale and sustainability in later chapters, but for now, know this: if you don't feel passion to crawl through glass for the cause, you will never enter the Goldilocks Zone. Keep exploring.

And remember this, too: you don't have to start your own organization to find and advance your passion. Quite the opposite, actually. There are almost two million nonprofits that already exist (and even more initiatives of other types of organizations) that address nearly every cause—and subset of causes—to which you can contribute your time, talent, and treasure in different ways. There's no requirement to be a founder of one to find your greatest opportunity, as we'll see in upcoming examples.

THE PASSION INSIDE YOUR ORGANIZATION

"Passion" is such a deeply human word that it may feel strange to apply it to businesses and other organizations. But on a practical level, we all know businesses have passions, and we notice those passions a surprising amount. Some "just have a feel" to them, exuding a lifelike culture or vibe—from Apple Stores to Disney parks and the cultlike obsessions around Trader Joe's and Costco. Passion abounds in businesses and organizations. Even so, we've all heard some businesses or organizations described as "having no soul" and we can feel that, too. Others take clear positions and embed their values directly into what they make, sell, and stand for—shaping how customers buy and how employees choose where to work. Whatever anyone's take may be about a business expressing its values, we know where Chick-fil-A, Hobby Lobby, Patagonia, Ben & Jerry's and the like usually stand. Even the Supreme Court reminded us, in its famous 2010 *Citizens United* decision, that organizations have the same free speech (and other) rights as individuals. So we might as well acknowledge that they can have passions, too.

When a company's founders, leaders, shareholders, stakeholders—including their teams and customers—care deeply about a cause, that cause often filters up, down, and throughout the entire organization. It is often—but not always—founder-driven, and is regularly demand-driven by employees and customers. Those who aren't as enthusiastic may opt out over time, and those who share and align their passion lean in more deeply—until a clear culture emerges, aligned around shared values and causes. When that happens, it becomes much easier for the organization to truly commit to doing Better Good.

Chobani, for example, is deeply committed to healthy ingredients and sustainable supply chains—both central themes in its philanthropy. And because supporting refugees is a personal cause of founder and CEO Hamdi Ulukaya, that, too, has become a signature part of Chobani's impact platform through its affiliated refugee-focused nonprofit, Tent.

Bass Pro Shops has a long-standing passion for conservation. Its founder and CEO, Johnny Morris, was honored with the National Audubon Society's Medal for a "lifetime passion for conservation and sharing the outdoors with everyone." That passion now shapes the company's broad investments in protecting forests and waterways across North America.

JPMorganChase has been a leading voice in the multi-stakeholder capitalism movement, a crawl-through-glass cause for longtime CEO Jamie Dimon, who has also chaired the influential Business Roundtable of Fortune 500 CEOs. And Apple, famously passionate about empowering creativity (poignantly established by its iconic "Think Different" campaign of the late '90s), has carried that ethos into its retail and community programming—using platforms like Today at Apple to open doors for the next generation of creators.

None of this is new. Companies have unapologetically aligned their operations with the values and causes they care about for as long as there have been companies. And examples my parents' generation regarded as new, are now known as classic examples (e.g., Patagonia, Ben & Jerry's).

None of this should be dismissed as so-called "woke capitalism," either. Bass Pro Shops is proudly conservative, and its founder has openly supported conservative candidates. And as this book went to press, Chick-fil-A—a company that openly grounds its culture in Christian values and is often held up as a conservative counterpoint in cultural debates—still maintained a public commitment to diversity, equity, and inclusion on their website, even amid the backlash against DEI initiatives. Because caring for employees, treating customers with dignity, and building workplaces where all people feel they belong are human instincts. They also consistently show up as durable and profitable business strategies.

Remember, all good is good, and real-life impact doesn't come with a purity test. Some of the most passionate conservationists I've met are hunters and fishers from red states. They care deeply about fertile farmland and clean water for fishing, drinking, and watering their crops and cattle. They care about the fields in which they hunt game and from which that game feeds, which need to be healthy, safe, and sustainable. When watering holes of cattle ranches run dry, or fire burns fields, farms, and family homesteads, environmental concerns become a passionate priority focus for anyone and everyone living with the land.

Passion doesn't follow party lines—it follows vision and values.

The key is this: corporate leaders can and should let their hearts and convictions shape their missions, visions, and values. But they must do it with clarity, which allows a passionate purpose to energize employees, inspire customers, and build alignment with those who believe in the same cause—and yes, also filter out those who don't. And lastly, a Better Good leader should learn about the passions of their teams and employees, and see how they can pour rocket fuel on those visions and values. Because if you're not listening to what the people you lead care about, they will make you listen. Just ask Maren Costa.

Employees Can Move Mountains

In 2019, a longtime designer at Amazon named Maren Costa, along with a few colleagues, started Amazon Employees for Climate Justice, a small internal group that began asking big questions. They were frustrated with Amazon's silence on climate action and wanted to do something about it. Within months, thousands of Amazonians had joined them—urging leadership to take meaningful action on climate change.

It worked. On the eve of a planned employee walkout, Amazon announced sweeping new commitments: a Climate Pledge to reach net-zero carbon by 2040, a fleet of 100,000 electric vans, and soon after, the Bezos Earth Fund—established with the largest philanthropic commitment ever to fight climate change and protect nature. One employee-led movement helped nudge one of the world's most powerful companies toward real change.

Now, none of this was without risk. Costa and another organizer were later fired for their activism—a decision the National Labor Relations Board eventually ruled illegal—but the point remains: employees inside one of the biggest and most complex organizations on the planet sparked a global climate commitment that reshaped Amazon's public posture and inspired similar efforts across the tech industry.

Fortunately, this isn't always how these stories end. At companies like Salesforce, employee advocacy around pay equity and ethical use of technology was embraced and institutionalized, shaping company policy and culture instead of ending careers. And at Microsoft, sustained internal pressure helped accelerate public climate commitments that leadership ultimately championed. Sometimes employee voices *are* punished. But other times they are absorbed, elevated, and turned into sound and lasting strategy.

The Amazon story isn't tidy, and the actions of Maren and her colleagues obviously had their limits. But it proves a point worth remembering: employees have power. A single voice, multiplied by many, can move even the most monolithic institutions to act. This work is hard, messy, and imperfect. Nobody said change would be easy. But growth—and Better Good—almost always lives on the other side of the hard things.

All of this brings us back to what Simon Sinek reminded us in *Start with Why*: People don't buy what you do. They buy why you do it.

KEY TAKEAWAYS AND ACTION ITEMS

Key Takeaways

- **Passion is a compass.** Passion points you toward what matters and gives you the energy to start (and restart) when things get hard.
- **Proficiency is your engine.** What you are good at, combined with your passion, is your Goldilocks Zone.
- **Not all passions are equal.** Use three tiers—Passing Concern, Consistent Care, Crawl-Through-Glass—to focus on passions that matter most to your efforts to do good and to right-size your efforts.
- **Strength Test Your Yes.** To determine how to right-size your efforts, use the filter "If it isn't a resounding yes, then it's a no" to protect your energy and keep you focused on the causes and efforts most important to you.
- **Organizations have passions, too.** When leaders focus and teams organize around passion, employee conviction and company capability can move even "unmovable" brands.

Action Items

For Individuals

- **Make your passion map.** List ten causes you care about. Sort them into Passing Concern, Consistent Care, and Crawl-Through-Glass. Highlight the ones that light you up most.
- **Inventory your proficiency.** Write five to seven transferable skills—leadership, fundraising, legal, operations, design, communications, social media—and star the two you love doing most.
- **Find the overlap.** Highlight the proficiency pieces where you can add outsized value fast and for a long time. That's your Goldilocks Zone.
- **Set a 90-day focus.** Pick one crawl-through-glass cause and one high-proficiency contribution to advance it. Add a recurring weekly task list item to ensure you move it forward.
- **Apply the "Resounding Yes" rule.** As progress and success create new opportunities, apply the rule that "If it isn't a resounding yes, then it's a no" (or "no for now"). Keep a "Later/Elsewhere" list for good causes that aren't your three passion categories right now. Pro tip: recommend others who might be a great fit for the invitations you decline!
- **Continue Curating.** Remain intentional about naming your causes and how you help as your work,

interests, and passions evolve with the causes you care about most.

- **Measure what matters.** Track three key factors: time invested, people mobilized, result achieved. Review monthly and adjust. This becomes an important part of your storytelling over time.

Action Items

For Organizations

- **Take the passion pulse.** Survey team members by asking: Which causes do we care about? Which skills can we offer? What impact do we most want to have? Share results transparently.
- **Build a skill bank.** Create a simple opt-in directory of team member strengths—leadership, logistics, design, data, languages—so teams can find and leverage key core talents.
- **Curate a Goldilocks Zone portfolio.** Choose one to three causes aligned with your core business strengths, stakeholder motivations, and core competencies. Say no to the rest for twelve months to focus effort and resources.
- **Offer time to act.** Pilot a "ten hours per quarter" or "1 percent time" volunteer time off (VTO) policy. Keep

it simple to use and track. Incorporate a method for capturing results for impact storytelling purposes.

- **Match giving that matters.** Implement, maintain, or grow an employee-matching giving program. If budget allows, provide tiered matching gifts—1:1 for any 501(c)(3), 2:1 for focus-area partners—capped per employee to maintain equity.
- **Model the cadence.** Encourage leaders to set the example: one service day per quarter, one spotlight post per month, one partner engagement (informational session; lunch and learn, etc.) per quarter. Right-size it for your organization.
- **Tell the story.** Publish a quarterly "Impact Note" that shows what was done, who it helped, and what's next. Spotlight employees, partners, customers, clients, and other stakeholders.
- **Measure inputs, outputs, and outcomes.** Track hours, dollars, and participation—but also report on meaningful results (clients served, tons saved, students tutored, etc.).
- **Make it durable.** Integrate purpose into onboarding, reviews, and partner renewals. Revisit and recommit annually. Tell your story to, with, and across stakeholder groups to ensure your commitments and your impact are known so that your example inspires and engages others.

PART III

WHAT YOU CONTRIBUTE: TTT

Now that you've explored *who you are*, it's time to focus on *what you can contribute*. Every one of us holds resources that can be used for good—no matter how ordinary they may seem. In this part of the book, we'll look at the three resources that matter most: your Time, Talent, and Treasure.

Your time is the great equalizer. You, Oprah, and José Andrés all start with the same twenty-four hours a day. Chapter 7 helps you use that time more mindfully and meaningfully, through a simple framework for how to spend it in service of good.

Your talent includes every skill, strength, and bit of expertise you can deploy to make a difference—even and especially the ones that don't come with a diploma or title. Chapter 8 helps you identify and apply those gifts, showing how transferable they are when you aim them toward purpose.

Your treasure is whatever financial resource you can give, raise, or redirect. Contrary to popular belief, you don't need extraordinary wealth to make an impact. In fact, those with the least often give the most. Chapter 9 helps you stretch every dollar of generosity—from one to one billion—showing that smart giving can amplify good far beyond its face value.

By the end of this section, you'll see that you already have everything you need to start making an impact. The challenge—and the opportunity—is to use it wisely.

CHAPTER 7

Your Time

What is it you plan to do with your one wild and precious life?

—Mary Oliver

THE OPPORTUNITY COST OF "I DON'T HAVE TIME"

"Hey Scott," said one of the world's top law firm leaders at the start of our call, "would you meet with my partner Jack? He's done it all—and now he wants to . . ."—*wait for it*, I thought—"give back."

I knew those last two words were coming. I'd heard some version of this request dozens of times. A senior partner, at the apex of a wildly successful legal career, gets the itch for more meaning and fulfillment and decides that they (finally) want to do more good.

Of course, I always say yes to the request to have these conversations. It's the only acceptable answer when a global chair of a top-tier firm makes the ask. These are the same firms that supported our work at the Clinton Foundation with millions in pro bono time and talent. And I'm always genuinely happy to meet anyone seeking to do more good in their life and work, especially when they're well-positioned to make a significant impact. But privately, I often find myself asking the same question out of mild frustration: "What were they waiting for?"

Most of the "Jacks" I meet are titans of their profession. They've built huge books of business, mentored waves of talent, and closed deals in the billions. And now—often approaching the third act of their career—they're ready to step into service. It's admirable. But it's also a missed opportunity.

Because they didn't have to wait. They could have done good all along.

In his book, *From Strength to Strength*, Arthur Brooks reminds us that in almost every high-skill profession, cognitive decline begins earlier than we expect, often in our late thirties to early fifties. He points out that even Charles Darwin spent his later years haunted by a sense of irrelevance. If it can happen to Darwin, it can happen to anyone. The better move is to pivot toward purpose earlier—ideally from the beginning, and before the peak passes. Because when you wait until your peak has passed, you may find yourself searching for meaning from a place of decline or fatigue rather than from a place of momentum and mastery.

For the Jacks of the world, that momentum can be found not just in the spare moments or on the sidelines of their lives, but at the center of their careers, if not at the outset. They could have modeled impact for peers and protégés, embedded purpose into firm culture, and spoken the language of service in client pitches, conferences, classrooms, and partner retreats. (In other words, they could have harnessed their profiles and platforms more purposefully.) They could have used their time to mentor changemakers, fundraise for causes, or organize firm-wide service efforts that created or amplified a culture of impact.

Instead, they waited. The perishable commodity of time was lost in the delay. And the opportunity cost of that delay is immeasurable. The missed mentorships. The unspoken invitations to younger lawyers to leverage their firms for Better Good. The culture shifts that never took root. The effects that never had a chance to ripple. The opportunity cost compounded rapidly in my head each time I spoke to Jack. And it's not just him. So many high-powered people like him are in an enviable position. They can use just a *tiny* amount of valuable time to leverage their profiles, platforms, and passions and make a huge—no, a massive—impact. A little piece of my soul dies every time I talk to one of the Jacks of the world.

Yes, true, it's never too late to begin. I agree—and we'll talk more about that soon—but the *earlier* you start, the greater the impact. As the proverb goes: "The best time to plant a tree was twenty years ago. The second-best time is now."

I'm not trying to guilt-trip anyone. But here's my point: you don't have to choose between professional excellence *or* personal purpose in terms of how you spend your time. This is a both/and, not an either/or. You can achieve more by integrating both.

The tools in this chapter are designed to make doing good a seamless part of how you spend your time, every day, throughout your entire life and career. You don't need to wait until you have "more time" to do good. You have time now. It comes in different forms, often right under your nose.

If you start now, you won't just catch up—you'll lead the pack. And your example will give others the permission and playbook to do the same, which is a force multiplier.

YOUR MOST POWERFUL RESOURCE

Time is the great equalizer: universal, nonrenewable, and profoundly precious. You can't earn more of it, buy it, sell it, borrow it, or save it for later. Every person and organization on the planet gets the same twenty-four hours each day. But you can choose how to use it, which makes time the most powerful—*and most accessible*—resource in your social impact tool kit. I know in the day-to-day hustle of life it doesn't always feel like that, but I've learned that the amount we can fit into our days is far more elastic than we usually want to admit.

This saying attributed to Jim Rohn holds true for most of us: "If it's a priority, you'll find a way. If it isn't, you'll find an excuse." Whether we're talking about getting to the gym, tackling a long list of tasks at home, making progress on that important-but-not-urgent volunteer project, or even just making an overdue call to a family member or friend, there's almost always a "good" reason we didn't get to it. Yes, we really are "busy." But we also *do* have time. Both can be true and usually are.

In the context of doing Better Good, and to varying degrees based on our circumstances, we all have a choice about finding the time necessary to increase our impact footprint. Like any muscle, the better and more efficiently we exercise time management, the stronger it'll get. Shifting your mindset about time gets exponentially easier the more you do it. And time is *most* elastic when it comes to the things that we're most passionate about.

In a world that glorifies wealth, status, and visibility, it's easy to assume you need more of something—more money, more talent, more connections, more professional success—to do good in meaningful ways. But even if you feel under-resourced in those areas, you are still fully equipped to make an impact, because your time matters just as much, if not more, than money and status. Whether you're volunteering, mentoring, supporting a cause, or simply using your time to more intentionally allocate your talent and treasure, time is the gateway to all of it. It's how good begins, expands, and gets better. You start by learning how to leverage the time you have into the impact you want. Using your time wisely—not just for productivity, but for purpose—is how everyday choices become lasting contributions.

Using our time to make an impact doesn't happen by accident. It happens by design. There's an extraordinary world of possibility you can access with some simple changes to how you see, approach, and manage your time for the purposes of doing Better Good. So, in the interest of the preciousness of time, let's dive right in.

WHEN MINIMAL TIME DRIVES MAXIMUM IMPACT

When former U.S. President Jimmy Carter passed away at age 100, his obituaries were filled with images of him in work clothes and a hard hat, hammer in hand, helping to build houses for Habitat for

Humanity. His long affiliation with Habitat was a core part of his identity, and you wouldn't be alone if you assumed he built houses all year long after leaving the White House.

So it might surprise you to learn that for more than thirty-five years, Jimmy and his wife, Rosalynn, usually spent just one week per year swinging a hammer and lifting plywood. Yes, just one week. This is not a criticism of their efforts; quite the opposite. It proves that their wise use of relatively modest bits of time made a massive impact, because the Carters always attracted media attention, donations, and volunteer sign-ups. They made the absolute most of a relatively minor—but meaningful—amount of their time.

Habitat for Humanity reports that since 1984, the Carter Work Project has built 4,447 homes through the efforts of 108,000 volunteers in 14 countries. But very few of those homes ever saw a nail hammered by the Carters themselves. That's an amazing ratio of impact to time.

Of course, regular people like you and me won't attract an enormous press contingent to cover our volunteer efforts, and we're unlikely to inspire thousands of volunteers and donors in a single week. But we can still learn a valuable lesson from the Carters' partnership with Habitat: don't assume that impact and time are directly correlated. You might be able to make a truly significant difference to causes in your Goldilocks Zone with a fairly modest (or even very modest) deployment of your time. We can think of this as *exponential time*—when the impact far outstrips what we think is possible with the hours invested.

Think about a time when you, your family, or your colleagues engaged in a volunteer activity. Perhaps you served meals at a homeless shelter around the holidays. Or maybe you and your colleagues donned matching T-shirts for a day out of the office cleaning up a park or running a 5K for a cause. These events—some of which may be *years* old by now—probably stick in your mind as noteworthy, maybe even as formative team-building and bonding activities. Not because they took a lot of time, or because you made the biggest difference, but because they were both feel-good activities and meaningful acts of service. And if you do such activities with your neighbors, family, and especially your children, you're likely to seed some meaningful core memories that will influence them for a lifetime. That's those happy chemicals at work again, creating the same bonds that have propelled humanity forward for millennia.

Now imagine those feelings being a more regular part of your life and work. Imagine you have these experiences twice as often per year, or per month. Or imagine making them part of your weekly or even daily routine in ways small or large. What starts as a little time here and there can ignite our passion and even more feel-good brain chemicals flowing. In turn, that drives purpose and fuels the confidence and desire to carve out more and more time for doing good. This is how you grow your impact exponentially in a way that is intentional and is more likely to be sustainable. But this snowball effect doesn't happen by accident.

Exponential time happens by design. And that's why having a system matters.

SYSTEMS OVER GOALS

One of the most transformational ideas I've ever come across is that we don't rise to the level of our goals—we fall to the level of our systems. This axiom, popularized by James Clear in *Atomic Habits*, changed how I think about almost everything. You can have the best of intentions. You can care deeply about making an impact. But unless you have a system—a structure—for making time for the things that matter, your good intentions will never be more than haphazard, or worse, steamrolled by the chaos of the day.

Distractions will win. Urgencies will hijack your priorities. And the good you intended to do will get deferred to "someday." But, as the saying goes, "Someday isn't a day of the week." The beauty of time management is that "someday" can literally start right now. That's what I tell the Jacks of the world who have kicked the can down the road for far too long and have come to regret it.

I've spent years experimenting with systems to manage my time with more purpose and observing how others do the same. I devour books and podcasts on time management and productivity. I download templates and tools and spend many Sunday nights mapping my week with online tools like Asana alongside old-school pen and paper to jot down my "Big 3" priorities for each day. Some of this is overkill, but if you're going to become a nerd about something, time management offers the greatest point of leverage when it comes to doing good.

There are hundreds (perhaps thousands) of systems, tools, and apps that can help you get better at allocating and protecting time. I'm agnostic as to whether you should try a digital system, a notebook, a wall full of sticky notes, or a large desktop calendar. Whatever works best for you to keep you grounded and focused. Just remember: what gets scheduled gets done. What gets measured gets improved. And what gets eliminated, automated, or delegated gives you back precious time you can allocate to what matters most.

Once you've gotten better visibility into how you are using your time and how much you want to carve out for doing good, the next step is figuring out where to start. Maybe you have thirty minutes a week or three minutes a week—either way, you have to decide how you are going to deploy those minutes to do the most good possible.

In the previous chapters you mapped out your profile, platform, and passion—giving you a sense of how to best leverage your time. Now it's time to delve a little deeper into how to *prioritize* it.

THE POWER OF THE EISENHOWER MATRIX

With all you have to do in the weeks and months ahead, you might feel overwhelmed. Most of us do. It's how people like Jack end up making great headway in one area of life while letting their desire to do good fall to the wayside. If we don't want to wake up decades from now wondering how the promise of our three P's never came to fruition, we have to get tactical.

Here's one of the most helpful concepts I've ever encountered for smartly prioritizing your time: the Eisenhower Matrix. It's a simple 2x2 framework that helps you distinguish what's urgent and what's important—which are *not* the same thing.

Here's one version:

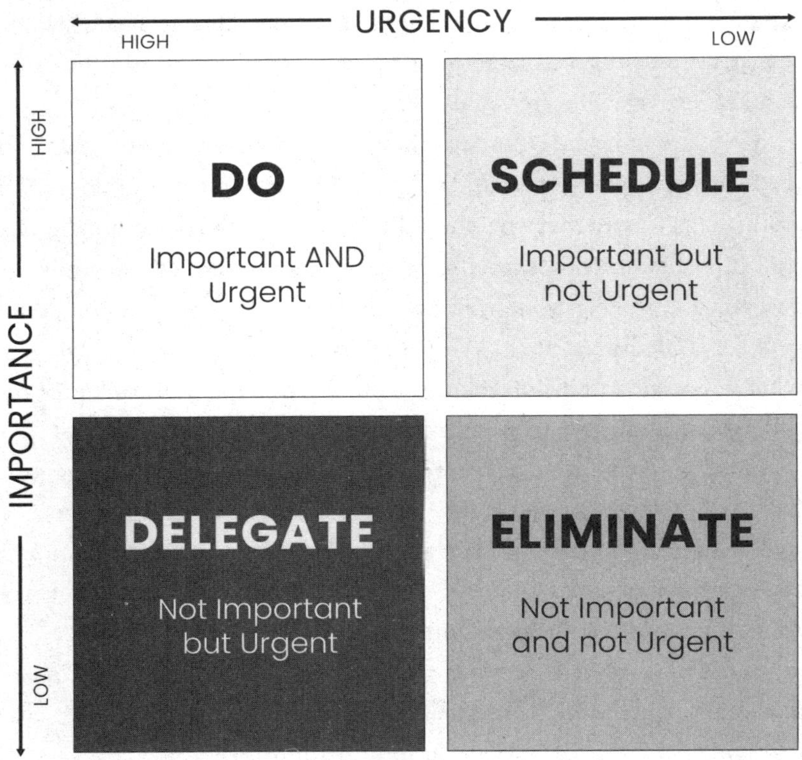

The Eisenhower Matrix simply helps you sort tasks and projects into one of four possible categories:

- Important and urgent
- Important but not urgent
- Not important but urgent
- Not important or urgent

Most of us rightly focus on the "urgent and important" quadrant, which includes time-sensitive priorities that have hard deadlines and serious consequences, like catching a flight for a work trip, getting a kid to an important soccer tournament, working on a major project with an approaching deadline, or even just replying to an important email from a supervisor, client, or colleague. You might block time for deep dives or fast sprints to get these tasks accomplished, ignoring all distractions or lesser priorities until those fires are safely extinguished.

Because our brains like to respond to the power of urgency, however, many of us are also drawn to the "urgent but not important" quadrant, the insidious enemy of well-managed time. It's human nature that urgency trumps importance. There's a lot of power and often a lot of intentional technological design behind the ding on your phone: the alert about a new comment on your post, the sound of an incoming text from a friend, or the sight of a newly arrived email from your boss. Even if none of these are *actually* important, their *apparent* urgency hijacks your focus. Resisting this hijacking requires intentional awareness and a bit of lifestyle design—silencing alerts for certain apps altogether, going on airplane mode, or just leaving phones out of reach to keep focus on what's actually important.

The "neither urgent nor important" quadrant is the junk food of your calendar: mindless social media scrolling, checking sports scores, binge-watching episode after episode, googling that actor you liked. When you fall into one of these rabbit holes of distraction, you will only find yourself losing precious time. Like Oreos or Doritos, these should be enjoyed sparingly—and never during your prime hours of mental acuity and energy.

And finally, we have the fourth quadrant: "important but not urgent." When it comes to doing good, this quadrant is the key to impact, scale, and sustainability. It's the quadrant that is simultaneously the most challenging and has the most potential to change your life.

Let me explain.

Without the urgency prompts that seek to constantly distract us by design, it's easy to neglect tasks and projects that are actually important to us. Ones that will contribute significantly to our success or our efforts to do good, but which lack external time pressure. If you've ever looked at important items on your task list with high levels of frustration that you *still* haven't gotten to them after months, because you "simply haven't had enough time," you know this category well. It looks like scheduling doctors' appointments, responding to that email from a friend or family member checking in on you, and getting back to the volunteer or service opportunity you've been meaning to prioritize. These are the tasks on our to-do list that haunt us every time we look at them and *still* haven't been able to check them off the list. These are the challenges of this important quadrant.

That said, the wins in this quadrant are impactful and have ripple effects. Because of the actual importance of these tasks and projects, we tend to feel great once we *do* get around to catching up with an old friend, scheduling the Salvation Army pickup for that growing pile of donation items, or going to a religious service for the first time in a while. When the feel-good chemicals kick in, they remind us of how important these tasks truly are, and we feel sheepish that it took us so long to squeeze them in. This tension is partly why the most successful people typically have a process for protecting and defending their "important but not urgent" time. This is where the intentionality comes in: They schedule time for self-care, planning, and deep work while blocking both online and offline distractions. They lock the door, go into airplane mode, put on noise canceling headphones, or all of the above. (What doorbell?) Understanding how easy it is to get swept up in urgency and distraction, *they* decide ahead of time how their time is used. And I can't recommend that enough.

Once you get familiar with the Eisenhower Matrix and start labeling how you allocate your time, patterns will emerge along with deeper understanding. You'll see that your "not-to-do" list is just as important as your to-do list. You'll be inspired to say no to the wrong things so you can preserve, protect, and prioritize the time you invest in the right things.

In the end, your goal isn't simply to be productive; it's to benefit from a system you thoughtfully design. And to make sure that how you spend your time reflects your true values.

But how?

THE POWER OF OVERMANAGING

Once you've used the Eisenhower Matrix to identify your "important but not urgent" tasks, you need a way to ensure they get the care and consistency they deserve. That's where a Disney practice called "overmanaging" can be especially valuable. It's a great way to protect and reinforce important but not urgent actions with intentionality and precision.

Overmanaging should not be confused with its less-positive cousin, micromanaging. Pioneered by the Disney Institute, the business consulting arm of the Disney Company, overmanaging is taught at the beginning of every Disney Institute course. It's a foundational principle behind "the Disney difference" that helps the company excel across all of its global business units—from entertainment to theme parks to digital streaming, consumer products, and beyond. (Guilty as charged: I love all things Disney, especially the cruises.)

Disney defines overmanaging as paying closer attention to small but impactful details that others either undermanage or overlook altogether. When you choose the right things to overmanage, you give yourself a significant advantage with a small investment of extra time and effort. And as it relates to doing good, this is one way to give yourself the gift of the "Jimmy Carter effect"—getting the biggest bang for your buck (or, in this case, time).

One visible example of overmanaging is found on every Disney theme park employee's shirt: the famous Disney name tags. Every name tag includes the wearer's first name only (even the CEO's) to keep everyone friendly, familiar, and on a first-name basis from the moment they meet. It also includes their hometown, to make it easy to forge a connection or start a conversation ("Hey, I'm from Chicago, too!"). And employees who are fluent in another language get a flag logo added, thus inviting guests to use that language with them.

All of these details are simple and fast to implement and don't cost a penny more than a standard name tag. But by overmanaging them, Disney makes bonding with guests significantly easier. Few ever realize that overmanaging is hiding in plain sight—in almost every aspect of their business—contributing to that "Disney difference" that is hard to put a finger on.

There are probably plenty of ways that you already overmanage in your own life or work to generate similar leverage. Maybe you overmanage your work efficiency by codifying best practices that help you focus when you're distracted; creating standard operating procedures for you and your team; or even just making sure your workspace is tidied at the end of each day. Or maybe you overmanage your family time by having everyone put their phones in a dedicated drawer for a couple of hours every night.

While overmanaging can be used in many areas of our lives (and I encourage it—it's magical), it's exceptionally helpful in our Better Good efforts. Overmanage your schedule to "find" time to volunteer at your child's school; overmanage your finances to contribute money more intentionally to causes you care about most; even overmanage your screen time to include a few minutes each week amplifying causes you believe in. Think of it as applying intentional care to the time you've already deemed important. The Eisenhower Matrix reveals the right priorities. Overmanaging ensures that those priorities are actually honored and acted upon. And putting the two together can reveal an entirely new world of opportunity.

THREE TYPES OF BETTER GOOD TIME

Even those of us who diligently apply the Eisenhower Matrix are still busy. Very busy, in most cases. Our jars are inevitably "full" with work, family, and everything else that life throws our way. But we sometimes surprise ourselves with what we can fit into even the busiest days, especially when purpose enters the equation.

In the context of doing Better Good, and to varying degrees based on our circumstances, we all have a choice about finding the time necessary to increase our impact footprint. Like any muscle, the more efficiently and effectively we exercise time management, the better we'll get at it and the more time we'll find. Shifting your mindset about time gets exponentially easier the more you do it. And time is *most* elastic when it comes to the things that we're most passionate about. You'll almost always find time for the things you care about.

Consider the three distinct types of time commitments each of us can make toward Better Good. This simple framework turns the abstract "elasticity" of time into something you can actually work with—like dials you can turn up or down as seasons change. Start small, stack where you can, and invest deeply when it matters:

- No Extra Time (NET) commitments
- Found Extra Time commitments
- Transformative Time commitments

Let's see how these strategies show up in life and work—for individuals and organizations alike.

NET (NO EXTRA) TIME

In this first category are the actions that take—almost literally—no extra time. For instance, do you ever listen to a podcast while on a walk or run, while mowing your yard, or on your daily commute? You're walking/running/mowing/driving anyway, so adding the value of absorbing the podcast requires literally no extra time.

Remember Lorenzo from Chapter 5—the barber who saw an opportunity for turning barbershops into safe spaces for comfortable conversation about mental health? Those conversations take No Extra Time for trained Confess Project barbers to have, but have a massive impact on his clients.

During the writing of this book, Taylor Swift casually wore a long-since-sold-out vintage sea otter T-shirt from the Monterey Bay Aquarium. Within hours, the aquarium reissued it and raised more than $2 million for sea otter conservation. A perfect reminder that No Extra Time moments—when paired with passion and platform—can spark substantial impact. Nice work to team Taylor and all the Swifties!

Here's a personal favorite example from the "overmanaging" Disney playbook that perfectly demonstrates an organizational No Extra Time commitment to do good. Disney trains everyone who works at a Disney theme park—at every level of position, regardless of rank or seniority—to help keep the parks clean by picking up any and every piece of trash they encounter, whenever and wherever they encounter it. And this isn't just to have pretty parks—Disney considers cleanliness a critical part of their commitment to safety. Clean parks aren't just more pleasant, they're intentionally designed to reduce hazards—slips, contamination, pests, and other risks.

For that reason, cleanliness isn't just the duty of their custodial team; it's an opportunity for *everyone* to be part of the mission of having the cleanest and safest parks in the world. So even if a ride operator is on her way to work a shift at an attraction (her actual role), if she sees a piece of trash, she knows it's part of "the Disney difference" to pick it up. She doesn't even notice the extra few seconds required.

Just like those theme park cast members, you can take virtually No Extra Time to stop and pick up a piece of trash on your walk, drop a can into a recycle bin, take a few extra seconds to hold the door open for someone, press "yes" when presented with the option to round up for charity at checkout, send a text to make a quick donation for a cause you care about, or even just speak up to advocate for someone in need. Or, you can dedicate your public transportation time or your lunch hour to swapping mindless social scrolling with intentional social media promotion of causes you care about, or connecting with fellow members of an organization you're committed to and have perhaps "needed to get back to" (important) but not on a specific deadline (not urgent). These are all simple opportunities to use your NET for good.

But don't let these actions stop at your commute, lunch hour, or social scroll! Perhaps while walking your dog, you consciously choose to pick up trash or have a brainstorming phone call with a fellow volunteer at a nonprofit organization. As small as these acts might seem, you are concretely doing good. Tiny investments of NET time add up. Using your NET to capture new opportunities effectively and efficiently is the way you get the Better Good ball rolling. Being aware it's there—and full of potential—is the key.

Found Extra Time

Next, you can build "found extra time" commitments into your day. These are opportunities that require a few minutes to a few hours a day, at most, or a commitment of modest chunks of time at various intervals. For example, you could identify specific days each year for grabbing lunch with a student or young professional about their career interests, or find an hour each semester to do two volunteer events with your kids' PTA, or ask your law firm to commit staff hours to reading to first graders (a real example of a top law firm's dedication of time—the precious commodity their business sells—as a meaningful part of their social impact footprint as a firm). Maybe you commit to a monthly shift at the local food pantry or homeless shelter, help organize an electronics recycling event in your community, or serve on a committee at church or on the board of a local nonprofit.

Such commitments are more of a time stretch than those in the first category, but all are doable if we're more mindful about overmanaging our schedules and finding opportunities to incorporate more good into the same twenty-four hours we all have.

Lawyers "find" time to do pro bono work in spite of their busy billable hour requirements. Whole businesses "find" a day or two per year to shut down for a day to devote team time to a worthy endeavor. When asked if they really "have" the time, or if there's a singular convenient time, most busy people and organizations would say no. But they find it. This is the essence of important but not urgent work. And when we overmanage it by scheduling it, protecting it, and prioritizing it with a firm calendar commitment, we feel more connected, engaged, and fulfilled in our work, organizations, and communities. We feel more connected to our causes of consistent care, and with others who share those causes. And for our crawl-through-glass causes? Watch out! We'll protect those entries on our calendar at all costs. It's remarkable how much time we can "find" when these opportunities are aligned with our passions and proficiencies.

Think about a favorite memory when, despite your usual busy schedule, you found time to undertake a volunteer opportunity, help a neighbor in need with a project, or show up for an important community meeting. Or that time you rushed to catch a train home in time to volunteer at a kid's school event, which had felt like a giant inconvenience when you looked at your calendar and inbox, but made you feel amazing. Finding time for those meaningful moments might require a cognitive override the moment you're scheduling it, but it's almost always worth it.

Transformative Time

The highest level of time commitment is called *transformative* time, because it requires rearranging our schedules in significant ways. We're talking about serious investments of time, either on an ongoing basis or in big chunks, measurable in weeks, months, or years. Such commitments shouldn't be undertaken lightly or without full consideration of their true requirements.

Transformative time commitments might take the form of life-changing decisions like changing jobs, shifting careers, going back to school, or otherwise meaningfully pivoting our lives toward good in seismic ways. You might choose to serve in a leadership position on a board, become an adjunct professor or substitute teacher, or take off on an AmeriCorps, Peace Corps, Teach For America, or similar long-term service opportunity. You might create a new project, organization, or initiative, whether nonprofit, for-profit, or social enterprise. You might even quit your law firm job to move to Arkansas for a masters of public service degree and a dramatic career shift. (I did, and it was transformative indeed!)

Sometimes an initiative to do good transitions from found extra time to transformative time, as initially modest efforts gradually become big efforts. This evolution typically occurs when you've aligned your commitment of time with your passions. It's the doing-good equivalent of lighting a fuse that results in a bigger boom the longer it burns.

A great example of this evolution is Nancy's commitment to what became Watts of Love, which began with awareness and fundraising and gradually evolved into a full-fledged nonprofit start-up, and eventually a big organization with a global footprint. Or David Fajgenbaum's unexpected transformation from doctor to patient with a rare disease, and then to leader of a global movement to find cures for overlooked diseases.

Evolutions can go the other way, too, when a life circumstance thrusts us into a transformative time commitment that evolves over time either because our participation becomes less important, or because we hand it off to others to manage. Marie Tillman created the Pat Tillman Foundation not long after her husband, Pat, a former NFL football player turned Army Ranger, was killed by friendly fire in Afghanistan. Marie's transformative time commitment turned Pat's legacy of service and sacrifice into a foundation that supports military veterans. Early on, Marie was the primary leader of this organization, committing transformative time for years before handing the reins over to various professional nonprofit leaders. She still remained meaningfully engaged, but spent more time growing her personal and professional pursuits outside of the foundation. There's no requirement to commit yourself to one form of time commitment in perpetuity. Time commitments can change and evolve.

Working the Mix: Design a Time Portfolio

If we want to avoid the "I waited too long" regret, we need to reassess how we use time—now. Look closely at where your hours go and make deliberate choices to squeeze more good out of your schedule. The shift is time well spent.

Here's a playbook for operating across NET, Found Extra Time, and Transformative Time:

- **Start now** (NET). Do one No Extra Time act today. Small, consistent moves build momentum.
- **Add one anchor** (Found Extra Time). Put a recurring, light commitment on the calendar (e.g., monthly mentoring, quarterly service day). Scheduling makes it real.
- **Open a window** (Transformative Time). When the season allows, plan a bigger block (board role, sabbatical, launch sprint). Use NET/Found Extra Time as on-ramps.
- **Work by season.** You won't run all three time commitments at full tilt. Life evolves in seasons and Better Good evolves, too. In busy seasons, protect a minimum viable mix (NET + one Found). In spacious seasons, expand.
- **Quick review, quarterly.** Schedule fifteen minutes every quarter to evaluate your time commitments (put these check-ins on your calendar right now): What energized you? What felt heavy? Right-size the mix for the next quarter or season.
- **Pro Tip:** When life throws you a curveball, borrow a lesson from improv. Performers are taught to *"accept the gift"*—to see whatever happens on stage as an opportunity, not a mistake—and then build on it with *"Yes, and . . ."* rather than shutting it down with *"No, but . . ."* Apply the same principle here: when life inevitably forces your plans to change, accept it as a gift. Say "Yes, and . . ." by finding a small way to keep your impact momentum going, even if it looks different than you expected.

Remember, you're not choosing a single time-portfolio strategy forever. You're choosing a mix for *this* season—and you can remix as life evolves.

ORGANIZATIONAL TIME: MAKING ROOM FOR IMPACT

The same systems that help individuals use time more effectively—clear priorities and structured goals—can be just as transformative at the organizational level. Every team, company, nonprofit, or public institution is made up of people who can choose—both individually and collectively—whether they want to reinforce business-as-usual or actively find time for doing Better Good.

For organizations, the most powerful impact opportunities often come not from adding more hours, but from using existing hours more intentionally. That might mean offering employees paid volunteer hours or weaving social impact into team retreats and training. It might mean creating space for cross-sector partnerships, pro bono service, or moments of reflection about how the organization shows up in the communities it touches. When organizations incorporate impact into their work, it becomes a cultural norm that reinforces shared values, attracts top talent, and unlocks meaningful engagement. The impact can be enormous.

The Newman's Own Foundation dedicates a portion of employee—and even consultant—time into mentoring their grant recipients and social entrepreneurs. I've participated in this directly and seen its impact firsthand. By baking these engagement opportunities into its annual rhythm, the organization ensures that purpose is part of everyone's job in ways that align with the mission and integrates seamlessly with the existing time commitments of team members. Encouraging teams to apply the Eisenhower Matrix to their shared work, and empowering them to overmanage key areas of impact, creates a culture in which doing good isn't an afterthought—it's a standard that is part of smart organizational design.

"What gets scheduled gets done" isn't just a productivity mantra for our individual to-do lists; it's also a strategy for aligning teams and entire organizations around purpose. When leaders signal that time spent on impact is time well spent, people listen. When leaders also model it—blocking their own crowded calendars to make room for volunteering, mentoring, or mission-driven projects—others in the organization feel they can, and should, do the same.

Of course, time looks different across different kinds of organizations. A law firm might dedicate billable hours to pro bono service. A retailer might incorporate cause campaigns into peak season planning. A nonprofit might give program teams time off—or even increasingly popular sabbaticals—to participate in continuing education or mission-related field work. (These three examples are Found Extra Time.) The forms may vary, but the principle is the same: doing good requires time set aside for the "important but not urgent" quadrant—together.

So, whether you're a CEO, department head, team leader, or just someone with influence on the culture around you, ask: "Are we making enough time for what really matters? Are we helping our people do good across the range of time commitments within our organization's mission and structure? Are we intentionally organizing our Better Good efforts in terms of our no-extra-time, found time, and even transformative time?" If not, start there. The results won't just show up in quarterly impact reports. They'll show up in collective morale, retention, innovation, and trust.

KEY TAKEAWAYS AND ACTION ITEMS

Key Takeaways

- **Time is your most accessible, powerful resource.** It's universal, finite, and the most accessible lever you have for impact—when used with intention.
- **Impact scales by design, not by hours.** Small, consistent choices can compound into outsized results ("exponential time").
- **Work a time portfolio.** Mix NET (No Extra Time), Found Extra Time, and Transformative Time—and let the mix shift with the seasons of life.
- **Systems beat willpower.** Protect "important but not urgent" work with scheduling, elimination, automation, delegation, and a simple weekly cadence.
- **Overmanage the right details.** Small, repeatable acts that streamline your efforts (and a "Yes, and . . ." mindset when plans change) keep momentum alive.

Action Items

For Individuals

- **Be aware of your mix.** Notice where NET, Found Extra Time, and Transformative Time already appear in your life—and remember, the mix will evolve with each season.
- **Start small, today.** Use a No Extra Time moment (commute, scroll, walk) to advance a cause or connect with someone doing good.
- **Anchor and expand.** Add one recurring Found Extra Time commitment (monthly mentoring, quarterly volunteer service) and protect it as a priority.
- **Design your system.** Block time for "important but not urgent" work, make a not-to-do list, and review your mix quarterly (schedule that review now).
- **Adapt with "Yes, and . . ."** When plans shift, accept the change as a gift and find one small way to keep your impact momentum alive.

Action Items

For Organizations

- **Treat time as a strategic asset.** Name and track NET, Found Extra Time, and Transformative Time across teams; expect the mix to shift; be the champion and facilitator.
- **Schedule and protect impact time.** Put service days, mentoring hours, or pro bono work on the calendar—and model participation from the top.
- **Build supportive systems.** Use tools like the Eisenhower Matrix to prioritize impact and eliminate low-value tasks.
- **Overmanage culture.** Celebrate time spent on purpose, share quick wins, and include "impact check-ins" in meetings.
- **Review and rebalance quarterly.** Reassess team time allocations, remove blockers, and keep the mix aligned with mission and momentum.

CHAPTER 8

Your Talent

Your talent is God's gift to you.
What you do with it is your gift back to God.
—Leo Buscaglia

THE TALENTS THAT CHANGE LIVES

When most people think of a global superstar like Will Smith, they think of his blockbusters and greatest hits—*Independence Day*, *Men in Black*, *The Fresh Prince of Bel-Air*, "Gettin' Jiggy Wit It" (na na na na na na na)—or, in more recent years, the headlines that have overshadowed those hits. But behind the lights and noise, there's another story that reveals something uniquely human that we all share: how people who've mastered one craft wrestle with how to use their profile, platform, passions, and talents for doing good.

After two decades working with high-profile artists, athletes, entertainers, and entrepreneurs, I've noticed that these stars often long for a deeper purpose they're not quite finding in the pursuits that made them famous. They're surrounded by systems that monetize attention but less frequently reward depth. And that tension can leave even the most accomplished people feeling strangely under-fulfilled. It's the celebrity version of what happens to the "Jacks" you met in Chapter 7. It's what Tony Robbins cautions in his oft-referenced axiom that "achievement without fulfillment is the ultimate failure." Many stars don't realize that their fans actually do want to see the good they do along with their other accomplishments.

That's what drew me to the work Will and Jada Pinkett Smith were doing through their family foundation. My friend and frequent collaborator Keisha Senter, who was working for their foundation at the time, called me one day to share how Will and Jada were developing ways to translate their success in the entertainment industry into access for others. They designed their marquee initiative, Careers in Entertainment (CIE), to open doors for young people from underserved communities who wanted to break into an industry that can seem impenetrable from the outside. CIE created studio-lot workshops, mentorship programs, and partnerships with major Hollywood institutions—teaching everything from camera operation to contract negotiation. The effort focused on empowerment, helping participants build lasting skills and networks that could carry them into the future. It showed Will and Jada applying the same abilities that fueled their own rise—storytelling, collaboration, and creative leadership—to create opportunities for others to thrive.

I had the privilege of advising their foundation during the exciting, active years of CIE, helping the team align strategy, governance, and goals around impact that could last. From that vantage point, I saw how seriously they took the mission. These were genuine, sustained efforts to use hard-earned talent to expand opportunity for others.

When I finally met Will during his 2021 book tour, in a backstage lounge at the legendary Chicago Theater, I shared a thought that had crystallized after years of working with his team to help him leverage his platform for purpose in ways I knew not everyone got to see.

"Your art is your gift to the world," I told him. "But your impact is your legacy."

He paused, nodded slowly, and said, "I like that, man. I really like that. Thank you."

That exchange summed up everything I believe about talent and smart use of platform. Whether you're a global celebrity or someone simply working to improve your own corner of the world, your greatest contribution comes from aligning your natural gifts with meaningful purpose for the impact you leave in the world. Will's talent—and his ability to share it on various and multiple stages, ranging from actual stages to screens big and small—extends far beyond performing. It includes connecting, mentoring, and creating possibilities for others. That's the kind of work we're all capable of doing when we operate in our own Goldilocks Zones.

You don't have to be as high profile as (or a triple threat talent like) Will Smith to make a lasting impact. And you don't have to be a consultant to someone's family foundation to feel that you've contributed in a meaningful way. More often, the talents that change lives are the ones you already have. The skills you've built, the instincts you've refined, the efforts people already count on you for. Your gifts.

THE POWER OF YOUR TALENT

In the world of doing good, few contributions will be as personal, important, and inspiring as your contribution of talent—the dynamic combination of skills, abilities, and life experiences that are uniquely yours to give. Among the three T's, time and treasure have narrower definitions and limited inherent uniqueness. Their application is effectively limited to amount and frequency. But contributions of talent can be a force multiplier in a uniquely impactful way. Deploying your talent for good is full of expansive possibilities.

This chapter builds on earlier ideas from the Profile chapter but takes a critical next step. While your profile is built on formal credentials and external identifiers—things like diplomas, job titles, and affiliations—your talent is more expansive, including the full terrain of what you're good at. Some of that may come from your professional life, but much of it lies beneath the surface, resulting from your life experiences and what makes you uniquely you. And when there's overlap between what you're good at and what you love doing, your Goldilocks Zone begins to clarify and even expand in exciting ways.

Talent includes what you've learned through life, as well as what you've learned through work. It includes what you've practiced, what you've survived, what others rely on you for, and what comes naturally to you in a crisis, a brainstorming session, or a group project of any and every kind. Talent is inclusive of your profile credentials, but it's also broader, deeper, more flexible, and more creative.

Not sure what counts? Your talents might include:

- Strategic thinking from years of corporate work.
- Project management from raising three kids or leading a PTA.
- Coaching and mentoring skills from your role as a manager, as an athlete, volunteer coach, or even as the oldest sibling.
- Communication, persuasion, or empathy honed over time and experiences.
- Creative problem solving from navigating change or adversity.
- World-class juggling, yo-yo, improvisation, stand-up comedy, singing, or any other unique skills with surprising application to any variety of social situations that make people smile. Because those matter, too!

Think about the people who inspire you through the good they do in life and work. How would you describe their talents? What do they do uniquely well? And how would those same people describe your unique talents?

THE THREE TYPES OF TALENTS

Most of us take too narrow a view of our talents, often reflexively defaulting to the credentials part of our profile, unaware of how our *uncredentialed* talents may be transferable to the wider world of doing Better Good. To avoid this pitfall, it helps to map your talents into three categories: Primary, Underlying, and Emerging.

Your **primary talents** are your most obvious skills and abilities—those in your profile, as well as those that you instinctively share during quick introductions when someone asks what you do. They are what you're known for at first glance. They're likely to come up in other people's answers about who you are and what your talents are. They are apparent during any quick analysis of your profile, platform, and known passions.

For example, I'm an attorney, a social impact consultant, a husband and father, with a passion for dog rescue. Which means I've got a talent for simplifying complexity, guiding mission-driven work to greater effectiveness, and helping others see how their work fits into something larger. Those are among the first things you'd learn about me if we've just met.

Your **underlying talents** are less obvious and more easily overlooked, but they're equally important abilities that stem from your lived experience across all dimensions of who you are. Similar to the informal credentials of our profile, underlying talents include the foundational soft skills that prepared you for everything that followed, even if there's no way to get a degree or other formal credential for them.

Maybe you grew up immersed in the arts or fascinated with science and technology before you became a marketing major, uniquely equipping you with creative or analytical skills that underlie your approach to all you do. Or perhaps you were part of an immigrant household, regularly translating between cultures, enabling you to serve as a world-class connector and bridge builder. Or maybe you were the peacemaker in a large family, the calm voice in every emergency, positioning you as the go-to voice of reason in times of trouble in your life and at work.

Those aren't just "soft skills"; they're real assets that you can leverage to make a tangible impact.

One example I love comes from Dina Benadon, cofounder of the nonprofit Walt Disney Birthplace. Dina's primary talents were forged over a lifetime immersed in storytelling, animation, and themed entertainment—first working alongside her father in Hollywood film postproduction, then through her own pioneering work designing immersive attractions for theme parks, museums, and science centers. But her most impactful contributions didn't come directly from acquiring the primary talents. They came from recognizing how her underlying talents—creative vision, collaboration, systems thinking, and a deep belief in the power of imagination—could be applied in an entirely new context. When the opportunity arose to acquire and reimagine Walt Disney's modest Chicago birthplace, Dina saw what others might have missed: more than just a historic home, she saw it as a living platform for inspiration and education. Then, by applying the same instincts she used to build world-class theme park attractions, she helped transform the Birthplace into both a physical destination and a globally accessible teaching tool about creativity and innovation for children, families, and communities. This opportunity revealed itself when Dina widened her lens and allowed her underlying talents to point her toward a cause that fit her Goldilocks Zone.

Your **emerging talents** are still works in progress. Because we tend to undervalue what we're becoming (hey imposter syndrome . . . you again?), it's easy to overlook talents that are in the process of leading us to new roles, hobbies, and opportunities. Maybe you've been mentoring junior colleagues but never thought of yourself as a teacher. Maybe you've become the go-to crisis person on your team, even though crisis management isn't part of your job description. These are clues! Emerging talents might lead to your next great act of service and an expansion of your impact footprint.

In Dina's case, her emerging talents came into focus only *after* she stepped fully into the work of the Walt Disney Birthplace. While her primary talents were rooted in immersive design and storytelling, advancing the Birthplace required her to grow into new roles she hadn't previously defined as "talents" at all. She found herself becoming a nonprofit leader, learning how to steward a mission-driven organization; a public storyteller, articulating why Walt Disney's early life still matters to children and communities today; and a fundraiser, building relationships and inspiring others to invest in a vision larger than any single attraction or site. These skills emerged through necessity, curiosity, and commitment to the cause. Dina didn't set out to become these things. She became them by following the work wherever it led and allowing her talents to evolve in the process. That's often how emerging talents reveal themselves—less of a dramatic pivot and more of an expansion of who we already are.

To see how all three types of talents come together, let me introduce you to someone who hides incredible talents under a seemingly average and unassuming surface. She's also one of my favorite people, for obvious Goldilocks Zone reasons.

THE FAIRY GODMOTHER OF DOG RESCUE

Do you have someone in your life who you just *love*—who always seems infallible, always motivated by good, and has no perceptible weaknesses, character flaws, or even bad habits? The kind of person who appears to seamlessly weave their life purpose, professional skills, and personal ethos together to be a shining example of goodness?

When it comes to my crawl-through-glass passion for dog rescue, that person is Donna Easley. Amy and I refer to her as the Fairy Godmother of Dog Rescue. She might look like any other sweet, white-haired but vibrant retiree in her seventies, but she's far from ordinary.

Donna was, as a young woman, one of the first "nontraditional" (i.e., female) AT&T employees to "work the line," climbing utility poles to restore service after outages. Over a decades-long career, she rose through the ranks, leveraging each hard-earned position into yet another one. She led mostly male teams of line-repair experts, inspected AT&T plants throughout the state of Arkansas, oversaw maintenance centers in multiple states, and eventually became a supervisor for placement of new facilities.

After retiring from her trailblazing career, Donna began to redirect her seemingly limitless energy into rescuing dogs that need immediate saving from kill shelters or the streets, including dogs with urgent medical needs. Using the same talents she previously applied to coordinating logistics for crews of linemen, she now facilitates and coordinates logistics for volunteer rescuers, veterinarians, and transport people.

She works phone lines in a different way—across her nationwide network of rescue organizations, foster families, and those willing to bring rescued dogs hundreds or even thousands of miles to a new home, by both ground and air. There's always another dog in need of immediate help, another vet who needs to give that dog urgent care and approval to travel, and another transport volunteer who needs help getting the dog from a kill shelter to a loving new family. (We've benefitted from her magic; Donna arranged for the rescue of not one but two of our special needs blind and deaf dogs, who you can meet at www.bettergoodbook.com/dogs.)

Donna draws on a lifetime of logistics and operations experience that has equipped her for exactly this unique role that she's created for herself. Those are her *primary* talents.

Her *underlying* talents are that she's always been an animal rescuer, a people person, a connector, a caregiver, and a natural leader. Until her retirement, she never realized how valuable that unique combination could be.

Her newest *emerging* talents, developing over the past few years, include fundraising. While she has always helped fundraise for some of the organizations in her ecosystem to meet immediate needs, she now more purposefully leverages her growing network of those who have benefitted from her help and now want to "give back." Donna finds herself increasingly raising both awareness and money for the many organizations inextricably linked with her work, especially to pay for essential medical treatments for animals she helps rescue.

(We'll learn more about Donna's growing philanthropy in the next chapter.) Concurrently, she's also emerging as an advocate and leader in the broader animal rescue community.

Donna exemplifies that we all have special skills and talents that can be leveraged to make an impact, even if we often don't always realize that we've been honing them for years or even decades. Donna certainly didn't know, during her trailblazing days at AT&T, that her ability to solve problems and coordinate nationwide logistics would eventually lead her to deploy those and other talents for some of the most fulfilling work of her life.

YOU CAN ONLY CONNECT THE DOTS LOOKING BACKWARD

Like Donna, Dina, Will Smith, and you, every one of us has a unique combination of talents that contribute to doing Better Good. Some of us know early in our lives what we want to do with our talents; we can draw straight lines from then to now. But even more of us embark on a winding, evolving, and even bumpy journey to discover how our core, underlying, and emerging talents can be harnessed in the service of doing good.

José Andrés began as a cook, then became a chef, then rose to fame as a celebrated restaurateur—a natural progression for someone with a primary talent for preparing food for others. Then he pivoted his passion for feeding and comforting people in need following the 2010 earthquake in Haiti, stepping into the new roles of crisis responder and nonprofit founder. His organization, World Central Kitchen, went on to redefine food relief and humanitarian aid around the globe, evolving its work in disaster zones, conflict regions, and communities on the brink. José discovered that his primary, underlying, and emerging talents could be used not just to feed people, but to lead, advocate, and shape the global conversation on dignity, justice, and resilience. And when you hear him, on stage or in private conversation, you get the sense that despite all he's done, he's still just getting started.

Nancy Economou began her career in the fashion and accessories industry, with an eye for beauty and design and a talent for selling products and being a dynamic family leader as the mother of five boys. It was only after her trip to the Philippines that she realized her underlying talents could also serve a deeper purpose. She drew on her entrepreneurial instincts, creativity, and capacity to engage, motivate, and manage people to launch Watts of Love and bring uniquely designed and sustainable solar light to families who had been stuck in darkness. Nancy cites her experiences in sales, as a mother, and as an active church member as fundamental to her emerging talents for sharing the Watts of Love story with new audiences, volunteers, donors, and corporate partners.

Marie Tillman found her talents as a nonprofit leader and veterans' advocate as a result of circumstance and experience that evolved over time. After initially starting out shy and spotlight-averse in the early years of the Pat Tillman Foundation, an organization that supports the next generation of military leaders through scholarships and leadership development, she is now an accomplished author and entrepreneur who chairs its board and headlines its events, where her emerging talents as a leader and speaker are on full display.

Even former presidents don't always immediately see how they can put their own talents to work. One of my favorite stories about Bill Clinton is how he discovered that he could combine his frustration with traditional conferences—where people "just talked and didn't do and then came back and did it all again the next year"—with his natural ability to convene and connect people with big ideas. That's the origin story of the Clinton Global Initiative's unique "commitment to action" model, which has transformed lives and communities around the world. Meanwhile, George W. Bush used his love of painting—initially just a hobby—to raise money to benefit veterans' causes dear to his heart. After working together on post-earthquake relief initiatives in Haiti, Presidents Clinton and Bush realized that despite their different political backgrounds and approaches, they could team up to equip and empower the next generation of leaders via the Presidential

Leadership Scholars Program, one of the preeminent leadership programs of its kind.

If even former presidents unexpectedly evolve into discovery of emerging new talents and opportunities to do Better Good, it's totally okay that the rest of us do, too. In fact, it should be relieving, exciting, and empowering. There's no single path. It's all inspiration, innovation, iteration, and a little bit (or a lot) of improvisation.

No matter who you are or where you are on life's journey, keep in mind a quote from Steve Jobs's 2005 Stanford University commencement speech: "You can't connect the dots looking forward; you can only connect them looking backward. So you have to trust that the dots will somehow connect in your future." This idea helps us make full sense of how our core, underlying, and emerging talents are fueling our future selves and the good we have done, are doing, and will do.

TALENT AT WORK: ORGANIZATIONAL IMPACT

Just as individuals often underestimate the value and range of their talents, so, too, do organizations. Every team—whether it's a start-up, a school, a global business, a law firm, or a local nonprofit—is made up of people with a unique and wide array of skills, both seen and unseen. The best organizations make the effort to uncover and activate these talents from day one, not just for productivity in the specific role for which they are hired, but for impact. People want to bring their whole selves to work, including their desire to be part of something bigger, and to do good while doing well. Failing to put team talent to work organizationally is a perilous oversight. But if engaged—and especially if overmanaged—it promises spectacular results.

In their book *Build the Life You Want,* Arthur Brooks and Oprah Winfrey argue that meaningful work is essential to a happier life. And work that engages team talent within team members' individual and collective Goldilocks Zones is a surefire way to build a sustainable and scalable culture for doing good. When people show up as the highest and best versions of themselves—doing work that draws on their true talents and aligns with their Goldilocks Zone—the satisfaction they find at work naturally spills into life beyond it. Brooks and Winfrey call it "work that is love made visible."

Encouraging employees or team members to inventory their talents across the three categories can be a powerful culture tool. Primary talents help teams better align roles and responsibilities; underlying talents help surface overlooked strengths; emerging talents help leaders recognize and support growth areas that can be developed for future impact-driven projects.

Organizations that embrace a talent lens for impact—along with time and treasure—are better equipped to fully unleash purpose in the workplace. Think about creating space for employee-led volunteer programs, pro bono talent pools, internal innovation labs, or talent-sharing partnerships across departments or sectors. These practices recognize that people want to use their skills to contribute beyond their job description—and doing so can deepen morale, engagement, and retention.

Whether you're a team member or a leader, begin by asking: What talents are we underutilizing? What unexpected skills are hiding in plain sight? And how can we create space to use them not just to perform, but to contribute?

Several law firms I know give young associates time each month to apply a skill they're excited about, like writing, speaking, or mentoring, to causes the firm supports. That one shift has unlocked a wave of pro bono and community service projects, ranging from reading to first graders to helping write résumés for single moms getting back into the workforce. More importantly, the program has unlocked awareness across the entire firm that it values their talents and contributions beyond billable hours. Other firms, like DLA Piper, have evolved traditional pro bono projects into entire nonprofit organizations housed within their firms that promote and strengthen rule of law and access to justice.

It's hard to overstate how important these efforts are—not only to workplace culture at some of the largest firms in the world, but as an example for other firms to follow. In an industry that sells time for money, voluntarily taking some of that commodity away from the billable category to dedicate to other causes sets a profound example, and happens to also be good for business. The smartest leaders know that investing in talent-inclusive impact is a wise business decision in the long run.

Outside of the legal field, impact-aligned businesses are finding ample ways to channel team talent into impactful service. Deloitte, one of the world's largest professional services firms and a "Big 4" accounting firm, channels its consulting, finance, and tech talent into community impact through its annual IMPACT Day. It closes its offices nationwide so its employees can contribute their expertise to a nonprofit or school. Projects have included strategy consulting for food banks, digital transformation plans for small nonprofits, and mentoring sessions with youth entrepreneurs. Their focus is on delivering high-value, skill-based service, not just physical labor.

JPMorganChase connects its employees' financial and business acumen with the needs of nonprofits and community-based organizations to provide pro bono consulting, financial coaching, and business development support.

On monthly "InDays," LinkedIn employees devote a work day to focusing their talents on advancing either themselves, their team, or the wider community. One available program for these efforts is LinkedIn Coaches, an initiative where employees can provide one-on-one coaching and résumé help to jobseekers facing barriers to employment, including veterans, immigrants, and the formerly incarcerated. This leverages LinkedIn's domain of expertise and crawl-through-glass cause of supporting career development.

The flagship program of PwC (formerly known as Pricewaterhouse-Coopers) focuses on financial literacy education. Employees volunteer their time to teach middle and high school students business and financial fundamentals using PwC's own custom curriculum.

These are just a few high-profile examples. In all of them, employees are doing more than just volunteering. They're using their day job skills to strengthen communities and model the kind of engagement we most hope to see, and increasingly demand, from major corporations.

These efforts and the work they entail also just so happen to be excellent for both employee and client satisfaction and retention. Greater connection with purpose at work is correlated with all sorts of good things: higher customer satisfaction, profitability, productivity and quality; lower turnover; less absenteeism; and fewer safety incidents. Would an organization really want to leave all those upsides on the table? And while one McKinsey study noted that upward of 70 percent of workers surveyed say their sense of purpose is tied to their work, only 18 percent feel they are actually getting as much purpose as they want. This reveals a huge opportunity for employers to find new and better ways to connect talent with purpose.

Your organization is likely full of potential for harnessing purpose in ways that keep employees engaged. After all, most organizations don't lack purpose or talent. They lack a framework for understanding (and systems for connecting) the two. That gap represents a huge opportunity for increasing impact in service of Better Good.

ANCHORS AND WINGS

The initiatives of Will and Jada Smith's foundation were linked to their talents as actors and producers, through the opportunities, networks, and influence their success created. They drew on the access, credibility, and influence those talents had earned. Their Careers in Entertainment (CIE) initiative created opportunities for young people without easy access to the entertainment industry, including students from Will's childhood neighborhood of West Philadelphia. CIE events around the country, including on Hollywood studio lots, drew on Will and Jada's powerful relationships, and networks built from their primary talents. Their presence and engagement also enabled them to serve as career inspirations for participants. CIE was praised for giving eager young people unique exposure to the industry that had given the Smith family their stardom.

When I left the Chicago Theater the night of Will's book launch event, I couldn't have been prouder to be connected to his foundation and grateful for the opportunity to connect with him, however briefly. Just a few months later, the instantly-infamous Oscar night slap unfolded in front of millions. It was an off script, unfiltered, and impossible to ignore blow to Will's nice-guy image. But from my perspective, it also aligned with the self-awareness he had threaded throughout his memoir. The story he had already begun to tell, about striving, stumbling, and learning, continues to unfold. And whatever mistakes he has made—or mistakes that any of us make—they shouldn't inhibit him or us from serving others.

Like Will, we are all still works in progress. There are times when we all stumble personally, professionally, and/or when trying to do good. Sometimes we stumble spectacularly. We can't predict the future, or how we'll ultimately be remembered. What matters is that we keep going, with a focus on our core talents guiding us through. And *that* will add up to a legacy.

In the wake of the 2022 Oscars, Will and Jada quietly closed their family foundation. But they haven't stopped their journey of doing good. And despite what some of the headlines implied, this wasn't a retreat, surrender, or failure. It was an opportunity for recalibration. Like so many public figures who start a foundation, they had learned what so many eventually do—that meaningful impact doesn't always require an organization. In fact, letting go of that particular structure can free up resources of time, energy, capital, and talent to flow more intentionally elsewhere.

Many prominent individuals actually discover—as I suspect Will and Jada have—that they can do Better Good in other ways, free from the constraints of an organization and its obligations. There's no shame in the pivot, and there should be applause for the pursuit.

Will's core talents for singing, acting, and entertaining are those to which he most immediately and understandably returned in the years following. This makes perfect sense for anyone seeking to realign with their truest sense of self. Seeking solace and growth rooted in our greatest talents fills us up. I suspect it will be the platform from which Will continues his evolving journey of discovery for the next phase of doing good in his life and work . . . for turning experience, even painful experience, into something that connects, moves, and inspires people. His primary talents continue to be his base for growth, resilience, and redefinition. And in his emerging talent as an author, I can't wait to read the next installment, which I'm certain will provide thoughtful insights about recent events.

What's most important, and what remains constant in work that scales, is deployment of talent in our Goldilocks Zone, or as close to it as possible, in whatever form that takes. We humans are never done developing and becoming something new. It follows then, that our pursuit of doing Better Good is also never done. And the more our social impact footprint aligns with our core, underlying, and emerging talents, the more scalable and sustainable our impact will be.

That's the final truth I hope you take from this chapter: our talents are not fixed points. They are foundations (that sometimes become actual nonprofit foundations). They are both starting blocks and safe harbors, both anchors and wings. Sometimes we build upon them. Sometimes we return to them. And sometimes, in our hardest moments, they return to us—reminding us who we are, what we're capable of, how much we still have to give, and providing a path forward.

The pursuit of doing good is an endless evolution of trial and error. And learning how to steer this evolution is a talent we hone over the course of our lives.

KEY TAKEAWAYS AND ACTION ITEMS

Key Takeaways

- **Talent is your most personal asset.** It's the combination of your skills, instincts, and experiences—what you're naturally good at and what you've practiced over time.
- **Talent comes in layers.** Your primary talents are the obvious ones, your underlying talents are the hidden ones that power everything else, and your emerging talents are the ones still developing and full of possibility.
- **Your Goldilocks Zone is where it all comes together.** When you align what you're good at with what matters most to you, impact and fulfillment reinforce each other.
- **Soft skills are real skills.** Empathy, communication, adaptability, and curiosity are often the very things that make your hard skills matter.
- **You're always becoming.** Talents evolve. What was once new can become core, and what's core can grow into something even greater.
- **Deploying talent is scalable good.** When individuals and organizations intentionally use their unique mix of talents for good, they multiply their impact—and everyone benefits.

Action Items

For Individuals

- **Inventory your talents across three categories:**

  Primary Talents—The obvious ones: What you're known for. What shows up in your job title, credentials, or how people introduce you.

  Underlying Talents—The hidden gold: What you've gained through lived experience, personal growth, or informal roles. These are often the most transferable—and undervalued.

  Emerging Talents—The "not quite there yet" skills that are just beginning to reveal themselves. Nurture them—they might lead to your next great act of impact.

- **If you need help: ask yourself five revealing questions:**

  What do people thank me for most often?

  What do I do easily that others find hard?

  When do I remember feeling truly useful?

  What skills am I using more and more lately?

  If someone shadowed me for a week, what talents would they notice?

- **Spot what stands out.** Star the talents that energize you most. Circle the ones that connect to causes or communities you most care about.
- **Apply your mix.** Look for ways to use your talents in real life—at work, in service, or through mentoring, board involvement, or other projects.
- **Share and refine.** Tell someone you trust what you've identified. Ask what they'd add or see differently. Repeat this reflection regularly given that your talents—and the ways to use them—will evolve.

Action Items

For Organizations

- **Uncover hidden talent.** Encourage team members to identify their Primary, Underlying, and Emerging talents. People want to bring their whole selves to work—make space for that.
- **Create opportunities for use.** Integrate skill-based service, pro bono projects, and internal or external social impact initiatives that allow employees to apply their expertise to meaningful work.
- **Align talent with purpose.** Match individual strengths with organizational goals and social impact priorities. The closer the alignment, the stronger the engagement.
- **Recognize and reward it.** Celebrate examples of employees using their talents for good—through stories, internal spotlights, or recognition in performance reviews.
- **Make it part of culture.** Build systems that support ongoing discovery and use of talent—mentorship programs, innovation labs, or dedicated time for purpose-driven projects.
- **Track and tell the story.** Capture, celebrate, and share the outcomes. When people see how their unique strengths contribute to something larger, motivation and impact compound.

CHAPTER 9

Your Treasure

I won't wait. And I will keep at it until the safe is empty.

—MacKenzie Scott, 2019, in her Giving Pledge letter describing her commitment to donating the vast majority of her fortune

THE BILLION DOLLAR QUESTION

"If I want to give away a billion dollars over the next ten years in a way that doesn't suck, what should I do?"

That was a real question I was unexpectedly asked by my billionaire officemate. (Yes, "billionaire officemate" is a strange pairing of words; explanation below.) This was long before I became a consultant and was expected to deal with such heavy questions. And at first, I was stumped. Was "doesn't suck" really the bar for success? If not, what should be?

I struggled to find the words to respond. Partially because of the foggy baby brain that came with having a newborn at home, but also because of the novelty of the question. I'd never had a billionaire ask me this question before.

While this particular billionaire wasn't my boss, he was a colleague and collaborator of sorts. Thanks to his affinity and support for the Clinton Foundation, he offered to provide me and a colleague space in his Chicago office. So we became officemates for several years, and I got to know him and the teams of his business and family foundation. The spirit of collaboration led to the day when he dropped in, asked if he could take a seat (his office, I noted, so of course he was welcome *any* time), and the ensuing billion-dollar question.

"Don't worry," he continued. "I'm not actually expecting you to answer that."

I relaxed a bit and exhaled. I knew that he employed entire teams of world-class experts and consultants to answer such questions—and so I found myself both surprised and somewhat humbled by the fact that he had asked *me*.

While the wheels spun inside my head, he added that this question was at the core of his family foundation's recent engagement with a top-tier consulting firm. He was holding their report and shared it with me. He noted that the firm's guidance was predictably *good* but not *great*, and certainly not exciting, inspiring, boundary-busting or needle-moving. He wanted more.

"Maybe you'll see something they didn't," he said, sliding the report across my desk. "Give it a read and let me know what you think." I told him I would, and he nodded, already half turned toward the door. "No rush," he added, "but I'm serious about wanting to get this right." Then he was gone.

What has stuck with me most about that conversation all these years later, and what I hope you'll find empowering, is that none of us—billionaires and world-renowned consulting firms alike—know the "right" way to deploy treasure for the most good. He was struggling with the same questions we all struggle with, just on a much bigger scale: *How much should I give? In what ways? On what time frame? To which causes? And how can I give in a way that "doesn't suck."*

Even those with nearly unlimited resources struggle to crack these questions. This realization should take the pressure off the rest of us. It gives us space to relax a little, take a calming breath, and begin to explore what works best *for us* and the causes we care about most. Getting this giving, donating, investing, and otherwise deploying capital for good "perfect" or even just "right" is like gripping a handful of sand . . . the harder you squeeze it, the faster it slips through your fingers. But when you relax the grip, you actually have more success in the effort.

Of course, most of us won't ever face the challenge of how to give away a billion dollars. But each of us should be just as thoughtful, diligent, and even a little impatient about how we deploy whatever amount of "treasure" we do have—each day, in the future, and beyond—in order to do the most good possible.

Most of the world sees treasure deployed for good almost exclusively through the lens of philanthropic giving. But as you'll discover shortly, there are more diverse and dynamic ways to deploy treasure beyond donations of cash.

THE BEST THINGS IN LIFE ARE FREE, BUT . . .

First, the obvious: money matters. It's not the *only* thing that matters—not by a long shot—but it's a powerful tool and part of everyone's social impact footprint and tool kit. It's often the first thing most of us think about when considering how to make a difference.

Deployed thoughtfully, money can accelerate change, expand reach, and unlock opportunities that time and talent alone can't. Whether you're supporting a local food pantry, seeding a scholarship, scaling a social enterprise, or funding an international NGO, family foundation, for-purpose business initiative, or impact investment, money moves needles.

And needles really need moving these days. We're living through a period of seismic recalibration in how society funds and sustains the common good. Government priorities and institutions are shifting (or being shut down altogether), forcing nonprofits and businesses to fill widening gaps, even as *their* own efforts come under new scrutiny or political attack. This often results in recalibration and slowing of their giving, which creates a domino effect throughout sectors, communities, and organizations impacted by this once-in-a-generation shift. The result is a complicated moment that demands clarity, creativity, and courage in how individuals and organizations alike deploy treasure for Better Good.

At the individual level, even small amounts directed to worthy causes help others feel seen, supported, or safe. At the organizational or systemic level, treasure fuels infrastructure, innovation, and impact. And at every level in between, it creates leverage—matching gifts, pooled investments, and ripple effects that can multiply the impact of every dollar spent, raised, or deployed.

The challenge is that nobody knows the "perfect"—or even the "right"—way to deploy financial resources for impact, not even the richest people in the world. Right is always subjective, and there's only so much any giver of treasure can do to ensure that their money will have the intended impact, or that the impact will scale or sustain. Still, some ways to deploy treasure are indisputably more effective than others. The key isn't how much you give, but how much awareness and intention you apply to your giving.

This chapter shows that ultimately, making an impact with your treasure isn't about how *much* you give, but how *well* you give it. The key question is the same whether your pool of resources is $1 or $1 billion: How do you get the most bang for your buck?

WHY SMALL GIFTS BUILD COMMUNITY, DEMOCRACY, AND RESILIENCE

In a time when our sense of community feels fractured, our democracy strained, and our collective resilience tested by crisis after crisis, deploying our treasure effectively matters more than ever.

When we give—even modest amounts—to causes connected to our communities of greatest concern, we're voting with our wallets *and* our values, declaring that we belong to something larger, that our community—our humanity—matters, and that shared systems that make up our society can still be shaped by our actions. As the CEO of GivingTuesday, Asha Curran (no relation) puts it: "Generosity is an antidote to fear, isolation, and division."

The data backs this up. Everyday donors—those giving less than $5,000 a year—are the backbone of nonprofit revenue and resilience. Organizations with broad bases of small donors ride out shocks and changes to systems better because they're not overrelying on a single funder.

Consider Team Rubicon, a veteran-led humanitarian organization that serves communities after disasters like hurricanes, tornadoes, fires, and floods. They curate a community of monthly small-dollar donors they call their "Support Squad," who provide consistent collective contributions that provide stability before, during, and after disasters strike. This model provides an immediate opportunity for affected communities—and those seeking to support them—to plug into.

Small gifts are the connective tissue of civic life. They hold communities together, sustain democracy through shared action, and build resilience amid turbulent times and in the face of change. In a world of widening divides and multiplying storms, everyday, community-driven generosity is one of the most tangible, actionable, and powerful forces we have to participate in and benefit from.

Now, let's explore strategies and tactics for deploying financial resources, whether you currently have a lot, a little, or even none at all. No matter your budget, you'll find power, promise, poignancy, and potential in every opportunity.

SURPRISE! LOWER INCOME GIVERS GIVE THE MOST—AND MAKE THE BIGGEST IMPACT

When most of us think of philanthropy, our minds go to news stories of the super wealthy pledging millions, or major foundations making big grants or seeding new billion-dollar ventures. And those *are* awesome, and worthy of the coverage they get. But the real story of charitable giving in America is both more surprising and more hopeful: it's driven by everyday people.

Study after study confirms that lower-income donors give a higher percentage of their income to charitable causes than wealthier donors. Households earning under $50,000 per year give between 6 to 8 percent of their income, while households earning over $100,000 give closer to 4 percent, with high-net-worth households (with income over $1 million) giving approximately 3 percent.

In fact, according to Giving USA, individuals accounted for 67 percent of all charitable giving in the U.S. in 2023 alone, totaling over $374 billion. When you include bequests and gifts from family foundations (which operate more like individual donors) the number rises to more than 80 percent. Corporate contributions, by comparison, accounted for just 4 percent.

This is not meant to be a guilt trip or a rebuke of the affluent, but a testament to the outsized generosity of those with smaller budgets. It's also a reminder of how much impact is made by those whose names don't appear on donor walls. Collectively, small dollar donors put more into philanthropy than big givers who usually get more praise and attention.

Let me be clear: both big and small donors are important to the philanthropy ecosystem, but everyone is already more aware of the big donor stories. Few realize the presence and power of the masses of small donors.

Having a clearer grasp of the giving landscape shifts power—or at least perceptions about power—back to all of us as individuals. It also reminds us that giving is not the exclusive domain of the wealthy, and we all can utilize our treasure in meaningful ways. Giving is a personal and deeply democratic act practiced by tens of millions of Americans every year. Likely including you.

NO MONEY? NO PROBLEM

Even if you have zero disposable income and a corresponding $0 giving budget, you still have important power related to treasure: the ability to raise awareness, motivate and mobilize, and create giving moments for others. *Everyone* now has the ability to become an awareness-raising fundraiser. With the technology in our pockets and on our desks, and our increasing digital interconnectedness, we all have the ability to promote causes we care about and connect our communities—local and digital—to them with the hope that those you reach may give. In this realm, you can:

- Use social media to spotlight local or global causes.
- Share campaigns with a personal note about why they matter, in real life and online.
- Organize fundraisers or workplace challenges.
- Offer a small donation match to invite and encourage others to join you.

And yes, you *do* have the skills for this kind of work, because of your profile, platform, and passion for the causes you care about. That's all you need to start, even if your giving budget is literally $0.

TRACK SMALL DONORS FOR BIG IMPACT

The average American donates about 2 to 5 percent of their income, which results in giving amounts averaging about $2,000 for those at the lowest income levels to nearly $50,000 for those making above

$250,000 per year. That's a LOT of giving on average, much more than most of us realize. Way to go, friends!

But wait . . . there's more! These figures typically don't include easily overlooked contributions we make (and are prone to forget or fail to track) in our daily lives, like rounding up at the checkout, dropping coins in donation jars, boxes, or kettles, making purchases from kids selling cookies or candy for a cause, and those "buy one, give one" purchases. Tracking these numbers doesn't just paint a fuller picture of our financial giving (and accurate reporting for tax returns), but also helps tell the true, full story of how you do good in the world. It's easier than ever to keep track with a financial tracker app, or even just using the notes app on your smartphone. Getting into the habit of tracking helps you capture a fuller and more accurate view of all the ways—and all the places—you are contributing treasure.

This important point bears repeating: these seemingly simple, almost "insignificant" contributions really add up. In fact, point of sale and "round up" donations at checkout raised nearly $749 million in 2022, up nearly 25 percent from just five years earlier. Even more surprising, the *average* total donation per shopper was $50 annually, proving that what feels like spare change can quickly add up to big change.

This generosity also shapes the future of philanthropy itself. One study found that one in three major donors began with gifts under $250. Small gifts are meaningful in their own right—and are full of potential. They often represent the first spark in a lifelong practice of giving that grows over time, in both scale and significance.

This is usually an eye-opener for both donors and fundraising professionals alike. Sometimes small gifts are the seeds that grow into much greater giving. They speak to the potential on both sides of the donor/recipient equation. Imagine telling a child, or a colleague, that their seemingly minor gift could be responsible for extraordinary outcomes? That's both inspiring and 100 percent true.

In fact, some of the most iconic philanthropic efforts in American history were powered by everyday donors. The Statue of Liberty's pedestal was completed not with one major gift, but through a public appeal that drew thousands of modest contributions from citizens across the country. A nation of small-dollar givers mobilized to purchase WWII war bonds, an early precursor of modern-day social impact bonds. More recently, GivingTuesday and GoFundMe efforts see millions of Americans mobilizing small dollar donations that collectively produce massive results and inspiring impact.

That same spirit is alive and well in every local fundraising drive, aid effort, and grassroots movement sustained not by large checks, but by collective generosity. All those pennies in kettles, dollars in donation buckets, and rounding up for a good cause truly do add up to incredible social impact. The takeaways from all of this are surprisingly simple and powerful:

- Most giving comes from individuals, not institutions.
- Lower-income households give more, proportionally, than the wealthy.
- Big donors often start small—proving that those early gifts matter.
- Small gifts support community, democracy, and resilience.

In a philanthropic ecosystem often skewed by headlines and high-dollar donations, these facts serve as a necessary reset for the rest of us who give more modestly and won't see any headlines or our names on plaques or buildings. The empowering reality is that giving is not a privilege reserved for the wealthy. It is an act of power, possibility, and purpose—available to all of us, every day, and present in every contribution any of us make, no matter how big or small. And given the data about how our collective contributions actually create the greatest impact, each of us should feel as much—if not greater—a part of the giving ecosystem as the giving that makes news. Because when you zoom out to look at the full picture, you discover a powerful truth: the charitable engine runs not on the fuel of a few, but on the steady, generous contributions of many.

Big gifts turn heads, but smaller-dollar donors crank flywheels that produce big results.

FOUND MONEY

There's another opportunity to "find" money that actually doesn't cost us anything extra but allows us to extend the size of our impact footprint even further. The world of philanthropy *loves* a good matching opportunity. You've probably heard many such pitches: "Give by [date] and [prominent person] will match your contribution!" This model contains both marketing genius and real opportunity. You can feel great about doubling the impact of your gift (even if you can't double the tax deduction . . . sorry). It's the same psychology at work when we know that "a portion of proceeds" benefits a worthy cause when we purchase a product we were going to buy anyway. Whether the cause is near and dear to us or not, it never hurts and often helps.

This is regularly the case with matching grants for nonprofits, during special times like GivingTuesday, year-end fundraising campaigns, events hosted by school alumni organizations, and even major donors of nonprofits who offer to match small gifts dollar for dollar. You get to double your personal impact, which will make you feel doubly good. The more you look for these types of opportunities, the more you'll find.

At work, those underutilized corporate matching programs allow employees to double their giving up to a certain amount. More than 26 million of us work for companies that offer such matching programs, but upward of 78 percent of eligible employees don't even know this opportunity exists, leaving somewhere between $4 and $7 *billion* of matching funds unclaimed each year. Imagine the impact the average person could have if even a portion of their annual giving were matched by an employer contribution. That's right: we can collectively unlock *billions* for philanthropy at literally no extra cost to us, other than the time required to ask if our employers match qualified donations. Worst case scenario: your employer doesn't offer a matching program. And best case of that worst case scenario: they start . . . thanks to you!

So just ask. Please. The ferrets and otters need you. And that type of advocacy won't cost you a penny.

SHOULD YOU SPLIT OR CONCENTRATE YOUR TREASURE?

Some people prefer spreading small gifts across many causes, while others concentrate their giving to one or two core areas where they want to go deep. Neither is right or wrong, provided you're intentional and strategic about aligning your giving with your values, goals, and passion.

Let's say you can afford $1,000 each year to give to worthy causes. That may sound like a lot, but it's actually well below the national averages that we saw above, meaning you're likely already giving in this range even if you don't realize it. With the Better Good Framework in hand, you could make (at least) two simple choices.

Option one: give $1 to 1,000 different causes, feeling good—no, feeling amazing—about supporting literally "thousands of causes" every year! One hundred percent true, and a cool story of doing good by deploying your treasure.

Option two: make an intentional choice to decline all the smaller giving opportunities that present themselves in daily life—a dollar here, a dollar there—and save it all for one annual $1,000 donation to your crawl-through-glass cause, feeling good—no, feeling amazing—about giving the most possible to *the* one cause that most fills your soul. Also 100 percent true, and an inspiring story of doing good by deploying your treasure.

Again, there is no right or wrong method. Broad support creates widespread awareness and momentum, full of opportunity to provide a little support to lots of causes, learn about the problems they address, and share their message with others. Focused giving can create sustained impact over time for a smaller number of causes that more closely align with your Goldilocks Zone causes, allowing you to dive deeper with them. Both options provide that Better Good high. You don't have to pick either of these approaches exclusively or forever.

Whatever path you choose, intentionally deploying your financial resources is often the first and most accessible step on the journey to Better Good. Once you realize exactly how much you may be giving in all ways, you and your family can make more carefully designed choices about future giving. Some people may simply be more excited to have a more accurate view and feel inspired to continue the giving they're already doing. Others may choose to be more selective about which opportunities they say yes to. Trading haphazardness for intentionality makes it much easier to prioritize your Goldilocks Zone causes. And sometimes, the best place to start being more intentional isn't in your budget—it's at your own dinner table.

MAKE GIVING A FAMILY MATTER

Whatever the size, scale, or scope of your giving, here's a simple, family-friendly way to level up your impact budget: a semi-annual impact check-in. In our family, we pull up a running list of causes we've recently supported (I keep it in a simple notes app), talk about which ones matter most—crawl-through-glass or otherwise—discuss our thoughts about the issues and organizations we support, and give everyone a turn to make their case for continuing or changing our approach. That short conversation sparks better thinking, surfaces fresh ideas about our goals for our family's social impact footprint, and ends with a shared decision about how we'll proceed with future giving. The ritual works with any budget, any giving strategy, and any definition of family. It even works inside organizations.

HOW TO BE A GREAT BIG(GER) DONOR

If you're in a position to give beyond smaller amounts, you can step into even greater intentionality and impact for your Goldilocks Zone causes, or those that your loved ones care deeply about. As capacity and budgets allow, you can move along the giving spectrum by expanding into:

- Strategic family giving: Establish a clear budget, shared goals, and documented priorities, and track the ways in which your household supports causes you care about.
- Donor-Advised Funds (DAFs): Manage giving across multiple years and causes without having to set up a separate entity requiring governance, compliance, management, and oversight.
- Estate planning tools: Ensure that your legacy of impact will outlive you (more on this below).
- Foundations or family offices: For those who have substantial assets, you may want a structured and legally formal approach to giving.

My family has adopted all but the last of these tools, and I've seen them all used consistently and comfortably by friends, family, clients, colleagues, and collaborators. You can adopt any one or more of these approaches based on your individual or family circumstances and goals. And here's an important reminder: "bigger" doesn't mean "big"—it just means bigger than where you are today.

Donna, our dog rescuer extraordinaire from Chapter 8, recently funded a scholarship for veterinary students committed to small animal care—her crawl-through-glass cause. She endowed the scholarship with an initial gift and also decided to further support and expand the gift in her estate plan. It was her way of planting seeds now and for the future. As the Greek proverb goes: "A society grows great when people plant trees in whose shade they shall never sit." Donna will continue her legacy of saving animals in need—and inspiring others to the cause to do the same—long after her own ability to do so ends. The force multiplier effect of one individual's example has no limit.

TOUGH TRUTH: YOU CAN'T TAKE IT WITH YOU

None of us get out of this life alive. As country great George Strait reminds us, "I ain't never seen a hearse with a luggage rack." We can't take any of our treasure with us, but here's the good news: preparation extends our ability to leave a legacy of impact, lengthens our social impact footprint, and sets an important example even after we're gone—for our children, peers, and communities we care about.

While it can be difficult to come to terms with the underlying realities of estate planning, it's a smart way to simultaneously protect your assets *and* advance and enhance your use of treasure for doing good, both while you're living and beyond. More good news: many colleges, universities, and nonprofit organizations recognize people *during* their lifetimes for making provision for future giving.

Amy and I were in our early forties, with two young kids at home, when we made a simple provision in our estate plans to provide for a portion to benefit the law school where we met. That percentage didn't have a value attached to it, given lots of variables involved in estate plans. In fact, there are some scenarios where it might have no value at all for the school.

But after casually mentioning this to the law school's development team when talking about our annual gift for that year, we were unexpectedly recognized as new members of a group of alumni who include the school in their estate plans: The Gunsaulus Society! We didn't even know such a thing existed, but we now display the corresponding gift—a little plaque with a clock (seems ominous in context, doesn't it?) and a picture of us at the event where we were unexpectedly recognized. We even got a write-up in the alumni magazine about our having "joined" the society through our "generous gift" . . . of potentially $0. Of course, all of this is designed to encourage other alumni to make similar arrangements in their own estate plans. There's a reciprocal benefit to all involved. We literally gave nothing at this point (and will be gone before we know the amount we *actually* gave, if any), but they reacted as if we'd dropped a fat check.

For us, recognition isn't a motivator, but those feel-good chemicals that this recognition elicits reminds us that our gift has value and impact, especially since we won't live to see the tangible impacts of our estate planning. Such planned future giving—whether through beneficiary bequests for specific simple investment or insurance accounts, or via more complex estate plans—is simply *another* way to deploy treasure for good and expand your impact footprint. Whether you crave recognition or prefer anonymity, it's worth at least asking the organizations representing the causes you care about if they are seeking provisions in estate plans. The clock is ticking . . . but in a good way. It means you have time to think about the legacy you'd like to leave and intentionally structure your finances for that legacy.

BEYOND GIVING: PURCHASING AND INVESTING FOR GOOD

Up to this point, we've been focused primarily on *giving* treasure—how to donate, match, or raise it. But giving is only one side of the coin. The other is how we spend and invest the treasure we use every day as consumers and investors. Each swipe of a card, click of a checkout button, or line in an investment portfolio statement is a potential act of influence and impact that can reinforce the world as it is or shape the one we want.

The "buy one, give one" models and "a portion of proceeds benefits . . ." campaigns have made doing Better Good part of daily commerce, often at no extra cost if you were planning to buy the product anyway. These purchases are easy to overlook, but also easy to track—and they count as part of your social impact footprint.

You have also likely heard of impact investing and social finance, which offer even more ways of deploying treasure for good. Major investment firms like BlackRock, Vanguard, Schwab, JPMorganChase, Morgan Stanley, Fidelity, and Goldman Sachs all offer social impact investment opportunities, ranging from exchange-traded funds (ETFs) to mutual funds for retail investors and more tailored opportunities for high-net-worth investors.

Despite the growing awareness and availability, some institutions are still catching up to this trend. One leader in tech and social impact told me a story that perfectly captured the tension between traditional finance and the evolving world of impact investing. She and her husband, both highly successful and deeply values-driven, had chosen a respected local bank for its community roots. They wanted to move their family's considerable assets into impact-aligned investments and repeatedly asked their bank to grow with them on that journey by diversifying their investments with greater impact-inclusive options. But despite multiple conversations about aligning their portfolio with their impact-driven values, the bank seemed unable or unwilling to grasp what they were asking for. They kept defaulting to traditional investment and giving strategies—tried and true approaches, but increasingly outdated models.

The bank's refusal to see this caused growing frustration for my friend and her husband. The breaking point came during a meeting when, after yet another attempt to explain their impact-driven goals, one banker smiled, patted her forearm, and said, "Don't worry, honey. We'll make such a great return on your investments that you can give whatever you want to charity."

Yikes. Patronizing. Tone deaf. Stuck in old language ("charity" is infrequently used in the world of impact) and completely missing the point. "We tried, but I've had enough," my friend told me. The family moved their assets elsewhere—a meaningful loss for the bank, given the scale of the family's success. The episode is a cautionary tale for any institution: in a world where capital increasingly follows conscience, banks and businesses that fail to understand impact investing and meet their clients' demand for offering related services risk watching their clients—and their treasure—go elsewhere.

Beyond impact investing alone, other daily purchasing behaviors that aren't directly linked to a social cause may nonetheless still have a positive social impact. Remember our discussion of concentrated laundry detergent in Chapter 1? You can easily seek out eco-conscious, planet-friendly, cruelty-free products; clothing made from recycled fabrics or materials; food items that are organic, sustainably produced, and free from added hormones, antibiotics, dyes, and so on. You can rent a home or office space in a LEED-certified or otherwise energy efficient building. From solar panels and electric vehicles to cage-free eggs and organic food products, the possibilities are endless.

Microloan outlets like Kiva.org allow individuals to become investors in global entrepreneurs by making small dollar investments via their online platform. Kickstarter similarly enables individuals to become seed stage support for start-ups, including social enterprises geared for good.

There is an increasingly wider array of treasure-related opportunities for good, if only we tune in and pay attention to them. As James Clear emphasizes in *Atomic Habits*, every choice is a vote for the kind of person we want to be. And it can be found not just at those obvious points of sale, but nearly everywhere we look. Every dollar you spend mindfully is a vote in favor of the kind of world in which you want to live and the good you want to do.

ORGANIZATIONAL TREASURE

Whether you lead a company, a team, or an institution, every organization can make a meaningful difference deploying treasure for good *and* by engaging your team members and customers alike in that pursuit. When done transparently and tied to mission, organizational giving programs are standard operating practice. They form the core infrastructure of modern corporate citizenship and remain durable across leadership changes, market cycles, and headlines. Common examples include:

- Employee matching programs that double team members' giving to causes they care about.
- Corporate foundations that financially support programs, projects, and causes important to the company.
- Product-adjacent initiatives that offer buy one, donate one opportunities to customers, such as those led by TOMS, Bombas, Warby Parker, and the like.
- Cause partnerships like the Ronald McDonald House or the Tent Partnership for Refugees.
- Referral bonuses for good that thank current clients for referring new ones by making a donation to a cause of both clients' choosing.

When organizations deploy treasure for good, the greatest return is the culture of generosity and agency that develops across the organization, rippling through the work that follows. This can take the form of anything ranging from a cause marketing campaign or a year-end giving campaign with a match from the organization to amplify the impact of raising funds for a favorite cause, or making a corporate contribution in the name of customers and sharing the impact story of that gift in a holiday card or annual report. Or it might manifest in other ways that amplifies the impact footprint of the organization. That's the best part of building a Better Good organizational culture: the diversity of opportunities available will surprise you.

Today's workforce increasingly wants to be part of something meaningful and tied as much to purpose as possible. With corporate profits dominating the news, counterbalancing narratives about greed is not only good for business, it reinforces a rosier view of human nature. Offering clear, consistent, and participatory pathways for giving and engaging organizational treasure—whether through matching programs, grants, community support, or cause-driven campaigns—signals that your organization walks the talk and isn't solely a profit-seeking endeavor. Organization giving and other efforts invite everyone from entry-level employees to C-suite execs to see themselves not just as workers, but as contributors to something much greater than the bottom line.

Customers and other stakeholders feel it, too. In a marketplace saturated with choices, people continue to gravitate toward organizations that share their values. In fact, across twenty-five countries, 70 percent of consumers say they buy from brands they believe reflect their own principles. Thoughtful, transparent deployment of organizational treasure can become a brand differentiator, a trust-builder, and a loyalty anchor. Whether you're a two-person start-up or a Fortune 500 giant, putting your money where your mission is does more than just help others—it's smart, sustainable business. Meaningful action in service of purpose cuts through noise, creates impact-forward attention, and engages stakeholders. Bottom line: it's good for business.

MORE BILLIONAIRES DOING BETTER GOOD

As for my billionaire officemate, he reorganized his family foundation and revised their strategies. He has also expanded his personal commitment to public service in several admirable and impactful ways that continue to unfold. I'm proud of him and grateful for his example at a time when billionaires in public service and social impact are a mixed bag to say the least. He's one of the good ones. Thankfully, he's got growing ranks of good company.

At a time when income inequality is a daily discussion in the news and the ranks and treasure of billionaires are growing exponentially, there are some signs of hope among other high-profile philanthropists and social impact leaders.

MacKenzie Scott (formerly MacKenzie Bezos) is surprising organizations and individuals that do extraordinary work with life-changing contributions, which often show up unexpectedly while she keeps an exceedingly low profile.

Melinda Gates is charting an independent course that blends the best of her prior philanthropic experience with unfolding independence as a social impact leader. She's regularly present on stages where she speaks to rally others to causes of great global concern. Her visibility matters and provides a model for others to follow.

Laurene Powell Jobs, the widow of Steve Jobs and an extraordinary success in her own right, has created a dynamic approach to impact through the Emerson Collective, which blends traditional philanthropy, social enterprises, media, and her own visible leadership as an advocate for Better Good in the world.

Whether a sign of the times or a reaction to it, even some of the usual billionaire suspects are showing signs of dynamic new innovation. The Gates Foundation sent shock waves across philanthropy in 2025 when they announced they would spend down their $200 billion endowment over the next twenty years. Not long after the announcement, Bill Gates joined several of his fellow billionaires, including Steve Ballmer, Charles Koch, Scott Cook, and John Overdeck, to announce that they were creating and seeding a new $1 billion initiative called NextLadder Ventures, which will explore how AI can support economic mobility for those most at risk of being displaced by the technology.

These and other examples will, I hope, provide a new model for the wealthy to follow. And given estimates that the further evolution of AI alone is likely to create hundreds of new billionaires in the coming years, these role models matter. With great power comes great responsibility. And as the pursuit, accumulation, and disposition of the almighty dollar remains a central focus in modern society, models of how to do better good among those with the most will be critically important.

YOUR GREATEST ASSET ISN'T YOUR BANK ACCOUNT

Despite our society's disproportionate focus on wealth, please remember that your net worth should have nothing to do with your self-worth. Some of the "richest" people I've ever known were quite poor financially but did extraordinary good and left rich legacies. As my friend Sam Horn says each time we catch up, she is "rich in all the ways that matter." That's an important perspective to keep in mind any time we fall into discussions related to treasure.

While financial resources are undeniably important, money is never the impact tool that matters most. So I'd like to leave you with a quote from the late comedy and acting legend Robin Williams, in his role as Mork on *Mork & Mindy,* from the final episode of the series:

> *I don't know how much value I have in this universe, but I do know that I've made a few people happier than they would have been without me. And as long as I know that, I'm as rich as I ever need to be.*

KEY TAKEAWAYS AND ACTION ITEMS

You'll notice that the Action Items for Organizations in this section break down by type of organization.

Key Takeaways

- **Treat money as a tool.** Used with awareness and intention, treasure accelerates impact at any scale.
- **Start where you are.** Small gifts count—and often spark lifelong generosity.
- **Power comes from many.** Broad bases of small donors build community and resilience.
- **Be intentional: wide or deep.** Support many causes lightly or a few deeply—choose on purpose.
- **Count the whole picture.** Track *all* contributions, including big and small donations, roundups at checkouts, cause marketing purchases, and peer-to-peer support.
- **Unlock "found" money.** Seek employer matches, challenge grants, and pooled gifts to multiply impact.
- **Align how you spend and invest.** Purchases and portfolios can advance your impact footprint and the world you want to build.

- **Plan your legacy.** Simple estate provisions can sustain your impact footprint long after your lifetime.
- **Build generosity where you lead.** Organizations that give, match, grant, and partner earn trust and loyalty.
- **Remember what matters.** Your net worth and how much you give should never determine your self-worth. How you deploy treasure is important to—but not determinative of—your impact legacy. Your real personal legacy is ultimately measured by impact made, not exclusively by dollars deployed.

Action Items

For Individuals

- **Take inventory of your giving.** Don't just count the big checks or annual gifts. Look at the micro-donations: rounding up at checkout, dropping coins in a jar, contributing to a friend's fundraiser, or sponsoring a walk or run. These small contributions add up—and often reflect your values more than you realize. Use a notes app, spreadsheet, or financial tool to keep tabs on your giving, spending, and investing. Awareness creates patterns—and patterns create potential for more purposeful deployment of treasure.

- **Evaluate your spending.** Where you spend is how you vote with your dollars. Look at your purchases: Are they supporting small businesses? Local makers? Purpose-led enterprises? Mission-aligned brands? Conscious spending is an important form of treasure deployment, too.
- **Review your investing.** If you have retirement accounts, brokerage accounts, or any investment funds, take a closer look. Are you aligned with principles or impact strategies that are important to you? Even if you don't manage your investments directly, ask your adviser—or switch advisers, bankers, and funds to those that align with your impact goals. You can support those that are building the world you want to live in, invest in, and leave behind.
- **Decide to go wide or deep.** You can support many causes lightly or a few causes deeply. There's no single right answer—but you'll feel better about your giving, and more motivated to give, when it's intentional.
- **Leverage "found" money.** Ask if your employer offers a matching gift program—or if they'd be open to starting one. Got cash-back rewards, referral bonuses, or Venmo birthday gifts? Consider directing a portion toward impact.
- **Build an Impact Budget.** Treat impact like any other meaningful financial priority—because it is.

Whether it's $5 or 5 percent of your income, decide what's doable for you and build this percentage into your routine budgeting and spending.

- **Make Giving a Fun Family Practice.** Sit down once or twice a year to decide together where your giving will go and assess where your impact spending has gone. Engage kids to help choose causes they care about, vote on options, or "sponsor" a project. Not only does this make giving more inclusive and joyful, but a family giving practice makes it stick. Turn deploying treasure into a shared habit that reflects family values and priorities while equipping your kids with a template for impact they can use for life.
- **Talk about it.** Share your approach to deploying treasure with friends, kids, and peers. Giving is contagious—and your transparency helps normalize generosity in everyday life and attract greater support for causes you care about.

Action Items

For Organizations

For grantmaking nonprofits (those deploying funding)

Focus first on charitable purpose. Evaluate whether your giving truly aligns with your charitable purpose and your organization's past, present, and future goals for making a meaningful difference in this moment and for the future you envision.

Fund operations, not just programs. Unrestricted giving is back in style and strengthens your grantees' ability to survive and scale, especially during turbulent times.

Streamline the process. Look for ways to simplify your application and reporting processes to reduce burden on nonprofits. Many are leading this charge, everyone should follow.

Be as transparent as possible. Publicize your giving approach and decision-making criteria to invite transparency and accountability. Celebrate grantee successes by telling the story of impactful grants—because their success leaves clues for others to follow.

For grant-funded nonprofits (those receiving funding)

Make your impact crystal clear. Put your purpose and your impact front and center—make what you do uniquely well your clarion call so that funders can find you in a crowded marketplace of giving opportunities.

Make giving easy and dynamic. Make it easy for donors to give in different ways—recurring gifts, matching gifts, estate gifts, peer-to-peer campaigns, and in-kind support.

Elevate and amplify your unique impact. Relentlessly track and share your impact clearly so that donors know how their treasure creates real change. Transparency and great storytelling builds trust and consistent support and engagement.

Steward all donors. Celebrate and steward small-dollar donors as intentionally as major ones—they're often your long-term champions and most reliable givers.

Partner with purpose and for greater impact. Explore partnerships with values-aligned organizations (including businesses) for cause campaigns or shared fundraising.

For Social Enterprises

Clarify your impact model. How does the enterprise create good in a way that is baked into the business? Be specific and transparent about what is product-linked (pricing, sourcing, supply chain), profit-linked (financial contributions to causes), or operationally embedded (policies, governance, partnerships).

Involve your customers. Empower customers who support the enterprise to share the role they play by supporting the business. Equip them with simple starter messaging or data they can share and ways to easily share using social handles, links, QR codes, or hashtags. Keep in touch with and update them often to maintain engagement.

Use your platform. Frequently communicate about the social impact side of your business to rally additional support for your efforts, keep customers and stakeholder engaged, and inspire others to do the same in their work.

Measure impact. Just like revenue, track the dollars or resources you're directing toward good—and communicate about this clearly to enhance the credibility of your example and encourage others to do the same.

For Businesses

Go beyond the 4 percent. Corporate giving only accounts for 4 percent of total U.S. philanthropy. You can help boost that number, your brand, and your impact.

Offer a matching gift program to your employees. If you already do, review its use, enhance awareness, and encourage more employees to use it. If you don't offer one, start one, start small, then scale.

Align giving with employee values. Engage your team in choosing causes, designing campaigns, or directing resources.

Lead by example. Encourage founders and executives to publicly support causes they care about—modeling generosity from the top down.

Think "and" not "or." Generosity doesn't have to compete with profits. Purpose supports loyalty, talent retention, and long-term brand value.

PART IV

NEXT-LEVEL IMPACT: SSS

By now, you've mapped who you are (*Profile, Platform, Passion*) and what you contribute (*Time, Talent, Treasure*). The next step is to expand your impact into something brighter, bolder, and built to last. This section shows you how to amplify your good through the three S's of impact: Scale, Sustainability, and Storytelling.

Scale asks the essential question: Why do some efforts grow beyond anyone's expectations while others stay small? Chapter 10 reveals what the most effective changemakers do differently—how they build momentum, repeat success, and expand reach without losing purpose.

Sustainability is what keeps good both grounded and growing. It's the art and science of staying the course—of doing good not just once, but again and again. Chapter 11 offers a practical framework to help you avoid burnout, stay resilient, and sustain your capacity for good through the long arc of your life and work.

And then there's Storytelling—the force multiplier that turns private progress into public inspiration. A great story turns witnesses into participants. Chapter 12 helps you share what you're doing, for whom, and why, in ways that attract allies, energy, and action.

Together, these three S's are how ordinary efforts become movements. They're how the good you start keeps growing—through others, across time, and into the future.

CHAPTER 10

Scale What Works

Never doubt that a small group of thoughtful, committed citizens can change the world. Indeed, it is the only thing that ever has.

—Margaret Mead

ONE STARFISH AT A TIME

You may be familiar with the parable of the girl and the starfish. It usually goes something like this:

> *A young girl was walking along a beach upon which thousands of starfish had been washed up during a storm. When she came to each starfish, she would pick it up and throw it back into the ocean. People watched her with amusement. She had been doing this for some time when a man approached her and said, "Little girl, why are you wasting your time? Look at the size of this beach! You can't possibly save all these starfish. You can't make a difference!"*
>
> *The girl seemed deflated. But after a few moments, she bent down, picked up another starfish, and hurled it as far as she could into the ocean. Then she looked up at the man and replied, "Well, I made a difference for that one!"*

Some versions of this tale end with the child's reply, which nails the truth that doing any amount of good, no matter how small, is valuable and admirable. But here's the version of the ending I greatly prefer:

> *The old man looked at the girl inquisitively and thought about what she had said. Inspired, he joined her in throwing starfish back into the sea. Soon others saw them and joined as well. Before long, all the starfish were saved.*

Suddenly, this becomes more than a parable about small acts. It's a parable about *scale*—doing the good we're capable of on our own, while also doing *more* and *better good* by raising awareness and inspiring others to join and multiply our efforts.

Scale as a concept can often feel fuzzy, clichéd, or only relevant to big, national, or global organizations. The concept can be both deceptively confusing and also deceptively simple. Applying it can feel intimidating, but it doesn't have to.

Skeptics might say that the starfish parable only works for the starfish on this stretch of beach at this specific moment in time—it doesn't speak to the vastness of starfish rescue on all beaches the world over, much less the wider issue of ocean health, or all animal rescue. True. But this chapter isn't about solving every problem, everywhere, all at once. Like the girl on the beach, we'll focus on scaling the good we're already doing to inspire others and achieve more.

It's easy to get overwhelmed by "scale." Don't. Our goal is simply to think beyond the one-offs of daily life and maximize our contributions over time. Hence, scale. And the only real definition of the "right" kind of scale is what works for you and your goals.

SCALE, SIMPLIFIED

I define scale as expanding the reach, depth, or duration of any effort that's already effective. It's not about doing everything—it's about doing the right thing, more often, for more people, or for longer. Remember this simple rule of thumb from Sara Blakely, the founder of Spanx: "Start small, think big, and scale fast."

Sometimes scale means going wider: serving more people, entering new communities, expanding volume. Other times, scale means going deeper: getting better results, increasing sustainability, building capacity, or strengthening influence. And often, scale isn't linear. It's slow, steady, and imperceptibly exponential.

Jim Collins, author of *Good to Great*, famously uses the flywheel as a metaphor for organizational growth. Think of the first couple efforts to push your bicycle's pedals. At first, progress feels slow and requires a lot of effort, but as you stay consistent and focused, you build momentum. Eventually, the wheel turns faster and faster with less effort, powered by the cumulative force of your early persistence. That's scale.

WHAT MATTERS MOST FOR SCALE

As with everything at the core of the Better Good approach, awareness and intent matter most in your pursuit of scale. The first step is becoming aware that we all have the opportunity to scale in our own way, as both individuals and with organizations we serve and support.

How can you move beyond transactional, one-off, intermittent, and inconsistent efforts to do something more sustained? Even as your social impact footprint evolves over time (new causes, new efforts, new organizations, and evolving roles within each), keeping scale in mind enables a long-view mindset for doing good consistently and repeatedly. Done well, this might even result in less effort and greater results as you crank your own flywheel of momentum.

By being intentional about scale as part of your goal, you can refine your actions, approach, and contributions toward a greater version of the good you already do. This works for both individual and organizational efforts. And when you incorporate a vision of scale, you create greater clarity of the long-term effort you envision and create an opportunity for others to see, support, and join your pursuit of that vision.

For example, as an individual working in and with organizations, when you keep scale in mind, you bring a vision for your contribution to that organization. You'll be more intentional about seeking opportunities to scale your efforts and potentially helping drive the organization's work to new heights. For instance, you might start as a member of a committee at a nonprofit with an eye toward chairing it in the future, then eventually becoming a board member of the organization, or perhaps pivoting to a similar role with a larger organization once you have more experience. At work, you might engage in the group volunteer activity with hopes to expand that effort in future years, either doing similar work more often, for a larger number of causes, or expanding your workplace's approach to that kind of work entirely. Have you ever joined a group, seen others in leadership positions, and thought "I could do *that*!"—"I'd make a great board member!" or "I'm gonna run this [place/committee/initiative] someday?" Those are all visions of scale! And that vision can propel your efforts over time.

As you'll see in the examples below, one of the great things about scale is that it almost never has an actual endpoint, meaning there's always more opportunity for continued engagement and growth, regardless of where we are at any particular point in our specific journey of doing good.

In other words, even after saving all the starfish on one beach, there will be more starfish on more beaches that need our help, to say nothing of the many other animals in peril. That can be frustrating for some, but it can also be a form of rocket fuel that sustains your motivation toward a vision of scale.

A TALE OF TWO DAVES

Remember David Fajgenbaum from Chapter 5? His founding of Every Cure, a nonprofit with the mission to use every existing medication possible to treat every disease possible, is worthy of its own analysis of scale. But let's focus on something else: the fact that Every Cure isn't David's first nonprofit. Or even his second. It's his third, and probably not his last.

David's mom died of glioblastoma, a fast-spreading brain tumor, when he was a college student at Georgetown. He could easily—and understandably—have simply done his best to get through the grief, finish college, and move on to medical school. Most of us would have done exactly that—maybe raising awareness through social posts or raising money for cancer research by running a 5K. But that's not where David stopped. Instead, he turned his devastating grief into action by founding his first nonprofit, Actively Moving Forward, to help other students navigate grief while in college. All while playing football and pursuing his commitment to a career in medicine in memory of his mom. His story could end there as an extraordinary example of scaling from personal loss and grief into creating a nonprofit to serve others. But it doesn't.

While in medical school six years later, David received his own devastating diagnosis of Castleman Disease, a rare immunodeficiency disease with no known treatment, resulting in his multiple brushes with death, including being read his last rites five times in three years. After surviving long enough to research his own blood while in medical school, discover a potential cure that had been sitting on the pharmacy shelf the whole time, and keep himself in remission now for over a decade, David started his second nonprofit, the Castleman Disease Collaborative Network (CDCN), which advances research and treatment. Oh, and David also wrote a book, *Chasing My Cure*, while running CDCN, practicing as a young doctor, and becoming a professor at the University of Pennsylvania to advance his research on both Castleman and other rare diseases.

Which *then* led him to a greater version of scale: not just treating Castleman, but using tech, data, and emerging AI technology to more rapidly discover treatments for *all* rare diseases.

David and his cofounders, Grant Mitchell and Tracey Sikora, launched Every Cure with $0 in the bank, three volunteer founders, and some pro bono outside advisers. Within three years they had secured funding in excess of $100 million and hired a staff of dozens working feverishly to save and improve lives. Their efforts have saved patients at death's door, helped previously nonverbal neurodiverse children say their first words, and discovered a tumor-shrinking treatment for breast cancer that was hiding in plain sight. And they're literally still just getting started.

David's multiple and evolving commitments to finding the highest and best use of his abilities on his multiple crawl-through-glass causes reveals how much is possible when we lean into our Goldilocks Zones. Simply find what works and grow from there.

Now, I can hear you saying: "Okay, Scott, that's great, inspiring, and amazing. But I don't have a profound personal story like David's. I don't have a through line of rare diseases and medical degrees that will catapult me into a rocket-fueled trajectory. Are there other examples of scale that feel more attainable?"

Yes. Meet another Dave . . .

If David Fajgenbaum is an example of global scale born from personal experience, pain, and endurance, Dave Humphreys is the hometown everyman version. He's the locally legendary kind of person who might sit next to you at your favorite diner, community concert, or library board meeting.

Dave lives in Downers Grove, Illinois, the same community where he was born, raised, and plans to stay for the rest of his days. Now in his eighties and living at Oak Trace, a nonprofit senior community, Dave is, technically, "retired." Yet he remains one of the most active, integrated, and inspirational do-gooders—and one of the best examples of a lifetime of service at scale—I've ever encountered.

Over the decades, he has been a musician, marketing executive, community builder, festival producer, and organizational backbone for just about every major civic and philanthropic initiative in our shared community. He served more than twenty years on the Downers Grove Public Library Board. He chaired the DuPage County Board of Health. He led its Mental Health Advisory Committee. He's helped run the Rotary Club's annual community festival, GroveFest, for more than a decade—personally booking the music lineup, serving as MC, running sound and lights, and helping the event raise and redistribute nearly $600,000 to local and global causes.

Inside his longtime church, Dave has served in leadership positions, on committees, as a youth group leader, a member of the choir, and serves as the church's official community liaison to other local civic organizations because he's so involved in the community. He helped launch and lead a beloved community-serving music venue adjacent to the church called Two Way Street Coffee House—created in 1970 to combine folk music with access to financial, medical, and legal support for young people. Music is the hook and attraction to community patrons. Connection and service have been his goal and output for half a century. If there's a church activity or church-sponsored community event in town, Dave's there.

And, like David F., he's not done yet. In his "retirement," Dave has become an informal ambassador, formal foundation leader, and music-making legend at Oak Trace, his senior living community. He runs events. He mentors others. He even travels to represent his fellow residents at national board meetings for the nonprofit that owns Oak Trace. Wherever Dave goes, the same pattern repeats: he is present, engaging, and continually leveraging, expanding, and evolving his time, talents, and treasure in contribution to Better Good.

Dave might never be featured in the *New York Times*, write a bestselling memoir, or start multiple nonprofits like David Fajgenbaum. But what he *has* done—day after day, decade after decade—is scale his TTT across a single community in more ways than most people think possible. He's proof that scale doesn't require a global platform, a scientific breakthrough, a massive bank account, or a new nonprofit. Sometimes, scale simply looks like saying yes again. And again. And again. Until your entire community carries your fingerprints in the form of music, memories, and meaningful connections.

Most of us probably won't have the opportunity to scale globally on humanity-level issues such as rare diseases like David Fajgenbaum. But everyone has the ability to make a local impact, where you might well have the chance to scale like Dave Humphreys. And in a world hungry for Better Good, making a local impact is more than enough. It's just what we need.

ME, THE MIDDLE MARKET, AND THE MAJORS

Scale doesn't just happen in one place, in one way, or at one time. It happens all around us—in different forms, in different phases, across the many ways we do good. Attempting to consider scale—and determine how we can right-size our own commitments—across the various and multiple types of efforts we engage with can become unwieldy if not downright hard, which risks confusion and overwhelm. That's why it's helpful to do two things—at least until you build the muscle and can comfortably apply the lens of scale more broadly.

First, *don't* apply scale to *everything*, at least not at the outset. Instead, start exclusively with your crawl-through-glass Goldilocks Zone causes. Quick example: I care about, regularly engage with, and financially support our church. But while it's profoundly important to our family, it isn't one of my crawl-through-glass causes during this season of my life. As a result, it's totally fine for me to care deeply about our church without regularly worrying about how to scale my commitment. I know what our commitment is. I evolve and grow it as opportunity allows. But I don't need to apply the scale lens to it at this time.

Second, think about the causes and commitments you *do* want to scale through a three-part framework of the *types* of efforts with which you might engage: *Me*, *the Middle Market*, and *the Majors*. Each represents a distinct path, and understanding their differences can help you be more intentional about how your efforts scale over time.

Me:

Individual Efforts (High Control, Personal Impact)

This is what *you* can do directly to make an impact. It is the scale of your individual actions—efforts that are fully within your control and aligned with your deployment of Time, Talent, and Treasure. This is where your personal effort has a direct impact in real time.

When you decide to commit to picking up trash on every walk you take for the pure satisfaction of having that direct impact on the world immediately around you (a real example I hear about all the time), you're engaging in direct impact in that moment. You're doing something meaningful and effective. There is a direct correlation between your intent, your effort, and your impact. That's individual scale personified. Your personal direction and focus are high. You're the only cog in a machine you create and control.

Dave Humphreys's commitments to direct service in his community—his volunteer hours serving meals to the hungry, for instance, or volunteering a shift as master of ceremonies at the local community festival—are great examples of direct individual actions of time and talent being deployed at scale over decades. Donna's scholarship is another great example of a treasure-focused personal effort that creates long-term ripples for future veterinarians and the animals they will serve. Scale in these contexts may not be grand, but they are immediate and direct and entirely within individual control of individual effort.

The Middle Market:

Community Efforts (Shared Direction, Community Impact)

In midsize "middle market" organizations, your contributions go toward efforts that are bigger than you, but still accessible. These include nonprofits such as schools, churches, libraries, food banks, animal shelters, and civic organizations in or around your community. They might also include local banks, bookstores, and businesses with social impact initiatives that regularly support causes of community concern and invite your participation and patronage.

Think of these organizations as your neighborhood allies (with "neighborhood" defined loosely, including online communities you are connected to). Middle market organizations are small enough to feel personal, but big enough to reach beyond whatever you could do on your own. They're where your time, talent, and treasure join with others to power something greater than your individual contributions could achieve alone. With these organizations, you're a key cog in a medium-size machine. You have agency, lots of opportunity for contribution and leadership, and your actions really matter. You also have many advantages that come from being part of a larger system with more people and partners also contributing.

The more aligned your efforts are with your passion and purpose, the more meaningful your contribution to this kind of system can be, even when your influence is shared. Think about engaging with the PTA at your kids' school when they're young, maybe volunteering at an event or two, growing the organization as your kids progress through school, perhaps taking on a leadership role in later years before you both graduate on to bigger things. After serving in these ways, perhaps your persistent vision of scale combined with your passion for service leads you to serving on a commission, running for the local school board or city council. This is almost always how those who serve in such roles began. Be like them by keeping the concept of scale front and center along the way.

As an organizational example, consider Watts of Love. What began exclusively as light deployment to a single community in its early years grew to global deployments and expanded financial literacy programming and disaster relief as the organization adapted and expanded.

That's scale in motion. And participating over time—whether as a donor, volunteer, or even in a leadership role—plugs into that momentum.

The Majors:

Institutions (Big Causes, Big Solutions)

The majors are where your individual contribution meets institutions working at national or global scale—national nonprofits, big foundations, and well-known movements. Think organizations like the American Heart Association, the United Way, St. Jude's, Feeding America, the Intergalactic Starfish Rescue Federation, and so on. Okay, I made the last one up, but you get the point. Your personal role may be small, but the issues are big, and your support joins with thousands (or millions) of others.

It's easy to feel like a drop in the ocean when you're in the majors. But your drop contributes to the wave of impact. Further, you get to "borrow the halo" of the big-name, big-cause organization, which can make you feel good. Whether you're donating to cancer research in memory of a loved one, running a 5K on Thanksgiving to feed the hungry, or volunteering at a huge event, you're part of something larger. Your scale here on a personal level is likely small, but the impact of the collective effort you're contributing to is larger and still matters.

I saw this all the time in the work of the various initiatives at the Clinton Foundation and later with clients like the UN Foundation, the Starbucks Foundation, and others. All grew from focused beginnings to expansive efforts by following their early wins and scaling what worked in communities around the world. Through their growth and global reach, each provided new opportunities for growing ranks of employees, volunteers, even contractors and vendors, to contribute to their work in dynamic new ways that were materially a part of their impact. These examples remind us of an important point: scale does not need to come from starting something new. It's often about plugging in and immediately contributing to a team or project that's already making a difference and helping it grow.

Understanding the ways in which your efforts scale across the three types of impact opportunities—Me, the Middle Market, and the Majors—helps you see your role and impact more clearly: where you have full control, where you have shared influence, and where you're part of a much bigger system. None is better than the other. All are essential. And when you're intentional about each, your impact adds up—in ways that are both personally meaningful and globally relevant.

BEYOND STARFISH: POOP BAGS AND PLASTIC BOTTLES

The allegory of the starfish is great, but not terribly practical. Most of us aren't walking on a beach and saving marine life on any given day. So here are two more examples from our everyday lives that further prove the point about how our individual efforts impact collective outcomes, for better or worse.

There are an estimated 65 million pet dogs in the U.S. alone, and every responsible dog walker you see on any given day carries plastic poop bags. I started to think about this every time I unrolled a bag to pick up after my own dog, and now I think about this every . . . single . . . time I walk my own dogs and see the other dogs walking. I began to seek out environmentally friendly alternatives, and discovered that while some poop bags are a little less awful than others, there are no truly eco-friendly ones.

Is it crazy that of all the environmental issues our planet faces, the one that discombobulates me most often is dog poop? No, because the math is truly enormous:

65,000,000 dogs x 1.5 bags / day x 365 days / year = 35.5 BILLION bags / year

It might be impossible (and unpleasant) to visualize 35.5 billion poop bags, but by any measure that's a *lot* of crappy plastic hitting our landfills. If you're an inventor or scientist with a passion for the environment, and you want to make the world better at scale, please (*please!*) invent an eco-friendlier poop bag. (Imagine my delight while writing this chapter to learn that Japanese scientists are developing plastic that dissolves in water within hours.)

Maybe someday we can make as much progress on dog poop as we have on water bottles.

Water bottles, you say? Yes, water bottles!

As kids in the '80s, my friends and I drank from the water fountains in school and other public places, as well as any hose or faucet we could find. Only fancy folks drank bottled water—with Perrier and Evian seemingly the only two brands during my youth.

Then came the bottled water boom of the 1990s, driven by a rise in health consciousness and questions about tap water quality, coupled with effective marketing campaigns. Even Pepsi and Coke got into the bottled water game via their Aquafina and Dasani brands, respectively. By the early 2000s, Americans were consuming over 6 billion gallons of bottled water annually. By the early 2010s, bottled water had overtaken soda as the #1 packaged beverage in the U.S., with more than *50 billion* single-use bottles sold per year. That's about thirteen bottles per month per person, mostly ending up in landfills rather than recycling centers.

Then something began to change. Awareness of single-use plastics began to rise, along with questions about the safety of plastics themselves, revelations that tap water is often better than bottled water, and that bottled water often *is* just tap water. These concerns created the perfect storm for the resurgence of reusable water bottles of every brand, stripe, and variety. From Stanleys to Yetis to Owalas and even Brita water filters in the fridge, new options to avoid disposable plastic bottles became more convenient, more accessible, and more eco-friendly. This sparked a shift in cultural norms.

My kids, their classmates, their teachers, and coaches rarely ever have a plastic bottle of water in hand. Instead, they carry around reusable water bottles as consistently as they carry their phones. They personalize them, use them, and rarely lose them, which I find as astonishing as their commitment to consistent hydration. I see this trend everywhere—with students I teach in my law school class, with other professors at the school, and with colleagues in offices, at conferences, and just about everywhere else. Backpacks, briefcases, hip packs, and even fishing gear all now have dedicated water bottle pockets, clips, and custom carabiners for reusable bottles. Airports, workplaces, and other public spaces have retrofitted their drinking fountains into bottle filling stations to avoid that impossible tilt, lean, and barely-fill-the-bottle awkwardness of old school drinking fountains.

An entire ecosystem around reusable water bottles has taken root and grown . . . at scale. The global reusable bottle market crossed $9 billion in 2023 alone—proof that personal habit shifts can drive major commercial and cultural change.

Poop bags and plastic bottles teach us that opportunities to identify, grow, build, and flex the muscles of scale can be found almost everywhere. There are so many things that we care about, things that drive us nuts, and things that we feel helpless to change. Even if in the moment, you don't think you can do anything about it, by staying engaged with the issues and aware of what's happening, you're keeping the door open for future scaling. In other words, sometimes your version of scaling can just simply be *awareness*. Because you never know when a poop bag is going to go the way of the reusable water bottle.

SCALE FOR ORGANIZATIONS

Scale is an area where established organizations often have an advantage, because they see growth and expansion as a fundamental part of their mission.

For start-ups, on the other hand—whether nonprofit, for-profit, or social enterprise—scale can be a steeper hill to climb. So many of an organization's more immediate needs can distract leaders from considering long-term issues of scale, which might seem like a luxury when they're simply trying to launch or survive. But failing to consider scale early may set the organization on a course in the wrong direction, whether social impact is your core focus (as for nonprofits and social enterprise) or part of what you seek to incorporate into commercial activities (as with for-profits). Worse, without a clear vision for scale, early-stage ventures often miss out on funding and partnerships, because capital and collaborators are drawn to efforts that signal how early momentum can turn into meaningful growth.

Aiming our efforts in the right direction is profoundly important at the outset. In *Atomic Habits*, James Clear uses the example of an airplane leaving Los Angeles en route to New York City. If the nose of the plane is pointed just 3.5 degrees off course (the equivalent of just a few feet at takeoff), it will end up hundreds of miles off target. This illustrates how small, seemingly insignificant changes in habits or direction, when sustained over time, can lead to dramatically different outcomes. Especially for organizations, early misdirection—or lack of clarity of destination—can result in a future that is wildly different from the original planned goal.

So, whether you're part of a scrappy start-up or a decades-old institution, it's worth stepping back to ask: *How are we thinking about our ultimate goals for impact at scale?* Not in terms of headcount or revenue alone, but in terms of how your Better Good can grow in its reach (who and how many you serve), depth (how far your contributions reach into the effort), or duration (how long the impact can endure without heroic effort). Just like individuals, organizations of all sizes benefit from a periodic scale check-in.

For "Me-level" organizations, such as founder-driven start-up nonprofits and solo entrepreneurs, individual impact efforts might entail codifying your vision for scale in your work so it's easier to identify, track, engage, and evolve as you build and grow your work over time.

For Middle Market organizations—especially community nonprofits, small businesses, or local initiatives—being attentive to your goals for scale over time might entail refining processes, investing in leadership, or replicating successful models or partnerships in new locations to engage and impact wider circles and larger numbers of stakeholders.

For the Majors—national or global institutions—a vision of scale often involves a focus on expanding your impact, replicating platforms for others to use, forging strategic partnerships, or decentralizing power to enable local adoption and scale of your efforts.

Regardless of size, the key question is the same: *Are we growing what actually works?* And more importantly: *Are we designing our efforts with scale in mind?* Without that lens, even the most heartfelt work for Better Good can stagnate—too dependent on a single leader, moment, or model without a clear vision guiding you toward greater growth and achievement.

AN EXCELLENT EXAMPLE OF ORGANIZATIONAL SCALE: CORE

Sean Penn's nonprofit, CORE (originally named J/P HRO), which got its start following the devastating 2010 earthquake in Haiti, focused primarily on disaster relief and recovery during its initial years. Following the devastation of Hurricane Irma in 2017, CORE's mission expanded beyond Haiti to assist with relief and recovery throughout the Caribbean region, and thereafter championed long-term disaster preparedness in similarly situated locations.

Widely known for moving quickly to help communities in emergency circumstances, CORE was tapped to help during the COVID pandemic in 2020, first with testing and later with vaccination locations throughout the U.S. While CORE had its customary share of challenges with this expansion—including the media scrutiny that comes with high profile leaders working on difficult issues in hard places, under ever-evolving, challenging conditions—its relentless focus on refining what worked brought about extraordinary evolution and impact over time. Over its fifteen-plus-year evolution, CORE has scaled in dynamic ways.

Beyond the organization itself, CORE's story also shows how personal growth can scale alongside organizational impact. Sean Penn and Ann Lee began as on-the-ground leaders in post-earthquake Haiti—immersed in the day-to-day realities of relief work. As CORE grew beyond its initial mission into new regions and new arenas like disaster preparedness and public health, Sean and Ann grew, too. Their leadership evolved from field-level response to strategic, global influence—helping shape conversations about philanthropy, humanitarian aid, and disaster resilience. Over fifteen years, the organization and its founders have scaled together, each reinforcing the others' growth. The result is a dual success story of an organization that scaled its mission and two leaders who scaled their own capacity to serve the world.

Similar examples of nonprofits that have successfully scaled include household names like the American Heart Association, Feeding America, the American Cancer Society, the Salvation Army, St. Jude's, the Red Cross, the United Way, and so on. These organizations represent the hopes and desires of most nonprofits to similarly reach such levels—and they've done so through consistency, clarity of mission, and relentless execution in service of ever-growing visions of scale for their work over time.

Many less-recognizable organizations have also succeeded and scaled around the world: groups like regional food banks, community health networks, local library systems, disaster-response coalitions, and local education and workforce initiatives. They are content to have less famous versions of scale, remaining more limited to specific communities, regions, and issues. For every CORE, Gates Foundation, or Red Cross, there's a local, state, or regional organization that isn't a household name but nevertheless succeeds in its own version of scale. Such organizations are happy to do what they do at the level at which they do it—they're able to quickly fill immediate, specific gaps and community needs that leave us all better off as a result.

BOTTOM LINE

To scale well is simply to continue to do more of what works. In service of this vision, stay curious, listen, evaluate, and collaborate. Then design and redesign as you continue to grow and learn. Always consider whether it is necessary to build something new, or whether bolting your (or your organization's) efforts onto existing efforts might take your work further, faster.

Because doubt tends to creep in for us all, and because the messy middle is always, well, messy, you're likely to encounter frustration and discouragement on your path to Better Good. You will likely question whether any of your efforts matter. Maybe even whether *you* matter in the grand scheme of it all. The answer to each is yes. Your efforts matter. You matter.

We *all* matter. And we can all make a difference, at scale.

KEY TAKEAWAYS AND ACTION ITEMS

Key Takeaways

- **Scale is the art of growing what works.** Whether through reach (who and how many you serve), depth (how far your contributions reach into the effort), or duration (how long the impact can sustainably endure), scale is about building on effectiveness to expand impact.
- **Intentional effort builds momentum.** Sustained, focused actions—especially when joined with those of others—create cumulatively greater impact over time.
- **Impact comes in many forms.** From personal habits to global partnerships, scale lives in individual choices (Me), community efforts (Middle Market), and institutions (Majors).

Action Items

For Individuals

- **Reflect on what's working.** Take stock of your social impact footprint and how you already deploy your PPP and TTT for meaningful good. What's working? How can you do more of that?

- **Apply the "Me, Middle Market, Majors" framework.** Think about how you're showing up in each category—what scale looks like for you individually, within community organizations, and alongside major institutions.
- **Look for your flywheel.** Identify the specific efforts that build the most momentum for you, especially within your Goldilocks Zone. What would happen if you gave those elements a few more strategic pushes?
- **Assess your organizational alignment.** If you're part of an organization, ask: Are we scaling what actually works? Are we coordinating with others and using our vision of scale to attract others to join or support our work? What should a future vision of scale look like if we are building on our greatest successes?
- **Zoom out, but don't drift.** Keep your long-term vision of scale in mind, but ground your daily efforts in intentional, incremental contributions to what works.
- **Avoid redundancy.** Before launching something new, ask: Is there already an existing initiative underway to which you can contribute your effort more effectively than starting something new or unnecessarily competitive?
- **Stay curious and adaptive.** Scale grows with you—keep learning, adjusting, and expanding your view of what's possible.

Action Items

For Organizations

For Nonprofits Grantmakers (those funding the work)

Invest in what works. Resist novelty bias and scale proven solutions. Ask: What needs to grow that works—not just what's new?

Fund operations and infrastructure. Scaling requires strong systems. Prioritize general operating support, tech upgrades, and leadership development. They matter, and you can't scale effectively without these fundamental tools in place.

Support model adaptation. Scaling isn't one-size-fits-all. Support efforts to localize or adapt successful approaches for new contexts, turbulent times, and shifting dynamics.

Share learning across grantees. Create communities of practice, case studies, and peer learning cohorts to help good ideas grow across the field.

Think long-term. Consider multi-year grants and strategic co-funding to help grantees move from early wins to sustained scale.

For Nonprofit Grantees (those doing the work)

Clarify your core model. What exactly are you doing that works—and how do you know?

Articulate precisely what past successes entail and how you plan to grow them as a future vision of scale so others can adopt, support, or fund it.

Codify before you grow. Document your methods, playbooks, and partnerships in ways that others can follow. Think tool kits, not just testimonials.

Pilot, then replicate. Prove your model at a small scale, then expand. Use a dispassionate focus on facts and data to determine when you're ready to grow—and where to go next.

Build capacity before you need it. Invest in systems, people, and infrastructure ahead of demand. Scale punishes underbuilt back offices, often brutally, and rewards those that are prepared for growth.

Keep funders and partners close. Share your story of scale—and your strategy for staying mission-aligned through future growth—with existing and prospective supporters. Invite them to scale with you.

For Social Enterprises

Clarify your scale story. Are you scaling process, product, profit, or impact? Be clear on which, and how they relate.

Document your model. Make your social impact model transparent, specific, and consistent. Scale requires clarity.

Refine before you replicate. Prove your model in one market before expanding.

Partner with purpose. Find cause-aligned allies—nonprofits, funders, influencers, even competitors—to collaboratively scale your model.

Use metrics that matter. Track not just sales, but lives changed, communities served, and other important metrics. Impact becomes exponential when it's measured, shared, and communicated via stellar storytelling.

For Businesses

Scale your purpose, not just your profits. Ask how your core business model can contribute to meaningful scale—at home, regionally, nationally, or globally, as the case may be.

Build from within. Start with employee engagement. Use your team and workforce as a force multiplier for scaled social impact initiatives. Take a successful office- or location-based initiative national (or global).

Design scalable giving programs. From matching gifts to paid volunteer time, build giving and service into the operating model—then expand what resonates and produces results.

Create signature initiatives. Anchor your social impact identity around a cause or campaign that can grow over time. Align it with brand values and market growth.

Elevate employee-led ideas. Some of the best scalable impact models come from within. Build systems to source, pilot, and scale internal innovations for good.

CHAPTER 11

Sustain for the Long Run

It does not matter how slowly you go
so long as you do not stop.

—Confucius

HOW MAKE IT RIGHT GOT IT WRONG

On any given day at the Clinton Global Initiative conference in New York, there is always palpable buzz throughout the venue. Once you pass through security and into the event space, you are surrounded by rock stars of every stripe: political, corporate, philanthropic, athletic, artistic, and even literal rock stars like Bono, Alicia Keyes, and James Taylor. Amazing do-gooders are around every corner, in every room, and sometimes right next to you.

But one day at the 2009 conference, the energy felt even more intense than usual. The narrow hallway outside a breakout session room filled with a crowd long before the session room doors opened, spilling back into the surrounding lobby. When the doors finally swung open, the crowd surged forward into the session room, with some literally running to grab prime seats. Within a minute or two it was standing room only. Who was everyone going to see?

Just a couple of do-gooders named Brad Pitt and Bill Clinton.

The subject was hurricane relief and efforts to rebuild homes for residents of the Lower Ninth Ward of New Orleans, which had been devastated by Hurricane Katrina four years earlier. Pitt had launched a nonprofit called Make It Right in 2007, partnering with world-renowned architects, designers, and suppliers who all committed to building homes that were beautiful, affordable, and cost-effective to maintain.

The panel, hosted by President Clinton, featured stories of this work as told by Brad himself, Make It Right CEO Tom Darden, and one of the Lower Ninth homeowners benefitting from their efforts, a hospice worker and mother named Dierdra Taylor.

Having purchased a home for her young family just a year before Katrina washed it away, Dierdra was a compelling, gracious, deeply human witness to the tragedy. She had a rare combination of humility and confidence, plus a quick wit and the ability to remain completely unfazed by a superstar actor and a former U.S. president. The audience was awed by Dierdra's resilience, gratitude, and excitement for her new home, and her testimony of how the Make It Right model was working for her community. She even explained that her new home was so low-cost to maintain that she was now exploring extracurricular activities for her kids that she couldn't previously afford, like soccer and karate. I, too, watched in awe as this extraordinary person stole the spotlight from Brad and Bill.

At the time of this door-busting session, Make It Right had built thirteen of its planned 150 homes. It would go on to build 113 in total. My wife, Amy, and I would tour several of them in 2015, when we visited our favorite city on the tenth anniversary of Katrina's landfall, which happened to coincide with our tenth wedding anniversary. The homes were as interesting and innovative as advertised. And Make It Right was starting to expand its work into other disadvantaged neighborhoods nationwide, including in Newark, New Jersey, and Kansas City, Missouri.

It seemed Make It Right could do no wrong. It was a juggernaut of a nonprofit equipped with the buzz, financing, and alliances it needed to achieve its rocket-fueled potential. The more its work grew and the better known it became, the more support piled on, propelling the organization further toward its goals. I thought the residents of New Orleans's Lower Ninth had finally found an organization with the will and resources to turn things around for generations to come, and in the process create a new, scalable, and sustainable model for many other such places.

But I was wrong—and the reasons why matter.

Despite exceptional efforts, legitimate early accomplishments, and sincere intent, Make It Right began to crumble. Sadly, so did many of the homes it built, along with the confidence of those involved. It turns out that neither the homes nor the organization were built to last. Within a few years of our visit to New Orleans, several homes were deemed uninhabitable and had to be demolished.

Meanwhile, Make It Right began receiving a litany of complaints, requests for repairs, and eventually lawsuits. Unable to keep up, it eventually shut down operations, but the complaints and litigation continued. In 2022, what was left of Make it Right agreed to pay over $20 million to settle a class action lawsuit brought by affected homeowners. It would later file its own lawsuits against architects and other partners it had relied on to execute its mission, as well as some of its own former executives.

When you compare the promise and potential of that buzzy 2009 CGI panel with how the initiative turned out, it's heartbreaking. But Make It Right isn't the only organization that has faced such a grim outcome. In fact, one-third of all new nonprofits fail within their first ten years. Some of them deserve to fail, due to fundamental flaws in their vision, leadership, and operations. Others are designed to have a limited lifespan. But many others *didn't* have to fail; they could have avoided the pains that tend to come with long-term growth, if only they had planned for sustainability much earlier and consistently throughout their work.

If the individual efforts of Brad Pitt, who was clearly committed, and the organizational work of Make It Right—with all of its resources and the support of so many partners—couldn't endure for the long run despite all of those advantages, who can?

You can. And the organizations you serve and support can.

For individuals and organizations alike, sustainability requires crucial upfront work at the outset, over time, and especially during periods of rapid growth. And you must be fully aware and intentional about the challenges of sustainability before you begin. And if you've already begun, now is the time to consider these crucial challenges.

THE T-SHIRT PROBLEM AND THE SUSTAINABILITY CHALLENGE

Is it better to burn white hot and then flame out, or to build a slow, steady fire with fuel for the long haul? This is the core conundrum of sustainability. Starting to do Better Good is easy. Enduring is hard.

Sometimes, we get super-committed to a new cause when we're inspired in the moment, only to find ourselves later thinking, "Oh yeah, I forgot about that." "*That*" being any number of important things that can't be overlooked. This pattern shows up even in some of our crawl-through-glass causes. And it's especially common with high-profile, shorter-term commitments that surge after an emergency, a natural disaster, or other major occurrence but fade once the urgency and headlines and our attention move on. I call this The T-Shirt Problem.

I've made many small donations, run 5Ks, and bought a drawerful of T-shirts to support a friend or neighbor battling a disease, or relief and recovery efforts following disasters, only to find those shirts at the bottom of a stack years later. And, of course, let's not forget the ferrets. Though I often *do* forget them . . . until I get the occasional email from the rescue organization reminding me of my fading fondness for the fuzzy friends.

Organizations experience similar evolutions over time, with some committing to a serious issue for sincere reasons at a particularly challenging or important time, but then evolving as priorities or other dynamics change. A delicate example is one I shared earlier in Chapter 3. After the murder of George Floyd in 2020, corporate America rushed to embrace anti-racism and DEI programs—but many quickly retreated when cultural, political, and legal backlash intensified. Most of the organizations that did this were new to the cause and therefore had shallower roots for sustaining the social, cultural, and even legal headwinds that began intensifying against such initiatives. To some, this looked like abandonment; for others, it was a necessary pivot to survive shifting forces. As with all things in social impact, there's no one-size-fits-all answer.

It's hard to refrain from judgment when we see an organization reverse course on an initiative like DEI or environmentalism. After all, it's a deeply American principle to be welcoming and inclusive of others and to promote liberty, justice, and opportunity for all. And we all care about breathing clean air, drinking safe water, and consuming food free of contaminants, which drives the core of environmental causes that literally every human should care about.

Even so, the hard truth remains that some organizations, despite even the best of intentions, are simply ill-equipped to sustain their commitments, especially when social, economic, or consumer sentiments shift. Sometimes these commitments end on purpose, other times by default, and occasionally just by chance or due to shifting winds that blow us in one direction or another while others more deeply rooted stand firm. The outcome of such initiatives starts to make sense when we understand the cyclical nature of sustainability.

THE CYCLES OF SUSTAINABILITY

Just as with scale, sustainability unfolds in cycles. Different causes in your life and work sustain in different ways, at different times, and for different durations. Understanding this cyclical nature reveals a middle ground between flaming out and enduring forever.

Many causes have a natural "season." They matter deeply for a time, then fade in intensity or close by design. Some are never meant to sustain beyond a certain point, like a short-lived nonprofit formed solely to raise money for a school playground. Once the playground is built and the ribbon is cut, the nonprofit shuts down. That's not failure—it's success. Sustainability beyond achieving a single outcome isn't a goal for *that* cause. These are the 100-meter dashes of doing good. The start and finish line are in close proximity, and you sprint to the other side.

Other commitments sustain for longer—but not forever—because they fit with certain circumstances of life. These causes burn brightly in a particular season, like going all-in on PTA activities while your kids are in elementary school, or donating and volunteering after a major natural disaster. These are the 4x400 relays of doing good, when we run hard for our stretch, knowing someone else will take the baton when we complete our leg.

Then there are causes that invite an enduring commitment—the ones at the core of our Goldilocks Zones. These are the marathons, endurance runs, or mud runs of doing good—the long-haul commitments that require persistence, pacing, and resilience. Sometimes we run faster, sometimes slower, sometimes we take breaks, or even get stuck, but we keep showing up, year after year, because the cause is woven into who we are.

The work is never really finished with many such causes, from persistent diseases, human conditions, or social causes like DEI. The American Heart Association will endure so long as heart health remains an issue affecting millions. Hunger relief efforts like World Central Kitchen remain important so long as there are hungry mouths to feed. As noted in Chapter 6, even Chick-fil-A's commitment to diversity, equity, and inclusion lives on amid the tumult of recent years about such work. Likewise, Bass Pro Shops and Cabella's joint commitments to conservation—which they proudly tout as "North America's largest conservation movement"— among other notable impact work, continues amid changes in the cultural landscape and attacks on environmentally-focused causes. Such work sustains because it is core to who they are.

Even the NFL, a visible and public target for DEI-related work, continues to navigate turbulent times without retreating from their efforts. Even though they have pivoted in tone from "End Racism" to "Choose Love" the message remains clear as they sustain their commitment to the core that is our shared humanity and a never-ending pursuit of liberty and justice *for all.* Just like Nancy's work for Watts of Love remains vital as long as any communities live in darkness. With anything commonly described as "a marathon, not a sprint," you don't endure such causes because it's easy. You endure because your effort matters, deeply.

Sustainability in this case isn't just about your effort alone—it's also about the *momentum* you build that others can carry forward. When you keep showing up, you sustain your own individual impact *and* you model an example that creates ripples of influence that help others sustain theirs. Momentum begets—and sustains—momentum.

As with every part of the journey toward Better Good, the key is awareness and intention: knowing which commitments are sprints, which are relays, and which are marathons—and adjusting your energy and expectations as your life and work evolve.

A FRAMEWORK FOR SUSTAINABILITY: FOLLOW THE ARC

So how do we build sustainability into our sprints, relays, and marathons? In my work with thousands of individuals and organizations, I've noticed a common trend among those that sustain the longest and through the most challenging of circumstances. None of them follow a single straight line from point A to point B with rigid consistency. In fact, many endure sharp ups and downs and often have to improvise. But over the long term, their progress and continuity take the shape of an arc that bends when necessary but doesn't break under inflexible rigidity. The acronym "ARC" (alignment, rhythm, capacity) offers a framework for analyzing how these efforts endure across all dimensions of sustainability.

Alignment:

Maintaining Clarity Around What Matters Most

Staying aligned with your Goldilocks Zone is the single best way to sustain. You're not forcing yourself to care; you're fueled by what matters most to you. Jack Canfield, author of *The Success Principles,* writes that "When you are in alignment with your purpose, everything flows." I'd add that everything sustains, too.

Alignment happens on multiple levels. For individuals, it means staying true to your values, passion, and proficiency—your Goldilocks Zone. For organizations, it's about keeping mission, methods, and operations pointed in the same direction, even as circumstances evolve. At its broadest, alignment also connects us to the communities we serve—ensuring our efforts match the real needs of the people and places we aim to help.

Alignment is why someone like Donna, the "Fairy Godmother of Dog Rescue," sustained decades of volunteer work. Some people call this alignment "being in the zone" or "firing on all cylinders" or "maximizing the flywheel of momentum." It's when your work feels comfortable, natural, and easy. For runners, the true "runner's high" doesn't hit them when a run is over, but in the midst of their maximum effort. It helps them reach their peak performance and keep going. That's what it feels like when you're aligned.

When you're in the zone, you don't just observe alignment, you *feel* it. The work is effortless, the burdens light, your commitment and enthusiasm high. You feel amazing about the work you're doing, to the point that it doesn't even feel like work at all. And conversely, whenever you feel unfocused, lost, or stuck, it's likely because you're out of alignment.

The remedy? Check in with yourself to ensure you're still working at the intersection of what you care about most, what you are uniquely good at, and what the world actually needs. Even a brief pause and reflection can give you an opportunity to recalibrate, to remain in alignment with your core causes of greatest concern. Remind yourself that you don't need to throw every starfish back in the ocean all at once. In fact, trying to do so is a recipe for burnout, not sustainable success. You need only to take the right actions, at the right times, and to whatever extent you're able in pursuit of your crawl-through-glass causes.

Here are a few pro tips to focus on as you seek alignment in your efforts.

Yes, and. First, remember the cardinal rule of improvisation: "Yes, and." You will almost certainly need to pivot throughout your evolution toward Better Good. Moving between and among various causes doesn't represent a lack of alignment. For example, I moved on from ferrets to dogs but maintained alignment with my crawl-through-glass cause of animal rescue. Similarly, when my kids were in elementary school, we were exactly those people who supported bake sales, bought wrapping paper, and ran 5Ks for the school's PTA. As they moved on from their grade schools, we did, too, ending our efforts on behalf of the PTA to remain aligned with their current interests and activities. These days, we put our time and effort into supporting the high school band and cross-country teams. Totally different activities, but the same alignment around supporting our kids and their peers.

Bottom line: it's okay to pivot. Treat the unexpected and evolving phases of your life as gifts and opportunities to improvise a bit. Be kind to yourself in the process and remember—there's no such thing as perfect, and "right" is only what is right for you.

Don't chase too many rabbits. A Chinese proverb says, "He who chases two rabbits catches neither." (Unless, of course, they're in need of rescue and you're all in on animal rescue. Then chase them both.) Ironically, the better you become at doing good, the more opportunities to do good will come your way. Because of your success, which may include becoming known for your dedication to one cause, issue, or skill set, others will ask you to bring that magic to the causes they care about. That's flattering. And enticing. Many of them will be interesting and worthy in their own right. But exercise caution, as these temptations may ultimately prove to be distractions from sustainable focus on your own crawl-through-glass causes.

For instance, I'm really good at (and love) helping nonprofit boards, so friends, colleagues, and collaborators frequently ask me to join the boards of their organizations. But I rarely accept those invitations, because their desire for me to help rarely aligns with my desire to do the deep work essential to being a truly committed board member. If I said yes to every invitation, I'd be serving on too many boards of organizations outside my Goldilocks Zone, thereby shortchanging my commitment to them. That's a perfect recipe for misalignment and burnout. Remember that your "not-to-do" list is just as important as your "to-do" list—if not more so. When it comes to remaining aligned, overmanage what you are committed to and be relentless about protecting your TTT for the causes inside your Goldilocks Zone. Think of this as the opposite of "Yes, and." In these instances, it's all about "No, but . . . thank you."

Rhythm:

Nurture Consistent Habits and Check-Ins to Maintain Alignment

You want to stay in the zone—cranking the flywheel, firing on all cylinders, finding a rhythm. A groove. A beat that keeps your crawl-through-glass causes fully integrated into your life and work. This is how to seamlessly align the good you do with the life you live.

Remember Jack from Chapter 7, the impressive lawyer who was finally interested in "giving back" later in his life and career? The Jacks of the world lack rhythm. When they find themselves in a midlife crisis of unfulfillment, they become textbook examples of what happens when you never develop an internal beat for incorporating good into your daily life and work: their efforts feel forced, fleeting, and frustratingly out of sync.

The antidote? Overmanage your commitment to the priorities revealed in the Eisenhower Matrix. That framework gives you a clear path to decide what to focus on, and when. Just as important, it clarifies what *not* to focus on. It's your guide for avoiding the trap of what's urgent but not important (or worse, neither urgent nor important).

Remember: what gets scheduled gets done. Scheduling what matters most—regularly, consistently, over time—is essential. Also remember James Clear's guidance that "You don't rise to the level of your goals, you fall to the level of your systems." Whether it's daily, weekly, or on some other rhythm, consistency in scheduling your commitment to the causes you care about most is key to sustainability.

Some rhythms are slow and steady like a long run (trying to get a beneficial law passed in your state); others are fast and frenzied like a sprint (raising, say, $1,000 from family, friends, and colleagues after a disaster), and many will change over time. All are good when they align with your Goldilocks Zone. Just keep the beat as you lean into the changing rhythms of life and work. Letting your rhythm evolve doesn't mean you've lost direction, sincerity, or scale. In fact, adjusting your rhythm may strengthen all three.

For instance, our family identifies as a rescue dog family. More specifically, a foster dog family. Often for special-needs dogs (elderly, blind, deaf, or even blind *and* deaf). In fact, we're an approved foster family for multiple rescue organizations. Despite this clear identity and commitment to this crawl-through-glass cause at the center of our Goldilocks Zone, we actually haven't fostered in a few years. The rhythm of our current life—spanning kids' activities, work and family travel, elder care obligations, and more—haven't allowed us to commit to fostering lately.

We haven't given up; we absolutely still identify as a foster family. But the *rhythm* of life hasn't allowed it for a stretch of time. It doesn't change our passion, our intent, or our commitment (especially among our kids, who want to say yes at every opportunity). We nonetheless have regular check-ins with our favorite rescue organizations, and with our shared family calendar. This pause in fostering is just for now, not forever. It's a season. But even that season still involves the rhythm of regular scheduled check-ins and calendar consults. That's important.

We see the same rhythm shifts everywhere. A teacher who tutored nightly during COVID lockdowns now mentors monthly and maintains a volunteer playbook for other teachers. A marathon fundraiser who can't train this season moves to sponsor outreach and donor thank-you calls for the same nonprofit. Different cadence, same cause, and similar, sustained impact that meets different seasons and circumstances of life.

Whatever the season of life or work you're in, commit to scheduling what matters most. Put it in your calendar. Make it real. That simple act may be one of the most powerful things you can do to sustain your good.

Capacity:

Build the Strength to Sustain What Matters Most

Rhythm is about consistency. Capacity is about endurance: to keep showing up—and to keep going—without running yourself or your cause into the ground.

Capacity is your ability to commit, engage, and endure. It draws on your reserves—emotional, mental, physical, and organizational—that generate the strength, stamina, and structure needed for sustained impact. Capacity builds on alignment and rhythm. When your alignment and rhythm are strong, your capacity to sustain grows naturally. When capacity runs low, however, even the causes you care about most can stall. Without capacity, you can't power your flywheel.

Most of us want to feel challenged in our work and rewarded for our effort. We crave personal growth. That word "growth" can be vague, but it includes *any* progress in your capacity, such as training to go "from couch to 5K," or even from lifting 5-pound weights to 10-pound weights. Like physical training, building your capacity for good is about being just a bit better today than you were yesterday. Then doing the same tomorrow. The mantra I use while running—which I learned from running and coaching legend Jeff Galloway at the start of a RunDisney half marathon—might help with this: "You can do this, you're doing this, you've done this."

You might start as a volunteer for a cause or in an organization. As you gain experience and become more technically skilled, opportunities to advance will appear. You might get a new degree or other credential, or advance your skills via promotion at work or at the organizations where you volunteer. Eventually, you upgrade from cleaning kennels at a shelter to managing its volunteer schedules, to joining its board. That's your capacity growing, building, and unlocking new opportunities over time.

This is a cycle without an endpoint. You may choose to level up (or not) and top off (or not) in one cause or position or another, and that's totally fair. Sustainability doesn't always require expansion. Sometimes, it simply means maintaining a level that is healthy and enduring. Other times, opportunity, experience, and growing capacity invite you to reach for greater heights—and that's fair, too. What matters most is staying aware of your limits and designing your rhythm around them, so your commitment lasts instead of burning out.

I think about this all the time in the context of my commitment to my church. With the hope I'm not damaging my chances of eternal salvation, I'm not actually looking to expand my capacity beyond sustaining a comfortable rhythm of attending as a parishioner, contributing financially as our family budget allows, and serving on a single committee at a time if it aligns with my interests (no Finance Committee for me—ew, spreadsheets!)—and that's enough for me.

Contrast this with my fellow parishioner, Dave Humphreys, who you met in Chapter 10. Dave is a legend in our church because he's always leveling up to another incredible commitment, contribution, or volunteer role. His indefatigable example makes me think about how I *could* seek to leverage my credentials and talents to work my way into helping with legal, program, or bigger board matters. But I'm not trying to advance my capacity to do the most possible with my church, at least not now and not the way Dave has.

In contrast, in other nonprofits I serve on a volunteer basis, like the Walt Disney Birthplace (run by Dina Benadon, who we met in Chapter 8), I do seek to deploy some of my growing capacity as a nonprofit expert. Because my alignment and rhythm with their mission are strong, I have greater capacity to contribute without feeling overburdened. That balance makes the commitment sustainable. Different causes, after all, require different levels of capacity at different times. I can easily see how the scale and sustainability of my commitment to these two organizations might flip in the years ahead as their needs and my circumstances evolve.

As always, in developing, strengthening, and following your ARC, awareness and intention remain key. Sustainable approaches require thoughtful planning, not hoping for happy accidents. The best Better Good happens by design, not by accident. You want the trajectory of your arc to be like a rocket in flight—on a clear path to whatever your destination may be.

HOPE IS NOT A STRATEGY: OVERMANAGING FOR SUSTAINABILITY

One of the best ways to unlock sustainability is overmanaging the design of any individual effort or organizational initiative early on—anticipating what's most likely to go wrong, then building protections to prevent or minimize those risks. This is no small task and it isn't glamorous work. But it is the quiet difference between a rocket launch that flames out and one that achieves orbit.

In the context of organizational work (especially for those in early stages or with limited resources), this point is critical. The Clinton Foundation, like Make It Right, started with all the advantages anyone would think a new nonprofit needs. But at an all-staff meeting during the intensifying runup to the 2016 presidential election, amid unprecedented scrutiny and politically motivated attacks on the foundation, President Clinton was asked what, in retrospect, he wished we had done differently from the outset. His answer surprised many in attendance. It wasn't about our global programs or fundraising; it was about our back-office operations.

He admitted that many of the unforced errors dogging the foundation under the glare of intense scrutiny were administrative. If we had invested earlier in finance, legal, and HR systems, we could have avoided the headaches that distracted from our mission. His point was simple: no matter how famous the name on the door, you can't sustain on star power alone. Sustainable infrastructure is essential.

President Clinton's words were music to my nerdy, back office–focused ears. They were also a powerful reminder that whatever advantages we start with, as both individuals and organizations, we can't assume those advantages will endure forever. And we can't hang on to a start-up mentality too long, believing that we'll get to "those other things" later, or hoping that they won't matter much. Hope isn't a strategy. And remember: *better* good—at whatever scale—happens by design, not accident.

The same lessons show up in the rise, fall, and survival of Livestrong.

Founded in 1997 by cycling champion and cancer survivor Lance Armstrong, Livestrong quickly became one of the fastest growing nonprofits in the world. In 2004, with Nike's help, Livestrong launched one of the most successful cause marketing campaigns of all time: the yellow silicone Livestrong bracelets. They sold for just $1 each, with proceeds going to help cancer patients. Almost immediately, they were everywhere—on athletes, artists, CEOs, politicians, teachers, and kids of all ages. More than 80 million were sold in less than a decade, raising $80 million for cancer research and family support, on top of Livestrong's other fundraising efforts.

I wore mine every day, in honor of my cousin Randy. Diagnosed with stage four colon cancer at 36, Randy fought valiantly but died at 38, leaving behind a wife and four young children. Every time I looked at the bracelet, or saw one on someone else, I thought of him. Years later, when I worked to facilitate Lance Armstrong's engagement at CGI events, I was delighted to be able to tell him about Randy and our appreciation for Livestrong's work. The bracelet was so much more than a trend—it was a tether to someone I loved.

But then, in 2012, this movement of magnificent impact began to fade when Lance was stripped of his Tour de France titles for using banned performance-enhancing drugs. He would never return to professional cycling, and his image as an underdog champion was left in tatters. As donations to Livestrong plunged, Lance quickly resigned as its chairman and later cut all ties to his nonprofit. But thankfully, this story doesn't go the way of Make It Right. Livestrong is still alive and relatively well.

While not as ubiquitous or well-funded as it was when it was a cultural phenomenon, Livestrong's work and infrastructure proved strong enough to survive Lance's scandal and departure, and eventually built enough momentum to stand on its own—outside its founder's shadow. You can still buy Livestrong bracelets on their website, and the organization is still supporting cancer patients and their families. And if you consider the downstream impact of the Livestrong phenomenon, the "cause bracelet" remains an incredibly popular fundraising and awareness raising tool for thousands of causes. That legacy alone is a huge accomplishment.

Yes, millions of Livestrong wristbands are no doubt in landfills or forgotten at the bottom of drawers. Mine are kept with other mementos and evoke bittersweet memories when they catch my eye. But they continue to serve as a reminder that sustainability can take many forms, and burning white hot for a period of time is far from the only model of success.

In fact, while writing this chapter, I saw a Livestrong wristband "in the wild" on the arm of someone holding a door at a store. It made me smile and think of Randy. I didn't think about Lance at all. Proof that missions can outlast their messengers.

REVISITING MAKE IT RIGHT: A CASE STUDY IN UNSUSTAINED GOOD

With all of this in mind, let's return to Make It Right and the Lower 9th Ward. There's no question the work was bold, visionary, sincerely intended, and passionate. And—at least for a time—it was effective. A new mode for cross-sector, community-centered recovery was created, homes were built, and homeowners, partners, and supporters were delighted. It all checked so many of the early boxes for rocket-fueled Better Good: celebrity-driven attention, cross-sector partners, smart design, immediate impact, and an inspiring narrative. But it ultimately faltered not from lack of intent or effort, but from a failure to prioritize sustainability.

Of course, hindsight is always 20/20, and Monday morning quarterbacking can be unfair. But there are lessons to be learned about the sustainability of such bold and consequential efforts. Make It Right offers a near-perfect example of why sustainability must be built into any model of better good from the very beginning—not bolted on later when problems arise.

Through the lens of the ARC framework, here's how we can analyze it:

Alignment: You'll recall that alignment works at multiple levels—mission, methods, operations, and connection to community needs. Of the three elements of the ARC, alignment was the strongest. The mission—rebuilding homes in the Lower Ninth Ward—was clearly aligned with urgent community needs. We'd have to get pretty technical to find any misalignment in mission. Ultimately, the only misalignment I can see was the speed (rhythm) of the effort and the quality control (capacity) needed to fulfill that mission at scale. The cause was right, but the implementation lacked the protections necessary to slow the work ever so slightly, both to avoid unforced errors and to plan for long-term sustainability of both the homes and the organization.

Furthermore, had they invested earlier in long-term operational alignment around critical functions like maintenance, repairs, and local capacity to identify and support evolving needs before they became catastrophic, Make It Right might have avoided lawsuits and eventual collapse. An earlier operational alignment check—looking at mission and methods—could have revealed the need to balance architectural innovation and fast construction with practicality, durability, and ongoing expert analysis to ensure long-term impact at scale.

Rhythm: The organization launched like a rocket with immediate success that attracted resources, partners, and fueled fast momentum. But it lacked the long-term rhythm of check-ins, accountability, and recalibration around quality and durability. The pace at the outset got the flywheel of momentum moving, but in hindsight, it was too fast a rhythm to provide the necessary focus on quality. Without a braking mechanism to slow the flywheel just enough to embed systems for ongoing maintenance, repairs, and the follow-up needs of homeowners, the initial momentum gave way to chaos. Moving just a bit slower to enable regular feedback loops, stakeholder community check-ins, partner audits, and post-occupancy evaluations and inspections might have helped surface and address issues quickly. Put simply, Make It Right just got ahead of itself, and sustainable quality control suffered as a result.

Capacity: The team had vision, star power, and resources at the outset but lacked the internal infrastructure necessary to scale sustainably and durably. It also appears that the leadership team neglected to build long-term operational, legal, quality inspection, and maintenance capacity. They needed some version of an independent quality control evaluator—an inspector of the inspectors—whose sole job was to anticipate potential failures and look for blind spots.

For instance, Make it Right hired "starchitects" from outside of New Orleans who didn't fully grasp how their designs would (or wouldn't) last in the realities of the Gulf Coast climate, with its heat, humidity, termites, and mold. Had they invested earlier in more careful planning and design, along with independent supervision and inspection—and perhaps more legal, compliance, property management, and long-term funding to troubleshoot problems—they might have matched their ambition and star power with staying power. There's no telling what Make It Right (and the Lower Ninth Ward) might look like today if they'd had greater internal capacity.

The big lesson of Make It Right isn't "don't be bold" or "don't try to tackle old challenges in new, dynamic, and innovative ways." It's "be bold, dynamic, and innovative when tackling old challenges *and* build wisely." Stay aligned, establish a rhythm, and grow your *capacity* in proportion to your ambition. Design for today *and* tomorrow. Make It Right's example demonstrates what's possible, as well as what's preventable, if we apply sustainability thinking from the outset. There's no telling what the Lower Ninth Ward might be like today had a simple tweak to their model toward true sustainability been made earlier in the process.

THE NEXT RIGHT THING

The path to sustainable Better Good doesn't require you to have everything figured out. It only requires that you take the next right step and follow the ARC toward sustainability with each step. Some causes—and the organizations committed to addressing them—sustain because the need is constant, but the efforts that actually last are the ones built with alignment, rhythm, and capacity. Hunger and disaster relief will always demand a response; what distinguishes those efforts that endure from those that fade is how they show up over time.

People like José Andrés and World Central Kitchen don't just respond to the urgency or magnitude of the need. They have built systems that allow them to show up again and again. The same is true of Nancy and Watts of Love, who continue to light the way when darkness persists, not because the path is easy or obvious, but because their work is designed to adapt and endure.

Many efforts, like the starfish parable, will never fully "solve" the problem in front of them. They sustain because people keep showing up—one starfish at a time.

In the pursuit of Better Good, you don't have to see the entire journey ahead, just the next right thing in front of you. As the *Tao Te Ching* reminds us, the longest journeys begin with a single step. And the good news is, you already know which first step to take. Keep your alignment, rhythm, and capacity in sight, and you'll then find the next right step is always waiting for you.

KEY TAKEAWAYS AND ACTION ITEMS

Key Takeaways

- **Sustainability is about designing commitments that can endure.** The goal of sustainability is to shape your efforts—individually and organizationally—so they can continue for as long as possible, without burnout or exhaustion.
- **Sustainable impact comes from being intentional.** Early enthusiasm or momentum alone rarely lasts long. Without a conscious focus on sustainability from the outset, even the most well-funded, well-intentioned efforts can falter over time.
- **The best way to sustain the good you do is to follow your ARC:**

  Alignment with values, passions, and real needs, so your efforts can last and grow in a clear direction.

  Rhythm in your habits, systems, and check-ins over time.

  Capacity that grows and evolves with your ambition and impact.

- **Boldness without infrastructure is a risk.** Scale and excitement are powerful, but they must be matched with structure, awareness, accountability, and steady operational muscle to last.

Action Items

For Individuals

- **Revisit your Goldilocks Zone.** Check in with your crawl-through-glass causes and make sure your current commitments are still aligned with what you care about most and do best.
- **Audit your rhythm.** Ask yourself: What systems (if any) do I have in place to sustain my work for good? Block time, build routines, and schedule what matters most.
- **Strengthen your capacity.** Invest in yourself—through learning, collaboration, or rest—so that you can show up for the long haul. Consider where your current limits are and what it would take to expand them.
- **Share your success.** Success leaves clues! Share your success stories—and the practices behind them—so you and those with whom you work can see what's succeeding and continue to reinforce and build on these practices in your future work.
- **Decline What Doesn't Align (protect your "not-to-do" list).** Distractions will come, but you can learn to

graciously decline the opportunities that don't align. Overextension is the enemy of sustainable impact.

- **Reflect on past flameouts.** What causes or efforts have you dropped, and why? Use those insights to recalibrate and recommit moving forward.
- **Seek Reinforcement.** Invite trusted friends, colleagues, and collaborators to provide feedback, reminders, and reinforcement about strengths, weaknesses, and opportunities for growth.

Action Items

For Organizations

- **Build for durability, not just visibility.** Make sure your internal systems (Finance, Legal, HR, Compliance, etc.) are resourced to match the scale of your ambition.
- **Institutionalize rhythm.** Embed regular check-ins, stakeholder feedback loops, partner evaluations, honest assessments, and data-informed quality control. Make sustainability a standing agenda item.
- **Plan for the full lifecycle.** Don't just plan to launch. Plan to support, grow, evolve, and—when appropriate—sunset your programs with integrity.
- **Match capacity to complexity.** Big impact demands big infrastructure. Invest in your people, tools, and

processes accordingly. Capacity-building is necessary for sustainable success.

- **Be transparent about sustainability.** Full disclosure is essential with your team, board, funders, partners, and stakeholders. Inform and engage them in efforts to create and evolve the vision for long-term sustainable success so that everyone has a role to play.
- **Invite honest assessment.** Invite others with expertise to help evaluate strengths, weaknesses, opportunities, threats, and especially blind spots. Think about independent advisers, evaluators, ombudsmen, or inspectors, whether in official roles or the casual equivalent.

CHAPTER 12

Tell Stories That Move the World

There have been great societies that did not use the wheel, but there have been no societies that did not tell stories.

—Ursula K. Le Guin

Far more profound than a theme-park ride, Spaceship Earth at Walt Disney World is a literal ride through the story of humanity itself. Inside EPCOT's iconic silver geodesic sphere you board a slow-moving "time machine" that glides through scenes of discovery and connection. Cave painters record their hunts in the glow of firelight. Scribes in ancient Egypt roll out papyrus and capture language for the first time. The Library of Alexandria burns, a devastating reminder of how fragile knowledge can be. Gutenberg's press begins to multiply ideas faster than any messenger could carry them. Then telegraphs click, radios hum, televisions glow, computers awaken, and the digital age is born.

Each scene feeds into a single, continuous narrative truth: the leaps of humankind correspond to leaps in storytelling. First by firelight, then in ink on paper, and now online. Our progress as a species is inseparable from our ability to tell stories, and each jump forward—whether in government, business, the nonprofit sector, science, or culture—depended on our capacity to share, to record, to remember, to imagine, and to reimagine.

When you step off the ride and back into daylight, you're reminded that the story of humanity is still being written. Every generation is an author, and those who tell the best stories steer our course. Governments, nonprofits, and businesses rise or fall on the strength of their narratives. As does your journey toward Better Good. This is why storytelling is the last (but not least) part of the Better Good Framework. Storytelling is what makes our good work visible, compelling, and contagious. It signals to others that they can join our work—that they have a role to play in the unfolding story of our shared human journey on Spaceship Earth. Without storytelling, even the best efforts risk staying hidden, overlooked, or forgotten. With it, they spark connection, inspire action, and multiply impact.

Today, stories live—and storytelling itself unfolds—inside crowded digital channels like social feeds, video platforms, podcasts, and newsletters, where attention is easily distracted and visibility is governed by algorithms, incentives, and speed. Those stories that spread shape what people believe, how institutions endure, and even whether democracy survives. In a time when disinformation, distrust, and division spread as fast as facts, mastering the art of storytelling for good is essential.

STORYTELLING AS A HUMAN CONSTANT

Stories tell us where we came from, who we are, what we value, where we hope to go, and how others can join us. They are used—for better and for worse—by those who seek to influence every facet of our lives and work. And once again, it's because it is how we're wired.

Neuroscience explains why stories matter so much. Stories light up more parts of the brain than facts alone. They activate empathy, trigger memory, and make experiences meaningful. They form the neurological connective tissue of how we relate to the world and each other and cause us to take action. In controlled experiments, neuroscientist Paul Zak found that when people watched or heard emotionally rich stories, their oxytocin levels rose—and they were significantly more likely to donate to a related cause or help someone immediately afterward.

This is why commercials of people suffering after a catastrophe or with scared puppies in shelters cause us to want to urgently donate.

Meanwhile, at Princeton, neuroscientist Uri Hasson discovered that as a storyteller speaks and a listener engages, their brain waves begin to synchronize—a phenomenon known as neural coupling. A good storyteller's experience literally transfers to the listener, creating a shared emotional reality. This is why Morgan Freeman's calm, warm, and authoritative narrations make us feel connected and capable as we learn alongside him in the documentaries he narrates.

Jonathan Gottschall, a leading authority on storytelling and human behavior, offers that storytelling is "the default mode" of the human thought. This framing explains why stories are central to Better Good: how humans process complexity, build connection, and decide whether (and how) to act. Relating to Better Good through story involves the same science behind the feelings we unpacked in Chapter 2. Our human bodies are a contained biosphere of goodness. We literally connect to others through stories that activate the same wiring and feel-good chemicals.

All of this hard wiring in our human brains and bodies is also why you still remember the parable, the movie scene, or the bedtime story long after you've forgotten some of the details. We relate to—and remember—it because we feel the power of the story. It's why you feel good rereading, rewatching, or just thinking about those moments or lessons again. It's why Better Good work thrives on stories. People aren't interested in just connecting to a cause alone. We want to connect to—and be part of—the human narratives that came before us and will evolve after us. Compelling stories motivate us to act as helpers, to contribute to a solution—and that is what most often moves people to give their time, talent, and treasure in service of change. This is why people give where they live and act on what they know and care about most. We are always living our own stories and being shaped by the stories and transformations we hope to see in the world around us. And as the world grows smaller through instant connection—to one another and to the causes that move us—we have more opportunity than ever to shape, and be shaped by, the stories we consume, participate in, and tell.

Storytelling isn't optional in our pursuit of Better Good. Our success depends on the quality of the stories we tell and how effectively we invite others to join our narrative and our Better Good efforts. When our stories connect, they deepen relationships and strengthen engagement, and ultimately unite us as individuals, families, coworkers, and communities.

THE BEST STORIES WIN

It is most often the case that those who tell the best stories win. Across our society, in government (and politics), in business, and in nonprofits, story is the engine of progress.

Governments paint pictures of their vision for society and the conditions it provides for life, liberty, and the pursuit of happiness. Every administration (and every candidate seeking to serve) asks citizens to believe in their vision—and corresponding story—of what the nation, state, or local unit of government can become, how it can serve, and how citizens can join in writing that next chapter.

Businesses similarly invite consumers, markets, and entire industries into their stories. Consumers aren't buying the product or service itself, they're buying the solution it provides to a problem they have and ultimately the story of a better life that results from it. Want clean clothes (of course you do): buy this laundry detergent. Want to get safely from point A to point B: buy this car. Want a computer that "just works" with less hassle and unlocks your true business brilliance or creative potential: buy this one. People's choices in the marketplace are based on the experience they expect to live on the other side of the purchase. Consumers buy the promising "plot" of a better life that surrounds the product or service.

Nonprofits tell similar stories about mobilizing resources to address a cause, right a wrong, or fix something that's broken to help improve society. Their form of buy-in to their stories shows up as funding from donors, as well as contributions of talent from workers, volunteers, and awareness raisers. Grantmaking foundations tell a story about the world they aim to improve by deploying their funds to support organizations and causes that align with their mission. Operating nonprofits tell stories about how they do the work to solve a particular challenge. When they do this successfully, they secure the attention and support of the aforementioned funders, other donors, volunteers, and the wider public who invest *their* time, talent, and treasure in that shared pursuit.

The goal is simple and serious: show the transformation you make possible, then invite people to participate in it. Over the years, I've seen this pattern play out again and again. Organizations often search first for the perfect fundraising strategy, firm, or individual to unlock new funding. While those tools have their place, they rarely outperform a compelling story told by those closest to the work—founders, team members, or those directly impacted—paired with empirical proof of progress. Across hundreds of organizations with which I've worked, the ones that break through are those that can clearly show what changed, for whom, and why it matters—*told via a clear and moving story.*

Using data and metrics strengthens these stories by showing where and how work is truly moving the needle—giving people confidence that their time, talent, and treasure are helping drive meaningful change.

Every mission, market, and movement depends on persuasion through narrative. The best story wins because it captures imagination and converts it into action.

EVERYONE CAN TELL A STORY, BUT FEW GET HEARD

Good news: today we live in an age when nearly everyone has access to tools of storytelling that those of past eras could barely have imagined. We can record our voices, capture images, shoot video, write long essays or short posts, publish instantly, and reach audiences across the globe in a flash. Social platforms, podcasts, blogs, newsletters, personal websites—all create a network of stages where ideas, efforts, and calls to action can travel quickly.

This democratization of storytelling in the age of social media, while a double-edged sword, is still ultimately good news. It means the playing field is more open than ever. Connection is possible across distance, differences, and divides. A tiny nonprofit with no budget, a small city government, even your grandma—all can share their voice online. When we use these tools with clarity and care, they allow us to coordinate, collaborate, organize, and amplify.

Of course, these same tools can be misused. Misinformation spreads as easily as inspiration, which is why clarity, authenticity, and evidence aren't just nice-to-have—they are necessary safeguards. They anchor Better Good stories in truth. They ensure that what spreads doesn't just get attention, but earns trust, the foundation upon which credibility and future engagement is built.

The democratization of storytelling also means that it's harder than ever to be heard. Abundance creates noise. About 5.5 billion people are on social media globally, with anywhere from a half billion to over a billion posts and streams being shared online on any given day. The result is fragmented audiences, shortened attention spans, and constant distraction.

On top of this, there's the challenge of third-party control over what is seen, by whom, and when, due to the all-powerful algorithms of the leading social media platforms. Algorithms sort, filter, and prioritize our feeds based on what *others* decide is most relevant or engaging. While not always malicious, they aren't neutral either. They are subject to the incentives, influence, and direction of those who design and oversee them, which means that the public sphere where we share our stories may not be as free and open as it appears.

The result? Even good stories get lost. You might write a post about inspiring good that only a handful of people see. You might produce a video that never gets the traction it deserves. As a result, you might feel like you're speaking into the void. Or worse, you might assume people don't care—when in reality they simply never saw it. That's the more dangerous consequence: it erodes trust in your audience, your story, and sometimes even yourself. When trust falters, stories collapse.

The important work becomes knowing what causes stories to fold and how to construct those that hold, so you can rise above the noise with impact.

STORIES THAT HOLD OR FOLD

Strong stories hold. Weak ones fold. The difference usually comes down to two things: promises kept and evidence shared.

When a story keeps its promise—when what's said aligns with what's done—trust takes root. When the bridge between words and results stays solid, audiences stay with you. We've all seen the opposite: elected officials who fail to deliver, products that don't live up to their brand promise, nonprofits that over-promise change they don't actually create. As those gaps widen, credibility erodes, and supporters drift.

Stories also hold when they're anchored in evidence. Strong, evidence-inclusive stories show real footing. They prove what changed, for whom, and by how much. In a noisy world, that clarity carries authority: *here is the work, here is the result, here is what comes next—and here's how you can help.*

But stories fold when that alignment breaks. They most often collapse under the weight of abstraction, clutter, or confusion. As Donald Miller says, "If you confuse, you lose." Most of the time, the work itself isn't the problem; the story around it isn't built to grab attention and keep it. The good news: stories fold in predictable ways—and they can be strengthened just as predictably.

Common Story Fails and Fixes

Time and time again I've seen stories fail because they confuse and overwhelm. Usually because of one or more of the following:

- **Too abstract.** Abstract or unclear stories confuse. Instead, keep it simple. Name one person, one place, one change.

- **Focus on activity vs. progress.** All activity, no progress makes the story busy but dull. Lead with the change your work makes possible.
- **Data dumps overwhelm.** One sharp proof point beats twenty soft stats.
- **Unclear call to action.** Vagueness about what the audience can do next is a flaw. A clear next step, link, or deadline drives action and engagement.
- **No compelling characters or case studies.** People love stories about people, so find great characters and narrate their journeys. Place your audience in the story to really compel them to see how their action can result in progress.

Choosing the Right Narrative

Strong storytellers also know *where* to begin. Not every story should start in the same place. The right entry point depends on your moment and your audience:

- **Founding / Creation.** Use compelling origin and founder stories when launching or rallying audiences and champions—explain the spark and the "why now" in ways they can understand and share with others. For example, David Fajgenbaum's origin story—about nearly dying five times in three years before discovering his own cure had been sitting on a pharmacy shelf the entire time—is a compelling founder's story.
- **Service / Beneficiary.** Relate the story to how those you serve are better off as a result of taking action. This is an important lead for donors, customers, and volunteers—center who is better off, how, and why this matters. When David shares the

statistic that a rare disease without an approved medication will affect one in ten of everyone you know, an abstract concept (rare diseases) becomes relatable quickly (this actually affects people you know and love).

- **System / Movement.** If a systems change or civic movement is at issue, explain it. Especially when policy, markets, or coalitions are key to success—with *elegant simplicity* show how rules/infrastructure are shifting and where the audience fits to make this change possible. David and Every Cure explain how generic drugs lack a profit incentive for drug companies to research them further, despite the promise of quickly repurposing many of them to save and improve lives, helping audiences clearly understand how Every Cure's work helps change a broken system.

Rotate your lead stories over time and across audiences so your narrative stays true, fresh and useful.

Telling the Right Story to the Right Audience

Even strong stories fail if they're told the same way to everyone, or the wrong way to the wrong audience. Great communicators modify the story for the audience accordingly. This is common sense. I bet you don't crack the same jokes around your closest friends as you do with other school parents who you don't know well. Select, adapt, and tailor. Here's a simple framework for doing so with your partners in pursuit of Better Good:

- **Funders/Customers:** Highlight repeatable results, efficient use of resources, and achievable milestones.
- **Participants/Community:** Emphasize belonging, immediate usefulness, and easy on-ramps for them to join or take action.
- **Board/Partners:** Transparently share strategy, risk, resourcing, and expected milestones.

In most cases, you'll tell the same story, just with a different emphasis. Tune the dial—don't change the song. Get the tune right, and people will remember—and repeat—it.

THE BETTER GOOD STORY RULES

Every leader and communicator faces the same challenge: we live in an era where attention is the world's scarcest resource. Good work disappears every day because its story never finds its audience—or never earns their belief. Getting it right matters. The stories that break through don't rely on luck or algorithms; they follow a pattern that captures hearts, minds, and momentum. That pattern can be learned, repeated, and mastered. It lives in what I call the Better Good Story Rules. I'll use the website for the microlending platform Kiva.org as an example throughout for demonstration purposes.

Origin Story

Begin with the spark that set the story in motion. A moment, a pattern, or a discovery that must be shared.

- **Example:** "It all began in March 2005, when the first loan on kiva.org was funded. Elizabeth, a woman in Uganda, used her $500 Kiva loan to expand her fish-mongering business, traveling to purchase fish by the basket to sell at local markets. That $500 changed her life."

Target Audience

Identify who needs to hear this story *right now*. Donors, policymakers, or other stakeholders served by the offered solution.

- **Example:** Kiva's home page targets visitors who are aligned with their mission and most inclined to lend using the platform with the following copy: "Real people, real solutions. Lend as little as $25 to create a more equitable world."

Transformation

Describe the transformation that your offered solution makes possible. Explain specifically how your individual action, organization's work, or audience's engagement can make this possible through your unique efforts.

- **Example:** Immediately below the headline above, Kiva features photos of a small number of funding recipients who are "Almost there!" and invite you to "Fund the last few dollars they need" (driving urgency) along with a brief description of how they'll use the funds, such as "$350 helps Juanito to purchase piglets to raise." When you click to learn more, the short paragraph specifically highlights Juanito's story and goal "to improve his livelihood in the future and achieve greater success."

Proof

Show that the transformation is real. Specifics build belief and help trust travel fast and far. Share data derived from past successes, analogous events, or similar opportunities. Share before and after results, testimonials, graphs, charts, or even, yes, spreadsheets.

- **Example:** Immediately after the section described above, you'll find a "Success Stories" section and the note that "100 percent of your loan goes to supporting borrowers" followed by pictures of real recipients of Kiva loans, which you can click to read about their stories and the transformation they experienced from the loan. Thereafter, three more simple data points appear explaining how Kiva lenders have helped improve livelihoods, including: 5 million people reached; $2 billion in loans funded; and a 96 percent repayment rate.

Call to Action

Invite people into a role that helps write the next chapter of the story. A clear call to action drives engagement—whether that's in the form of donations, participation, volunteering, partnership, or raising awareness.

- **Example:** Buttons inviting visitors to "Support Kiva" or "Choose a person to support" are found throughout the site, providing a clear call to action for visitors to either learn more or take action by lending.

You may recognize several of these storytelling tactics from other organizations that take a similar approach, use similar frameworks, and invite engagement using similar language. It almost looks formulaic, for good reason. These structures work! Whether you're crafting fundraising platforms for an organization like Kiva, designing marketing materials for a nonprofit seeking support, or writing annual reports of businesses or impact reports of governmental agencies, you can leverage the Better Good Storytelling Rules in your work. Success leaves clues. There's no trophy for reinventing the wheel, and leveraging these patterns of storytelling success provides clarity, comfort, and confidence for your work ahead.

MEASUREMENT: PROVING THE STORY AND THE WORK

Two questions appear most commonly in our work for Better Good: "Is the work working (i.e., changing lives or improving the world)?" and "Is our storytelling moving people to join us?" The first question measures impact. The second measures influence that drives others to contribute in some way. Both matter because impact without influence remains small and influence without impact fades fast.

In the world of impact, measurement and metrics can get complex (and confusing) quickly. Dashboard, frameworks, evaluations, spreadsheets and the like are tools with real value, especially for technical domains and high-stakes initiatives that require them, and many do. And for those organizations that need them, entire industries have developed to meet those specialized needs. But most individuals and organizations in pursuit of Better Good benefit from a simple but effective starting point that keeps story and evidence connected.

In December 2006, I graduated with the inaugural class of the University of Arkansas Clinton School of Public Service. President Clinton delivered the commencement address. He was on the ascendancy of his post-presidential leadership—brilliant, widely well read, and famous for making complex ideas clear. He could have given us a master class on impact measurement, metrics, and analytics to match the masters degrees being conferred that day. But he didn't. Instead, near the end of his remarks, he offered a single sentence that summed up the heart of impact measurement: *"At the end of it all, if you can say the people you sought to serve are better off when you stopped than when you started, it will all have been worth it."*

That simple, effective line strips away the jargon and goes right to the heart of impact. I use it with clients regularly and nobody has ever objected to it as the alpha and omega of impact measurement. Measurement should serve the story, not smother it. And the simplest, most powerful claim you can make is exactly that: because of this work, people are better off. Start there. When things get complicated, come back to that measure and build from it.

Of course, details matter. Numbers matter, especially if you're working in a technical domain, on high-stakes initiatives, or when investors or donors demand detailed proof. In those cases, you'll need tighter methods and deeper data.

For most of us, the work is simpler: support credible organizations, advance practical efforts, and tell honest stories about what changed. Borrow their data. Cite their results. Keep your own notes on the change you're seeing. Go as deep as your audience invites or requires. But start simple, then open the aperture—and develop additional metrics, measurement, and data—as interest or need requires. Most audiences prefer clarity first and detail upon demand. So if this is new to you, follow a simple process for keeping the Better Good Storytelling Rules and evidence aligned:

- **Name the change:** Who or what is better off?
- **Show a proof point:** numbers, photos, quotes, before and after data, graphs, or images.
- **Connect the dots:** how your time, talent, or treasure helped make that change possible.
- **Invite the next step:** what you're doing next, and how others can join.

When storytelling is grounded in evidence, no matter how basic or advanced, credibility grows. People believe you. They'll join you. And they'll support the work.

Good data reinforces good stories. And clear stories ground data in lived experiences that are easy to understand. They become the record that shows what mattered and how far we advanced. Show your audience that indeed, as President Clinton said, the work is worth it.

EVERY CURE'S POWERFUL STORYTELLING

Remember David Fajgenbaum, the college quarterback turned doctor-in-training who nearly died five times from a rare disease, before discovering a decades-old generic drug that saved his life? His personal story was so dramatic and inspiring that it greatly expanded his profile, landing him a featured session at the CGI conference, a TED Talk, and national media coverage. That story then became the seed of a much larger one—the story of Every Cure.

In marketing materials about its work, Every Cure pivots from David's astonishing personal story to some equally staggering data points. There are about 14,000 known human diseases, but we only have FDA-approved drugs to treat about 4,000 of them. That leaves 10,000 diseases—"rare" individually, but common in the aggregate—without a single approved therapy. Yet within those 4,000 existing medicines lies untapped potential. If a drug made for one condition could save David, how many more hidden cures might already be sitting on the shelves of our corner pharmacies?

By skillfully blending David's story of a single individual's survival with those easy-to-digest statistics about millions of others in the same boat, Every Cure began to quickly and steadily gain supporters, donors, and its own media coverage. From there, more stories began to unfold. Patients who were about to go into hospice care and saying goodbye to their families are now alive and thriving because of treatments identified and advanced as a result of Every Cure's work. Children with neurodevelopmental disorders who were once told they'd never speak are now saying their first words to their parents, thanks to repurposed therapies discovered through the work of Every Cure. Even simple, inexpensive medicines like lidocaine—already in operating rooms worldwide—are being used in new ways to improve cancer treatment and reduce mortality, thanks to connections sparked by Every Cure.

David's story has created a growing family of *new* stories.

Each of these breakthroughs tell stories far beyond clinical achievement and medical progress. They are poignantly human stories—of daughters who still have fathers, of parents who finally hear "I love you" from their child, of patients who are alive long after doctors prepared their families to say goodbye. Stories like these attract attention because they are surprising; they inspire engagement because they are personal; they move others to action because they show what's possible when science, data, and human emotion come together.

This is what Better Good storytelling looks like at its most powerful. One person's story gives rise to an organization; data transforms into connections; and individual lives are renewed in ways that ripple outward, like a boulder dropped onto a placid lake. Every Cure is proof that when stories are clear, evidence-backed, and deeply human, they don't just spread—they save lives.

STILL WRITING THE STORY OF SPACESHIP EARTH

Narratives now shape markets, movements, and even elections. That's why clarity and credibility have become moral imperatives, not just communications tactics. But in recent years, even our shared sense of what is *real*—what counts as a fact, or even as science—has come under strain.

The more our content consumption moves into a smaller number of digital platforms, the more a few corporations—and sometimes just a few individuals—control the outlets, platforms, and algorithms that determine what stories we can share and see. This is risky for obvious reasons. When power over information concentrates, manipulation and distortion follow. And when facts themselves become optional, story becomes a weapon instead of a bridge.

The bedrock of storytelling is *shared truth.* It's the common language that allows us to connect, relate, and make meaning together. When that shared foundation erodes, so does our ability to understand one another, solve problems, or build anything lasting. Better Good depends on preserving that common ground—on insisting that facts remain verifiable, that science remains respected, and that truth remains something we can still agree upon.

While I don't know where this will end, I do know this: your voice—and the story you tell about the kind of world you want to live in—matters. It matters in what you post, what you share, and what you demand from those who hold power over the platforms we use. The survival of civilization depends on how well we sustain *shared* stories of truth, empathy, and the common good. And that depends, in no small part, on you.

The chapters we add through our own work matter—not only for us, but for those who come after. Stories are how we pass on legacy. The next chapter is yours to write.

KEY TAKEAWAYS AND ACTION ITEMS

Key Takeaways

- **Storytelling is a human constant.** Storytelling is humanity's oldest tool for making meaning and remains essential today.
- **Technology has democratized storytelling.** The technology we have at our fingertips makes it easier than ever to connect, raise awareness, and collaborate.
- **But not without some risk.** On the other hand, the abundance of modern online tools creates tremendous noise.
- **Clarity stands out in the noise.** To overcome that noise, clarity and authenticity matter more than polish.
- **Data and evidence enhance credibility.** Stories of promises paired with credible evidence multiply impact and build trust.
- **Story is essential to Better Good.** Storytelling completes the Better Good Framework by making all the other elements visible and contagious.

Action Items

For Individuals

- **Write your impact story.** Write your Better Good story in one paragraph: what you care about, why it matters, what you're doing about it, and how others can join you in the effort.
- **Share it!** With one person this week, online or offline. Momentum begets momentum and sharing with at least one person is a great way to get started.
- **Incorporate data.** Pair your story with a simple proof point: Who is better off because of your action?
- **Make it personal.** Add a personal touch to one of your storytelling efforts—a note, a call, or a face-to-face conversation.

Action Items

For Organizations

- **Clarify your organizational impact story.** Be clear about who you serve, why, what difference it makes, and how others can join you.
- **Check and update your story often.** Use the Better Good Storytelling Rules to consistently audit your storytelling across platforms to ensure consistency and reach.

- **Use data to enhance impact.** Pair every report or campaign with both data and human stories.
- **Tell your story often (especially as it evolves).** Build a rhythm of storytelling so it compounds over time.
- **Keep it fresh.** Revisit and refine your story (at least) annually to reflect growth and change and refine it for different audiences and stakeholder groups.

PART V

FROM VISION TO ACTION

Everything you've read so far has been building toward this moment.

You've seen how good works, discovered who you are, identified what you have to offer, and learned how to maximize your impact. Now it's time to bring it all together and put it to work so that you're no longer just falling into patterns, but are following the framework and charting an intentional path forward. Chapter 13 introduces the Better Good action plan, a simple but powerful tool that ties together the framework of your Profile, Platform, and Passion with your Time, Talent, and Treasure, and then shows you how to Scale, Sustain, and tell persuasive Stories about your impact.

This is where vision becomes a movement. The Better Good action plan helps you see your full footprint, build it against the framework, and realize your full potential to translate it all into action—step by step, choice by choice, and moment by perfect moment. Because there will be perfect moments in front of you when you least expect them.

CHAPTER 13

The Perfect Moment Is Now

The perfect moment is now. Be here.

—Dan Millman, *Way of the Peaceful Warrior*

CalArts grad student Nirvan Mullick didn't set out to change the world; he set out to replace a door handle—and walked straight into a perfect moment.

In the fall of 2011, Nirvan stopped by a used auto parts store in East L.A. to get a part for an old car he wanted to sell. As he walked inside, something unusual caught his eye: a homemade cardboard arcade—complete with ticket dispensers, prizes, and even a security system. It had been built, it turned out, by a nine-year-old boy named Caine Monroy, whose father ran the shop. Caine had spent his summer break pouring his imagination into creating a fully operational arcade out of recycled boxes. He now staffed it on afternoons after school. Most customers walked by. Some smiled politely. But Nirvan stopped. And marveled.

He asked Caine questions. He stuck around the arcade, bought a "Fun Pass" (it was either four plays for $1 or 500 plays with a $2 Fun Pass, so Fun Pass it was!) and played. And in that moment—without fanfare or planning—the world began to change for both Caine and Nirvan.

Nirvan would have been justified in simply smiling at the cute kid project and walking on. But he followed a flicker of curiosity using what he already had: a few spare minutes, innate curiosity, a human impulse to connect, and a storyteller's instinct.

Nirvan talked with Caine's dad, who revealed that Nirvan was Caine's very first customer. Seeing genius in the boy's creativity, Nirvan thought others should see it, too. He arranged a time to return, organized a flash mob to surprise Caine with customers for his arcade, filmed the moment, and shared the video on YouTube. For Caine, the day felt like a dream come true—real customers, real lines, real joy. When you watch the video, you can literally see the change on Caine's face as he processes that his dream is coming true right in front of him. It became one of the internet's first viral videos for good. And the world responded.

Millions watched. Donations poured in—over $220,000 for Caine's college fund. Teachers reached out. Kids were inspired. Soon, Nirvan started a nonprofit—the Imagination Foundation—to harness this momentum to foster creativity and entrepreneurship in other children around the world. That foundation eventually merged with Two Bit Circus Foundation, where its mission continues today. (Full disclosure: I proudly served on its board for years.) All of that was sparked by a single decision to stop and take a closer look.

THE UNDERLYING FRAMEWORK FOR BETTER GOOD

Nirvan's story—which unfolds further below—proves an important point. The Better Good Framework (PPP+TTT+SSS) that we've been exploring throughout this book comes intuitively to many people. To a degree, it's simply human nature.

Though he didn't know it at the time, Nirvan fell into the same pattern as so many before him when he decided to help Caine. He naturally brought his Profile as a filmmaker, his online Platform (including Reddit,

YouTube, and social media channels), and his Passion for telling stories. Then he used his Time to return and film the flash mob, his Treasure to fund the incidentals of it all, and his Talent for editing and sharing the story with the world. He had a vision for Scale in how he could bring more customers to Caine's Arcade by producing the story of that day for others to experience. He saw how he could help Sustain the impact of these efforts to support Caine's creativity by creating a scholarship to fuel Caine's future and a nonprofit to advance the wider mission. And Storytelling was woven into every step of the experience. The Better Good Framework was right there, operating naturally within Nirvan's approach.

With heightened awareness of this framework, and an intentional effort to embrace it, we can make more of moments like these, more often, and rely less on luck. Yes, a dash of serendipity, good timing, or happy accidents play a role in having an impact. In fact, this is the most common pattern for people seeking to do Better Good, whether they join or support existing causes, or try to create their own effort. There's always an element of luck, trial, and error. As with all things in life, the twists and turns of fate inevitably play a role.

Privilege plays a role, too. Those with more resources start with certain advantages and therefore tend to start further along or make progress faster. They may have more PPP + TTT, more familiarity with SSS, and more access to experts—strategic planners, consultants, lawyers, accountants, etc.—who provide advice, guidance, and tools to achieve Better Good more quickly and efficiently than those with less access and fewer resources. If you can start with millions of dollars, a high profile, a big platform, and all the opportunities that these advantages allow, wonderful! You can burst out of the gates on the path toward Better Good. No shame in that game, but it's not essential or required.

As you've seen in many of the stories throughout this book, starting with many of the elements of the Better Good Framework doesn't guarantee success or better outcomes. Resources without a plan are like fuel without a destination. In Chapter 9, we saw that even billionaires with significant financial resources, entire teams, and the best consultants money can buy can still come up short.

Meanwhile, the likes of Nancy Economou, Donna Easley, David Fajgenbaum, and Dave Humphreys all prove that you don't have to start with a lot to achieve a lot. In fact, you can start with very little—almost nothing at all—and with the right approach, achieve extraordinary results.

Regardless of their starting circumstances, those who achieve the greatest good tend to use a greater concentration of the same elements—Profile, Platform, Passion; Time, Talent, Treasure; Scale, Sustainability, Storytelling—whether they start with billions or with cardboard and tape.

Beyond early wins, the difference between short-term achievement and long-term success almost always comes down to how you leverage the three S's of the framework: Scale, Sustainability, and Storytelling. Those that persist and succeed over time do so because they scale and sustain their work, and tell the stories that keep others who are essential to that success (donors, supporters, and other stakeholders) engaged over time.

In my work over the past twenty-five years, I've seen this pattern repeat time and again. When organizations are struggling, the struggle is almost always quickly and easily found in this framework. The organization already has several elements, but they're usually missing one or two of the others. Once you see that this pattern is at work in all efforts for Better Good, you, too, can see—and help others see—where the framework is working, where it isn't, and where it can be amplified.

So what happens when we don't let any part of the framework fall away—when PPP+TTT+SSS are all plugged in and working together? What happens when we don't just "fall into" this pattern, or merely hope that we get some elements of the Framework right? (Remember, hope is a bad strategy.)

We start spotting more perfect moments, acting with purpose, and making our own luck. Because perfect moments are where awareness meets intention, and they're all around us.

FROM VISION TO ACTION: THE BETTER GOOD ACTION PLAN

By now, I hope you're seeing new possibilities for how you can do Better Good in the world—whether through everyday choices or bold, far-reaching change. The question, of course, is how to turn that vision into action.

To make your pursuit of Better Good simpler, clearer, and actionable, I've created a simple tool you can use—the Better Good action plan. It distills the shared framework beneath the world's most effective changemakers—famous or not—that you've read about throughout this book. It ensures you start with the framework of this book and stick with it. Think of it as your guide for the journey ahead: see where you are, name where you want to go, and choose the clearest path to get there. Every journey is better when we have a map. Now you have one to use as you go on your continued journey toward Better Good.

And go you must. Knowledge without implementation is useless. Holding a map in your hand is of limited use if you don't embark on the journey. The Better Good action plan helps you put your knowledge of the framework you've learned to work so that you can confidently take the next step, and endure on the path to Better Good, whether you continue on the one you know, or venture toward new destinations.

Using this tool helps you turn vision into momentum. It moves ideas from imagination to execution—getting big visions for Better Good out of your head and onto the page so you can see, at a glance, both your full potential and the immediate actions that can move you forward. The action plan brings clarity to your path, expands what you see as achievable, and amplifies your ability to make the good you do clearer, stronger, more scalable, and more sustainable.

You'll find the Better Good action plan in the back of this book, and online at www.bettergoodbook.com. There are two versions: one for individuals and one for organizations. It will walk you, your family, and/or your team through questions that help you more fully discover:

- **Your Profile:** who you are and how you show up.
- **Your Platform:** the spaces, relationships, and influence you already have.
- **Your Passion:** the causes that matter most—the ones you'd crawl through glass for.
- **Your Time, Talent, and Treasure:** what you can realistically bring to the table.
- **Scale:** how you can grow wisely, building on what works.
- **Sustainability:** how you can endure for the long run.
- **Storytelling:** how you share your story to spark connection, inspire action, and multiply impact.

If you've been underlining passages, taking notes, or inventorying along the way, you've already started. The Better Good action plan simply helps you gather your notes about the framework in one place and prompts you to think bigger. Complete it once for immediate clarity, then return to it as you grow. Like your work for Better Good, it's never really complete; it will always be evolving, growing, and changing. And the more it works, the more it works (say that again). This is where inspiration becomes action. And as you use this tool, keep scanning for perfect moments—the small, generous chances to act in the moment—because the action plan helps you recognize and multiply them, for yourself and others.

The power of pursuing Better Good doesn't come from waiting for the perfect conditions to arrive at some future point. It comes from truly noticing and inventorying what's in front of you, using what you have, and taking the next right step to grow further. And repeating and continually elevating that process as you go. That's exactly how Nirvan sparked a global movement from a cardboard arcade in the office of a junkyard. And it's how you can begin your own version of Better Good, starting now.

The Better Good action plan works for everyone and for every organization, no matter where you are on the spectrum of experience. If you're newer to this path or unsure of next steps, take some pressure off. You don't need it all figured out—Nirvan certainly didn't. The work is to notice, to explore, and to act. The framework helps you see; the action plan helps you advance.

If you've been at this for a while—wins, misses, and lessons learned included—the action plan sharpens focus and alignment so you can turn good into Better Good.

There's magic in this tool and what becomes possible when you use it, revisit it, and bring it to life in all you do. To see how, let's return to Nirvan's story.

FINDING MORE PERFECT MOMENTS FOR BETTER GOOD

A few months after the video first went viral, Nirvan presented the story of Caine's Arcade at the Social Innovation Summit in Mountain View, California. That evening, at dinner, he noticed President Bill Clinton at a nearby table. Barbara Bush, daughter of President George W. Bush, who had seen Nirvan's talk earlier that day, introduced him. Nirvan shook President Clinton's hand and quickly snapped a photo of him holding one of Caine's cardboard "Fun Passes."

Then came a tap on his shoulder. A large man, whom Nirvan assumed was Secret Service, pulled him aside. "That's for personal use only, right? We wouldn't want to see that photo online. We'd hate to get our lawyers involved."

Nirvan nodded politely. "Of course. Totally understand."

But something tugged at him. He turned back and explained, "That Fun Pass is from a film I made about a boy who built a cardboard arcade."

The man's expression softened. "Wait—you made *Caine's Arcade*?"

When Nirvan nodded, the man put a hand on his shoulder. "That video made me cry. Go ahead and post the photo."

And he did. President Clinton holding a cardboard arcade Fun Pass—one more improbable ripple in a story that began with a junkyard car part and a kid's dream. And for the record: that man wasn't Secret Service. He was my friend Jon—appearing burly and protective at times, but kind and quick to offer a genuine smile. And the "lawyers" he referred to? That would've been me.

Like millions of others, I had seen Nirvan's video when it first went viral and started following him online. When I saw Nirvan post about the Clinton encounter, I smiled. I knew the people involved, so I had a strong sense of how it would unfold. I knew how kind President Clinton is. And I knew that I was the lawyer Jon meant. I would never have sent a letter.

Months later, knowing that Nirvan would be attending a Clinton Global Initiative meeting in Chicago, I reached out via email to invite him to connect. This was not my usual practice as a staff member, so I was hesitant to do so, but I was also in the early stages of beginning my transition away from the Clinton Foundation. I wanted to start making meaningful connections with people in my orbit who inspired me or from whom I thought I could learn. I also had a lingering question I was eager to ask him.

To my delight, Nirvan replied warmly, saying he'd be happy to connect in Chicago if the scheduling stars aligned. They did. What started with a quick hello in the hotel lobby bar—the unofficial gathering place for most CGI attendees—turned into a four-hour late-night conversation. It was a humble meeting. Just two guys drinking water, talking about CalArts (the college Walt Disney started and Nirvan attended), storytelling, creativity, failure, and the strange ways paths cross and the universe responds when people choose to pay attention. We stayed up chatting past 2 a.m. We remain good friends today.

At one point I asked Nirvan the question that had stuck in my mind since I first saw the viral video: "Why did you bother to stop that day? Why, when you were broke and exasperated and just needed a car part, did you choose to stop and engage with a kid? You were having a bad day and had every reason to just go about your business."

Nirvan unhesitatingly answered with two words. "Perfect moments."

He explained that, as a film student at CalArts at the time he met Caine, he was working on an assignment to create a one-second film about a perfect moment.

He further explained that one second includes twenty-four frames of film—an entire world packed into a blink. He shared how that idea stayed with him, elevating his own awareness of what's possible in every second of every day, and how perfect moments can be found even in just a single second at any given time. When he met Caine that day in East L.A., Nirvan wasn't having a perfect day. Not even close. And he wasn't out to change anyone's life, let alone the world. But he sensed that he could create a perfect moment for someone else and do Better Good in a single, simple moment. Little did he know that the lesson he learned in that film class would create a huge ripple effect for his own life, for Caine, for me, and maybe now for you, too.

WHAT IS POSSIBLE FOR US ALL

That night in the hotel lobby bar, Nirvan shared a concept that transformed how I see the world and has underpinned this entire book: every moment contains possibility. Every interaction contains potential. Every one of us—regardless of our status, schedule, or stage of life—has the ability to create ripples of good that reach farther than we may ever see. And we don't have to wait to get started.

This isn't a story about cardboard arcades, filmmaking, or going viral online. It's not about perfect plans. It's about what's possible when we show up, pay attention, and use what we have at any given moment. It's about how momentum builds after the simplest steps. It's about how too many of us wait for some bigger moment, some grand gesture, or something more perfect on some other someday.

Ordinary moments are filled with extraordinary opportunities. They, too, can be perfect. And we don't need more of something before we act. Not more time, more money, more standing, more confidence, more stature, or more connections.

When Nirvan met Caine and set a series of events in motion to change his and Caine's lives, he didn't have extra money—he was actually in need himself. He didn't have extra time—he just "found" some. He didn't have a big profile or platform—he simply leveraged his reach on Reddit. Nirvan wasn't at the apex of his life and work—quite the opposite. And the list of things he *didn't* have all would've made compelling reasons *not* to engage with Caine.

On the other hand, more compelling than what he didn't have is what he *did* have.

Nirvan was more prepared than most because he had the two core elements this book encourages you to discover: awareness and intent. Awareness of the opportunity to do good in any moment of our lives. Intent to do that good when a perfect moment arises. Nirvan noticed that perfect moment and made the intentional choice to lean into the inherent goodness of our human nature.

And let me be clear, had he simply just played Caine's Arcade that day and never returned, that would have been good on its own. That he *did* choose to do more is what led him toward Better Good.

There were no guarantees that Nirvan would succeed with his plan to arrange a flash mob to delight and inspire Caine with real customers. No assurance that anyone would respond when he posted on Reddit . . . or that anyone would show up on the day of the flash mob to become customers of Caine's Arcade . . . or that the video he posted to YouTube would go viral . . . or that anyone would support the scholarship fund for Caine . . . or that the Imagination Foundation would sustain after the viral success of the moment faded, after Caine grew up, and as the world moved on.

Nirvan's story reminds us that possibility doesn't wait for perfect circumstances, but life can give us perfect *moments*. Every moment contains the potential of a gift, and perfect moments are often hiding in plain sight—in a cardboard arcade, in a single second, or in the smallest choices we make to engage. When we encounter one such moment, we can say, "Yes, and . . ." to the opportunity, and expand the experience into an even bigger moment—maybe even a movement. The Better Good Framework is simply the foundation beneath it all, one that lets you see what's possible sooner and act on it with greater clarity. And the Better Good action plan is a simple tool that allows you to build on that foundation.

You don't have to stumble into this pattern the way Nirvan and countless others have. And you don't have to wait until you have "more." Because you now know that "more" isn't a requirement—or a guaranteed recipe—for success, and may even leave you doubting yourself more than those who have less.

The Better Good action plan meets you where you are and gives you a way forward. Whether you start with billions or with cardboard and tape, the pattern is the same: Awareness. Intention. A willingness to act using your PPP+TTT+SSS.

Perfect moments don't wait for perfect conditions—and now you have a map to meet them when they appear. With awareness as your compass and intention as your guide, the Better Good action plan helps you start, sustain, and share the good that only you can do—again and again.

KEY TAKEAWAYS AND ACTION ITEMS

Key Takeaways

- **The framework has always been there.** This book revealed the pattern beneath every story you've read—PPP + TTT + SSS at work, whether someone started with billions or with cardboard and tape.
- **The action plan operationalizes it.** Resources and good intentions are raw material; the action plan turns them into clear next steps and repeatable progress.
- **Perfect moments are your entry point.** You don't need perfect conditions—just the awareness to notice a moment and the intention to act.
- **No waiting necessary.** You don't need to wait for more money, more time, or more status. With awareness, intention, and a willingness to act, the action plan shows you how to begin today.

Action Items

For Individuals

- **Complete your Better Good action plan (print or digital).** Capture your awareness and intention;

your Profile, Platform, Passion; your Time, Talent, Treasure; and your plans for Scale, Sustainability, and Storytelling.

- **Inventory what you already have.** List the strengths, resources, and opportunities already present in your daily life and work—no matter how modest they may seem.
- **Look for "perfect moments."** Train yourself to notice small opportunities to act with awareness and intention, just as Nirvan did with Caine.
- **Revisit your action plan regularly.** As your life and impact evolve, update it to reflect new passions, emerging talents, or fresh opportunities.
- **Share your action plan with a trusted friend, colleague, or collaborator.** Accountability and conversation will help you refine your thinking and spark new ideas.

Action Items

For Organizations

- **Create an organizational Better Good action plan.** Convene key people to complete it together and capture your shared PPP, TTT, and vision for SSS. Use it as a tool to drive your efforts for Better Good forward together.

- **Start where you are.** Identify how your current organizational impact footprint already connects with your mission, vision, values, and daily operations. Use it to spot gaps or areas where your impact could be even stronger.
- **Engage your people.** Once your core impact team has developed your action plan, invite other employees, volunteers, or stakeholders to review and contribute their insights, so your action plan reflects the full breadth of your community. You'll likely discover more impact-oriented team members in the process.
- **Integrate the action plan.** Use it as a living tool to guide strategy, set priorities, and evaluate opportunities for growth and partnership.
- **Return to the action plan often.** Just as individuals and journeys evolve, organizations evolve, too. Revisit your plan periodically to keep your impact intentional, scalable, and sustainable.

CONCLUSION

We Are the Helpers

Do all the good you can,
By all the means you can,
In all the ways you can,
In all the places you can,
At all the times you can,
To all the people you can,
As long as ever you can.

—John Wesley

The world's problems never fully go away, but I'm writing this in particularly difficult times. It's almost too much to process: civic unrest on previously peaceful city streets; wars and conflicts displacing millions; climate disasters arriving faster and fiercer than predicted; economies teetering; institutions tested and transformed; truth itself contested. Division, polarization, fear and fatigue cut across our neighborhoods and around the world. In the U.S., the institutions of government, nonprofits, and businesses that provide the pillars of civil society are strained like never before.

It can feel relentless and paralyzing.

And yet, if history shows us anything, it's that the darkest moments are also when the need for light is greatest. It's in times like these that we most need to remember where to place our attention, and what to do with our individual and collective capacity for being good neighbors to one another, both in our local communities and in pursuit of leaving our world better than we found it.

THE LIGHTS IN OUR NEIGHBORHOOD

The morning of September 11, 2001, began like any other—and then, within a couple of hours, nothing was the same. Terror. Confusion. And the sense that the world we knew had permanently shifted. For weeks and then months, we lived in shock and disbelief, unsure what to feel or do. Most of us were scared, overwhelmed, and searching for a sign that things could someday make sense again.

People shared various reassuring quotes (mostly via email in those days before social media), and one that spread widely was by Fred Rogers, the iconic and recently retired host of *Mister Rogers' Neighborhood*. For three decades, Mr. Rogers's calm demeanor and simple decency had been a fixture in our homes, teaching millions of children how to name their feelings, face their fears, and simply be kind. To me and so many other kids, his presence had always been as comforting as our favorite blankets.

Now, as adults, we were once more—when we needed it most—reassured by his simple words:

> *When I was a boy and I would see scary things in the news, my mother would say to me, "Look for the helpers. You will always find people who are helping." To this day, especially in times of disaster, I remember my mother's words, and I am always comforted by realizing that there are still so many helpers—so many caring people in this world.*

In that dark season—and in this one—those words comfort and guide us. They remind us to shift our focus from horror to humanity, from the haze of chaos to the hands reaching through it. They tell us that light always exists, even when it is hard to see.

That simple instruction—to *look for the helpers*—is good advice for frightened kids. It's also wisdom for all of us any time when the world feels uncertain and overwhelming. It invites us to notice the ordinary people who step forward when things feel like they are falling apart. It reminds us that courage is the map out of despair, and that doing good, doing more good, and doing it better can empower us when the world feels broken. It teaches us where to focus our attention, and how to begin again when everything feels impossible.

In a time as noisy and chaotic as this one, voices like his—rooted in quiet, unwavering, decency—risk being drowned out by louder, sharper ones. That's why it matters to keep surfacing them, to pass them forward, to keep them alive as part of our storytelling, our culture, and our shared work for Better Good.

In the fall of 2001, when Mr. Rogers and that quote resurfaced to reassure us, I was twenty-four years old, in my first year as a corporate lawyer, trying to find my footing as an adult. The time I got that message from Mr. Rogers was about the same time I got that first message from Norm asking about helping the ferret shelter—one of my earliest invitations to step into doing good in a new way. A small act that would turn out to be a formative one on a journey still unfolding. That lesson—about the power of taking a small step toward Better Good during a particularly difficult time in the world—has never left me. It's guided how I've tried to serve: as a counselor, strategist, and companion to people and organizations striving to do Better Good in heavy times. The wisdom Mr. Rogers offered then still feels like the right guidance now. For those who remember it, as reassurance; and for those who haven't heard it before, as a compass that might guide us all.

Because the truth remains: the helpers we're looking for aren't only "out there."

They're us.

WE ARE THE HELPERS

It's tempting to believe the helpers are always someone else—the professionals, the leaders, the activists, the people whose names make the news and whose credentials suggest they are more qualified than us. And yes, many of them *are* helpers.

But so are you. Helpers are not a separate class of people. They are ordinary people who choose, in a given moment, to act with extraordinary awareness and intention in service to others.

We've seen it throughout this book. A busy mother of five who sees a clear opportunity to deliver light, love, and opportunity to remote communities living in darkness. A chef who refuses to let the hungry wait. A neighbor who connects abandoned dogs with loving families. A community member and parishioner who keeps showing up, quietly, faithfully, week after week. A young doctor who refused to accept "we've tried everything" and discovered a new path to saving and improving lives. A filmmaker who stopped for a cardboard arcade and sparked a global movement.

Each of them began as an "ordinary" person without extraordinary resources. Each of them looked at the need in front of them and simply chose to help.

Their stories remind us that progress doesn't come only from grand gestures or public victories but instead comes in steady, everyday acts of compassion and courage. In showing up when it's hardest. In choosing to believe that the long arc can still bend toward justice through the small actions of many, one day at a time, creating a collective and cumulative wave of Better Good.

When we look for the helpers, we can't just look outward. We must also look inward. Into the mirror. Into our own neighborhoods. Into our own circles of influence, however wide or narrow they may feel.

SOMEDAY STARTS NOW

Remember this: you are more ready than you may think. You've been wired for this since the day you were born. You've been doing this, you're doing this, you've done this.

The stories you've read in this book are stories of helpers. They are stories of ordinary people choosing to act with awareness and intention.

They are stories of what happens when "someday" becomes "today."

Now it's your turn. You don't need to be extraordinary to begin. *Beginning is what makes you extraordinary.*

You don't need to wait for permission.

You don't need to wait for perfection.

You already have enough. You already *are* enough. And you already know enough.

So let this be your moment. Your invitation. Your call to action.

Someday isn't coming.

Someday starts now.

All these years later, I know Mr. Rogers was right. The helpers are not only "out there." The helpers are *us*. He gives us permission to look at ourselves anew, as the helpers we need to see when times are difficult.

I hope this book does the same for you. The best time to start was yesterday. The next best time is now.

APPENDIX

Better Good Action Plans

BETTER GOOD ACTION PLAN FOR INDIVIDUALS

A simple tool to move from intention to action

Complete the action plan here in these pages that follow or online at www.bettergoodbook.com/actionplan to save, download, and revisit a digital version. For your convenience, each of the component parts of the action plan are included in the following pages for ease of completion. Revisit, revise, and update your Better Good action plan often to maintain your momentum and a clear view of your evolving Impact Footprint.

PPP	TTT	SSS
PROFILE How I show up to do good in the world **Credentials:** Education, training, and expertise I offer: ______ **Connections:** Networks and relationships I can activate: ______ **Character:** The traits, spirit, and values that guide me: ______	**TIME** Overmanaging time to maximize impact Actions I can take requiring No Extra Time: ______ Opportunities to make an impact using Found Extra Time: ______ Big impact goals that will require Transformative Time: ______	**SCALE** Doing more of what's working What is working that I am excited to do more of: ______ Individual, community, and larger efforts I want to grow: ______ Ways I can keep scale more top of mind as I grow my impact: ______
PLATFORM The places and spaces where I have impact The physical places and communities where I reach others: ______ Industries, organizations, and associations I connect to: ______ My online platforms, communities, and digital reach: ______	**TALENT** Using skills, abilities, and experiences for good Primary skills I can deploy right away with ease: ______ Underlying talents resulting from lived experiences include: ______ Emerging talents I might use for good are: ______	**SUSTAINABILITY** Creating impact over time The causes I'm most motivated to engage with over time are: ______ The things I love doing to support them even when hard are: ______ The ways I remain motivated when things get tough include: ______
PASSION The causes that motivate me most The causes I care about: ______ The causes I will crawl through glass for: ______ **My Goldilocks Zone:** What I'm best at and excited to do: ______	**TREASURE** Mobilizing financial resources to make impact Ways my current spending or giving already creates impact: ______ Cash, budgets, or investments I can deploy include: ______ Matching programs or influence I can activate: ______	**STORYTELLING** Telling the impact story and inviting others in The impact story I can tell now is: ______ Data I can use to tell my story and other places I can share it: ______ Who I'll seek to invite to join the story as it unfolds: ______

WHO YOU ARE: PPP

PROFILE
How I show up to do good in the world

Credentials: Education, training, and expertise I offer:

Connections: Networks and relationships I can activate:

Character: The traits, spirit, and values that guide me:

PLATFORM
The places and spaces where I have impact

The physical places and communities where I reach others:

Industries, organizations, and associations I connect to:

My online platforms, communities, and digital reach:

PASSION
The causes that motivate me most

The causes I care about:

The causes I will crawl through glass for:

My Goldilocks Zone: What I'm best at and excited to do:

WHAT YOU CONTRIBUTE: TTT

TIME
Overmanaging time to maximize impact

Actions I can take requiring No Extra Time:

____

____

Opportunities to make an impact using Found Extra Time:

____

____

Big impact goals that will require Transformative Time:

____

____

TALENT
Using skills, abilities, and experiences for good

Primary skills I can deploy right away with ease:

____

____

Underlying talents resulting from lived experiences include:

____

____

Emerging talents I might use for good are:

____

____

TREASURE
Mobilizing financial resources to make impact

Ways my current spending or giving already creates impact:

____

____

Cash, budgets, or investments I can deploy include:

____

____

Matching programs or influence I can activate:

____

____

NEXT-LEVEL IMPACT: SSS

SCALE
Doing more of what's working

What is working that I am excited to do more of:

Individual, community, and larger efforts I want to grow:

Ways I can keep scale more top of mind as I grow my impact:

SUSTAINABILITY
Creating impact over time

The causes I'm most motivated to engage with over time are:

The things I love doing to support them even when hard are:

The ways I remain motivated when things get tough include:

STORYTELLING
Telling the impact story and Inviting others in

The impact story I can tell now is:

Data I can use to tell my story and other places I can share it:

Who I'll seek to invite to join the story as it unfolds:

BETTER GOOD ACTION PLAN FOR ORGANIZATIONS

A simple tool to align intention, strategy, and impact

Complete the action plan here in these pages that follow or online at www.bettergoodbook.com/actionplan to save, download, and revisit a digital version. For your convenience, each of the component parts of the action plan are included in the following pages for ease of completion. Revisit, revise, and update your Better Good action plan often to maintain your momentum and a clear view of your evolving Impact Footprint.

PPP

PROFILE
How we show up to do good in the world

Credentials: Expertise, experience, and assets we bring:

Connections: Networks, partners, and stakeholders we activate:

Character: The principles that guide how we operate:

PLATFORM
The places and spaces where I have impact

Communities and markets where we reach others:

Industries, sectors, and ecosystems we influence:

The physical, professional, and digital stages we have:

PASSION
The causes that motivate me most

Issues that align with our mission and strategy include:

The causes our team will crawl through glass to impact:

My Goldilocks Zone: What we're best at and most excited to do:

TTT

TIME
Overmanaging team time to maximize impact

Actions our team can take that require No Extra Time:

Initiatives we can undertake with Found Extra Time:

Strategic impact efforts that will require Transformative Time:

TALENT
Using team skills, abilities, and experiences for good

Core team competencies we can deploy immediately:

Organizational talents shaped by our history and experience:

Team capabilities we can grow or acquire to increase impact:

TREASURE
Mobilizing financial resources to make impact

Ways our current spending or giving already creates impact:

Additional budgets, assets, or investments we can deploy:

Matching, other funding, or partner capital we can activate:

SSS

SCALE
Doing more of what's working

What is working that we should grow and expand:

Initiatives we can grow locally, nationally, or globally:

Systems that ensure scale is embedded in impact decisions:

SUSTAINABILITY
Creating impact over time

Core impact priorities we commit to sustain over time:

Activities we can continue even during downturns or pressure:

Structures protecting this work in leadership or market shifts:

STORYTELLING
Telling the impact story and inviting others in

The impact story we can credibly tell today:

Metrics and evidence that supports our story:

Stakeholders we will invite into the story:

WHO YOU ARE: PPP

PROFILE
How we show up to do good in the world

Credentials: Expertise, experience, and assets we bring:

____

____

Connections: Networks, partners, and stakeholders we activate:

____

____

Character: The principles that guide how we operate:

____

____

PLATFORM
The places and spaces where we have impact

Communities and markets where we reach others:

____

____

Industries, sectors, and ecosystems we influence:

____

____

The physical, professional, and digital stages we have:

____

____

PASSION
Causes that align most with our mission

Issues that align with our mission and strategy include:

____

____

The causes our team will crawl through glass to impact:

____

____

My Goldilocks Zone: What we're best at and most excited to do:

____

____

WHAT YOU CONTRIBUTE: TTT

TIME
Overmanaging team time to maximize impact

Actions our team can take that require No Extra Time:

Initiatives we can undertake with Found Extra Time:

Strategic impact efforts that will require Transformative Time:

TALENT
Using team skills, abilities, and experiences for good

Core team competencies we can deploy immediately:

Organizational talents shaped by our history and experience:

Team capabilities we can grow or acquire to increase impact:

TREASURE
Mobilizing financial resources to make impact

Ways our current spending or giving already creates impact:

Additional budgets, assets, or investments we can deploy:

Matching, other funding, or partner capital we can activate:

NEXT-LEVEL IMPACT: SSS

SCALE
Doing more of what's working

What is working that we should grow and expand:

Initiatives we can grow locally, nationally, or globally:

Systems that ensure scale is embedded in impact decisions:

SUSTAINABILITY
Creating impact over time

Core impact priorities we commit to sustain over time:

Activities we can continue even during downturns or pressure:

Structures protecting this work in leadership or market shifts:

STORYTELLING
Telling the impact story and Inviting others in

The impact story we can credibly tell today:

Metrics and evidence that supports our story:

Stakeholders we will invite into the story:

ACKNOWLEDGMENTS

This book reflects people doing good long before me and from whom I have had the privilege of learning. Any contribution I bring here is simply a reflection of those who offered opportunity, encouragement, mentorship, coaching, and friendship along the way. I'm deeply grateful to those who helped me complete this book, those featured within it, and the much longer list of people who inspired it. I've tried to acknowledge some of them here, though far from all. Any omissions are my error.

To my family. Amy, Ray, and Asprey: you are the best Better Good I've ever been part of. Thank you for the space and grace to write this book, and for being the heart of all the good I get to do. I love you.

To my parents, Lois and Chris; all my siblings (Steve, Sean, Paul, Petrea, Chris Jr., and Melanie) and their spouses; my nieces and nephews; cousins; extended family; and my far-reaching family of friends, thank you for a lifetime of love and encouragement. To my grandparents, especially Ray and Lorraine Wagoner, whose examples loom large in all I do. To all my aunts and uncles and our entire Asprey Family near and far. And to my Aunt Yasuko, Uncle Ken Wainwright, and their boys Bill ("Willie") and Kenneth, for showing how rich life can be in the ways that matter most. To my in-laws, Bill and Glenda Cobb, who have lived lives of service that inspire; Adam, Ann, and Rylan Cobb; and our extended family in Oklahoma, I'm so glad to be part of your family. To Karime Valencia and Francisco Mendez, thank you for being part of our family and for all you do for us.

To lifelong friends: Joe Wenckus, Mani Oller, Phil Cisco, Stephanie Begy, Howard Doberman, Gretchen Boerwinkle, Wendy Overend, Dave "Scrappy Doo" Metzger, Eric Lazzari, Jeremy Dershow, Christopher Leslie, and Pam and Sandeep Devata. To family friends, including the Boothbys, Harms, VanDerPuys, Paynes, Schieds, Fureys, Mayors, Dubois, Buttells, Molises, Forcashes, Smiths, Carrs, Weinshenkers, and so many others from all the neighborhoods and communities of my life. And to the many more friends from college, law school, grad school, and the school of life along the way. I wouldn't be who I am without you, and I'm so grateful.

To my teachers and coaches who modeled goodness and lifted others as they led, thank you. And to my forever guidance counselor, Cheryl Krauspe, and my forever coach, Dave Jackson, for the early lessons that still guide me.

To the StanFam, including the Peckenpaughs, Jill Stewart, Rita Vogel, the Montagues, Enoses, Seraponases, Swansons, Miss Marge, and our extended Downers Grove community, it's great to be part of your village and to have you as part of mine. To all the Pine Parkway neighbors, and families McCoy, Snyder, Jacobs, McGady, Mrjenovich, and Levine.

To the entire Beyond Advisers team, thank you for championing this work and supporting me through the journey. Zayneb, for sharing my brain and making it—and my life—better long before Beyond and every step since, and to the entire Shaikley family for welcoming us as your own. Joe Ballard, for a friendship that began the day we met and has been filled with wit, wisdom, and fun ever since. Jim Jacoby, without whom Beyond, MoCo, and so much more likely would not exist. Your confidence and encouragement have made an enormous difference. Dave Horwich, for being a rare friend, colleague, and collaborator. Fins up! Scott Taitel, for the early conversations and all the ones since about how to grow careers and impact with intention.

To my book team, I've been writing all my life, but I've never written like this. Thank you for helping me along this journey. These words are better because of all of you who made this book possible. Steve

Rinehart, for steady guidance, encouragement, and friendship from the earliest stages. Fred Lebron, my earliest creative collaborator on this part of the journey. Celeste Fine at Park & Fine, for responding to my query and opening doors. Jaidree Braddix, my agent, for helping me see the bigger book and traveling this road with me. From Margaritaville to countless collaborations, I'm grateful. My editor, Kimberly Meilun, and her team at Simon & Schuster for consistent and unwavering support and insights in pursuit of the best *Better Good* possible. Will Weisser, my writing partner and friend. Your calm, kindness, patience, and persistence were exactly right and this book is a reflection of that. Lauren Hamlin at Splash Literary, for sharpening stories at an important moment. Aaron Shulman, for helping me find the alpha and omega of this book's current form, for friendship, and for helping me explore what's possible in the expanding universe of Better Good. Kieron Banerji, for joining the fun through podcasting and bringing creativity, insight, and patience along the way. Brooklyn Huang and Markie Johansen for showing up at just the right time in all the best ways. Sam Horn, for extraordinary generosity, guidance, and friendship. From beachside conversations to lasting collaboration, you are a gift. Chris Vogler, for early encouragement. Steve and Liz Berry for kind guidance along the way. The Kauai Writers Conference, and Jane Green and Patti Callahan Henry, for wisdom, kindness, and making the new guy feel welcome. Thanks also to Pete Garceau for your cover design and to Rebecca Austin and Darlyn Simbulan for your design help.

To the team at Patzik, Frank & Samotny, thank you. Chad Buttell, for the interview that turned into a lifetime of mentoring and friendship, and to the entire Buttell family. Dirty buggies. Sheryl Halpern, for saying yes to helping the ferrets and showing the way. Steve Prebish (Preebs), for introducing me to improv and encouraging me to make time for it. Alan Patzik for unwavering support. To MZS, JGS, JP, MAX, DJS, Erica, Smilie, and the entire team at PFS for the encouragement, examples, friendship, and good counsel.

To everyone at the Clinton School, I'm grateful for the graduate program that sparked a career pivot of a lifetime, from the inaugural classroom experience to field service in the Mississippi Delta and a summer internship that opened the door to the Clinton Foundation and everything that followed. Thanks to Senator David Pryor and Dr. Tom Bruce for their leadership and mentorship; Bob Torvestad for the first tour that changed our lives; Dr. Mike Hemphill for leadership, guidance, and friendship; and to the faculty, staff, volunteers, partners, and community members who made those early years so welcoming. To Dean Vicky Soto and the current Clinton School team, thank you for supporting students past, present, and future on their journeys toward Better Good.

To the many Clinton Foundation friends, thank you for a career ride of a lifetime. Bruce Lindsey, for the first doorway conversation and enduring mentorship and friendship that followed. It has been the privilege of my career to work with and learn from you. Stephanie S. Streett, for modeling selfless mentorship and always lifting others higher. Your friendship is a gift. Trooper Sanders, for early opportunities and introductions, including putting Nishant and me together at that folding table and proving that working with friends on important issues is one of the best things in the world. Nishant Roy for being an extraordinary friend from day one and every day since. You are nice! Marc Gross for the friendship and collaboration from that first brown bag lunch to the most recent butter service. Eric Nonacs, for encouragement and collaboration over many years. Keisha Senter and Courtney O'Donnell, for proving that working in the trenches (and stairwells) with friends is work worth doing. Penny Abeywardena and Daniel Schaefer, for rock-solid friendship and collaboration at every stage that continues on. Greg Milne, for being a dear friend, a great thought partner, and constant presence and support. Bob Harrison, for guidance and friendship from the earliest days and collaboration that continues today. Terry Sheridan and the HR team for being in it together. Ginny Ehrlich, Julie Satterwhite, and the original Alliance team. To Andy Kessell for good grace and good humor for a decade. To the entire legal team over the years for all the effort, support, and friendship.

To everyone at the Clinton Presidential Center, and the entire Clinton Foundation community of board members, initiative partners, and supporters. What a privilege it was to work, learn, and grow with you. To the leaders of the PLS program, its partners, and scholars for modeling impact that brings all people together in ways that really matter, especially now.

To the Clintons themselves, with my deepest gratitude. President Bill Clinton, for a vision of post-presidential service that changed my life, for countless kindnesses large and small, and for showing that presence, care, and gratitude always matter. Secretary Hillary Clinton, for leadership, grace, and humor in ways seen and unseen. Chelsea Clinton, for trusting, challenging, and creating space for others to shine.

To our family of friends from Little Rock, including Erica Lawlor, Erin Robinson, Sarah Roberson, Paige Thurmond, Hannah Vogler, Tisha Gribble, Ellis Martin, Paul and Linda Leopoulos, Miss Lynda, Miss Betty, Sasha and Zach Cerrato, Jay Barth and Chuck Cliett, and all our friends and neighbors.

To Beyond Advisers clients, collaborators, and supporters past and present, for imagining and articulating audaciously bold goals and then always continuing with "and beyond." Too many to list, but including special thanks for the inspiration and partnership in recent years including Carmen Rojas, Zeeba Khalili, Hannah Nichols, Dan Gould, Ian Fuller, Rami Nashashibi, Melody Barnes, Stacey Abrams, Alex Amouyel, Emily Yu, David Fajgenbaum, Grant Mitchell, Tracey Sikora, Mary Zuccato, Juliana Jackson, Deb Roy, Tatiana Ivancevich, and all others who have offered the opportunity to be part of your work over the years.

To collaborators and friends including Chris Kelly, Ron Kertzner, JB Pritzker, Jana Babatunde-Bey, Jeff Noel, Christopher Frederick, Warwick Sabin, Jeff Leitner, Zeev Klein, Mel Ochoa, Ed Foster-Simeon, Jon McCoy, Becky Endicott, Julie Confer, Joan Garry, Glennda Testone, and the We are For Good, Nonprofit Leadership Lab, Social Innovation Leadership Council, BoardSource, and U.S. Soccer Foundation teams and communities.

To the many social impact lawyers who have led the way and supported this work, including Lee Miller, Jay Finkelstein, Renee Schoenberg, Lisa Dewey, Gene Takagi, Marc Lane, Lesley Rosenthal, Jerry Jones, Ameena Majid, Skye Perryman, and the innumerable others who continue to guide and inspire. To the Chicago-Kent College of Law community past, present, and future and to all the students who have taken my class. I've loved learning with you.

To Chris Fisher, Katie Gillman, the entire ISTO team; and Anthony Bertucci and team, thank you for all you do for my work and my family. To Pastor Scott Oberle and our church family at First Congregational United Church of Christ Downers Grove, for being a model of Better Good for so many.

To the Molis Coaching family, including my friend and business partner Ryan Molis, the entire Molis family, the Molis Coaching team, including Matt Hicks, Jenna Gillen, Sharon Mozes, Stacie Berndt, Michele Buralli, Kristen Lopez, Rechelle Dimmick, all our friends and partners at Align Technology, the MoCo Faculty, all of our members, and especially our Mastermind members, thank you all for your extraordinary efforts to make dreams come true for so many.

And to every individual and organization referenced throughout this book, and the teams behind them: your work is an important beacon in the world. Keep going. You are the best of Better Good and the world needs you now more than ever.

NOTES

Chapter 2:

Humans Are Wired for Good

Psychologists also call it: Zak, Paul. *Trust, morality-—and oxytocin?* Video on TED.com, https://www.ted.com/talks/paul_zak_trust_morality_and_oxytocin.

Sinek notes that oxytocin's effects: Simon Sinek, *Leaders Eat Last: Why Some Teams Pull Together and Others Don't* (New York: Portfolio/Penguin, 2014), 54–56.

In his book: Jim Collins, *Good to Great: Why Some Companies Make the Leap . . . and Others Don't* (New York: HarperBusiness, 2001), 14.

Chapter 3:

Doing Good in Groups: Government, Nonprofits, and Business

A 2020 Deloitte study: Deloitte, *2020 Global Marketing Trends: Bringing Authenticity to Our Digital Age,* December 1, 2020.

And Edelman found that: Edelman, *2020 Edelman Trust Barometer Special Report: Brand Trust in 2020.*

A famous business saying . . .: Ridgway, V. F., 1956. "Dysfunctional Consequences of Performance Measurements," *Administrative Science Quarterly*, 1(2): 240–247.

Chapter 7:

Your Time

Carter Work Project: https://www.habitat.org/carter-work-project.

But as the saying goes: Denise Brennan-Nelson, *Someday Is Not a Day of the Week* (Illumination Arts, 1996).

Chapter 8:

Your Talent

No matter who you are: Jobs, Steve (June 12, 2005). "'You've got to find what you love,' Jobs says," Stanford Report, https://news.stanford.edu/stories/2005/06/youve-got-find-love-jobs-says.

Chapter 9:

Your Treasure

As the CEO of GivingTuesday: GivingTuesday's State of Generosity. The State of Generosity in 2024–2025: Generosity as Resilience, https://stateofgenerosity.givingtuesday.org/.

Households earning under: 2018 Online Giving Statistics, Trends & Data: The ultimate list of giving stats. Nonprofits Source. (n.d.), https://nonprofitssource.com/online-giving-statistics.

In fact, according to Giving USA: A Look at American Philanthropy in 2023. LendingTree. (n.d.), https://www.lendingtree.com/credit-cards/study/charitable-donations.

The average American: How much does the average person donate to charity? Miami County Community Foundation. (2025, September 21), https://micocf.org/blog/how-much-does-the-average-person-donate-to-charity/.

In fact, point of sale: Major checkout charity campaigns grew 24% from 2020 to 2022. NonProfit PRO. (2023, May 31), https://www.nonprofitpro.com/article/major-checkout-charity-campaigns-grew-24-from-2020-to-2022/.

One study found that: How small donors become major donors: Analyzing major donor pathways. CCS Fundraising. (2022, April 28), https://www.ccsfundraising.com/insights/how-small-donors-become-major-donors-analyzing-major-donor-pathways/.

More than 26 million of us: Weinger, A. (2025, September 30). 19 matching gift statistics every nonprofit should know. 360MatchPro, https:/360matchpro.com/matching-gift-statistics.

In fact, across twenty-five countries: Willage, A. (December 17, 2021). People prefer brands with aligned corporate purpose and values. World Economic Forum, https://www.weforum.org/stories/2021/12/people-prefer-brands-with-aligned-corporate-purpose-and-values.

"I don't know . . .": Mork & Mindy, Season 4, Episode 22, "The Mork Report," aired May 27, 1982.

Chapter 10:
Scale What Works

Imagine my delight: Wang, I. (2025, June 4). Scientists in Japan develop plastic that dissolves in seawater within hours | Reuters, https://www.reuters.com/sustainability/climate-energy/scientists-japan-develop-plastic-that-dissolves-seawater-within-hours-2025-06-04/.

By the early 2000s: Shoumatoff, A. (2007, May 1). An ecosystem of one's own. *Vanity Fair*, https://www.vanityfair.com/culture/2007/05/greenguide200705.

By the early 2010s: Staff, Earth Day 2022 (2022, March 29). Fact sheet: Single use plastics. Earth Day, https://www.earthday.org/fact-sheet-single-use-plastics.

The global reusable bottle market: Pangarkar, T. (2026, January 15). Reusable Water Bottles Statistics and facts (2026). Market.us News, https://www.news.market.us/reusable-water-bottles-statistics/.

Chapter 11:
Sustain for the Long Run

As noted in Chapter 6: How is Chick-fil-A advancing diversity, equity and inclusion?: Chick-fil-A. (2025, August), https://www.chick-fil-a.com/customer-support/who-we-are/our-culture-and-values/how-chick-fil-a-is-advancing-diversity-equity-and-inclusion.

Likewise, Bass Pro Shops: America's largest conservation movement: Bass Pro Shops. Bass Pro. (2025, June 5), https://about.basspro.com/conservation/.

Chapter 12:

Tell Stories That Move the World

1. *In controlled experiments:* Paul J. Zak, "Why Inspiring Stories Make Us React: The Neuroscience of Narrative," *Cerebrum* (Dana Foundation, 2015); and "Why Your Brain Loves Good Storytelling," *Harvard Business Review*, December 16, 2014.

2. *Meanwhile, at Princeton:* Uri Hasson et al., "Brain-to-Brain Coupling: A Mechanism for Creating and Sharing a Social World," *Trends in Cognitive Sciences* 16, no. 2 (2012): 114–121.

3. *Jonathan Gottschall, a leading authority:* Jonathan Gottschall, *The Storytelling Animal: How Stories Make Us Human* (New York: Houghton Mifflin Harcourt, 2012).

4. *As Donald Miller says:* Donald Miller, *Building a StoryBrand: Clarify Your Message So Customers Will Listen* (New York: HarperCollins Leadership, 2017), 12.

Chapter 13:

The Perfect Moment Is Now

1. *He arranged a time to return:* To see Nirvan's original Reddit post and all that transpired, visit www.bettergoodbook.com/nirvan.

Conclusion

1. *When I was a boy:* Rogers, Fred (2006). *Wisdom from the World According to Mister Rogers: Important Things to Remember* (Peter Pauper Press).

INDEX

ABOUT THE AUTHOR

Scott M. Curran is a social impact lawyer, strategist, author, and founder and CEO of Beyond Advisers, a consulting firm that helps foundations, nonprofits, businesses, law firms, and social entrepreneurs turn good intentions into meaningful impact.

For more than twenty-five years he has worked at the intersection of the private, public, and nonprofit sectors, advising organizations ranging from hometown nonprofits and emerging social enterprises to major foundations, Fortune 500 companies, and global initiatives.

Scott previously served as general counsel of the Clinton Foundation, where he worked alongside world leaders, philanthropists, and entrepreneurs on initiatives spanning economic opportunity, public health, climate, education, and global development.

He is also an adjunct law professor, speaker, and host of the *Better Good* podcast, where he explores the ideas, stories, and strategies behind meaningful social impact. Across his work, Scott is known for helping people make sense of complicated challenges and translating big ideas into practical action.

At its heart, *Better Good* reflects a lesson Scott has learned repeatedly from extraordinary leaders and everyday changemakers alike: doing good is a skill that can be learned, strengthened, and scaled. Every person has the capacity to create positive change, and every organization has the opportunity to become a force for good.

Scott lives outside Chicago with his wife, Amy, their two children, and their rescue dogs.

To learn more, access additional resources, and continue the conversation, visit www.scottmcurran.com.